# SHIRLEY MACLAINE MEETS THE PLEIADIANS

by
Timothy Green Beckley

**Additional Material by Sean Casteel**

Conspiracy Journal
PRODUCTIONS

**Shirley MacLaine Meets The Pleiadians**

**Timothy Green Beckley**

**Sean Casteel**

This edition Copyright © 2015 by Global Communications/Conspiracy Journal

All rights reserved. No part of these manuscripts may be copied or reproduced by any mechanical or digital methods and no exerpts or quotes may be used in any other book or manuscript without permission in writing by the Publisher, Global Communications/Conspiracy Journal, except by a reviewer who may quote brief passages in a review.

Revised and Updated Edition

Published in the United States of America By
Global Communications/Conspiracy Journal
Box 753 · New Brunswick, NJ 08903

**Staff Members**
Timothy G. Beckley, Publisher
Carol Ann Rodriguez, Assistant to the Publisher
Sean Casteel, General Associate Editor
Tim R. Swartz, Graphics and Editorial Consultant
William Kern, Editorial and Art Consultant

Sign Up On The Web For Our Free Weekly Newsletter
and Mail Order Version of Conspiracy Journal
and Bizarre Bazaar
www.ConspiracyJournal.com

**Order Hot Line: 1-732-602-3407**
**PayPal: MrUFO8@hotmail.com**

## CONTENTS

Introduction—Tim Beckley ............................................................................. 1

Enter Shirley MacLaine ................................................................................. 6

Shirley MacLaine—A Dweller In Two Worlds—Sean Casteel .......... 9

Did Russell Crowe Photograph a UFO? ................................................. 22

Sightings Among The Stars —Tim Beckley ........................................... 32

The Entertainers ............................................................................................ 70

The Comedians ............................................................................................ 132

Muhammad Ali ............................................................................................ 151

Directors, Producers, Glamorous Model ............................................. 160

Presidents, Politicians and a Conquering General ........................... 177

Astronauts, an Anthropologist and an Ace Aviator ......................... 194

Author Biographies .................................................................................... 221

# SHIRLEY MACLAINE MEETS THE PLEIADIANS

## THE UFO EXPLOITS OF SHIRLEY MACLAINE AND OTHER CELEBS

### By Timothy Green Beckley

During the mid-1960s it was not unusual for me to hop a southbound Amtrak and head to the nation's capital. In those days D.C. was among the highly-charged hubs of UFO activity and interest. There was still lingering fascination with the time during the summer of 1952 that the saucers had buzzed the White House and agitated officialdom – especially the CIA – so much that they had had to form all manner of "scientific" panels to try and squelch public interest in the subject.

My main contact in the District during this period was a gentleman who ran a clearing house which he called *"The Little Listening Post." "The Little Listening Post"* was actually a very gossipy monthly newsletter published by World War II Vet Harold Salkin, who opened up his home to anyone passing through town who was remotely connected with the subject – in particular those associated with the contactee movement – and included the likes of George Adamski, Major Wayne Aho, and Woody Derenberger. Salkin had inherited a sprawling townhouse from the late Clara John, who had started the *"Listening Post"* and had been a ghost writer and editor for George Adamski. Few people know this, but John and Salkin were among those who helped found the National Investigations Committee On Aerial Phenomena (NICAP). Salkin also assisted in the writing of Major Donald E. Keyhoe's initial article for "True Magazine" and kept NICAP afloat with numerous donations. Keyhoe and the high mucky-mucks of NICAP were loath to credit the guiding forces behind *"The Little Listening Post"* as being their benefactors due to John and Salkin's close association with Adamski and the like.

Among those that Salkin hooked me up with in those early days was a gentlemen by the name of Paul Dicky, who worked for various branches of the federal government over the course of his extensive service to his country, primarily as

# SHIRLEY MACLAINE MEETS THE PLEIADIANS

an aerospace communications specialist. Dicky was a witness to numerous UFOs around the Washington beltway. Some of his sightings were in the company of various government employees. An hour-long retrospective interview, which I conducted at his retirement villa outside of Tucson, Arizona, decades after those heady 1960s, can be viewed on YouTube under "Startling UFO Sightings of a Washington Whistle Blower."

(https://www.youtube.com/watch?v=i6SE1YftqfY)

Eventually, the old guard of the UFO movement began dying off and the neighborhood where *"The Little Listening Post"* was physically located started sliding downhill as the criminal element started to encroach on what was once a clean, middle-class community.

Tim Beckley first met Washington, D.C., UFO whistleblower Paul Dickey in the Sixties.

Paul Dicky

I had just started to establish myself as a promoter in Manhattan, putting on regular UFO and occult meetings as well as an occasional rock concert. I also had a prototype for a magazine similar to *"Fate,"* which I was going to call *"ESP,"* and I was hopeful we would get the needed financing and distribution. I suggested that Salkin move to New York and reinstate himself here. Salkin was a motiva-

# SHIRLEY MACLAINE MEETS THE PLEIADIANS

tional whirlwind. Besides being a freelance journalist (he had been an AP reporter in the Pacific during WWII) and publicist, he seemed to know everybody. If he didn't know someone and wanted to meet them, Salkin could track them down. Together we started ACI – Artists and Celebrities International – with clients like musician Les Paul and psychedelic artist Peter Max. And anytime anyone involved with UFOs or the paranormal was passing through the Big Apple, we took them on as "clients" pro bono, hooking them up with an assortment of talk and variety shows like the Long John Nebel "Party Line," the Barry Farber program, and Joe Franklin's "Memory Lane," to name only a few.

One of the first things Salkin and I did together was collaborate on a blockbuster article for the nationally-distributed men's action magazine, *"Saga."* We had spent five days at NASA's headquarters in Washington and gone through every transcript from all the Apollo and Mercury flights, plucking out episode after episode where our astronauts had encountered an assortment of UFOs while in space. We found they would use code words like "Santa Claus" or phrases such as "It's just the wind in the rigging" when communicating with Houston Ground Control and trying to hide the true nature of their conversation.

Publisher Beckley stands with the 1970s staff of his Global Communications as they proudly hold an issue of the "Enquirer" showing a headline story based on their journalistic coverage, which garnered them an extra bonus. They wrote many of the celebrity UFO pieces for the tabloids during this period.

# SHIRLEY MACLAINE MEETS THE PLEIADIANS

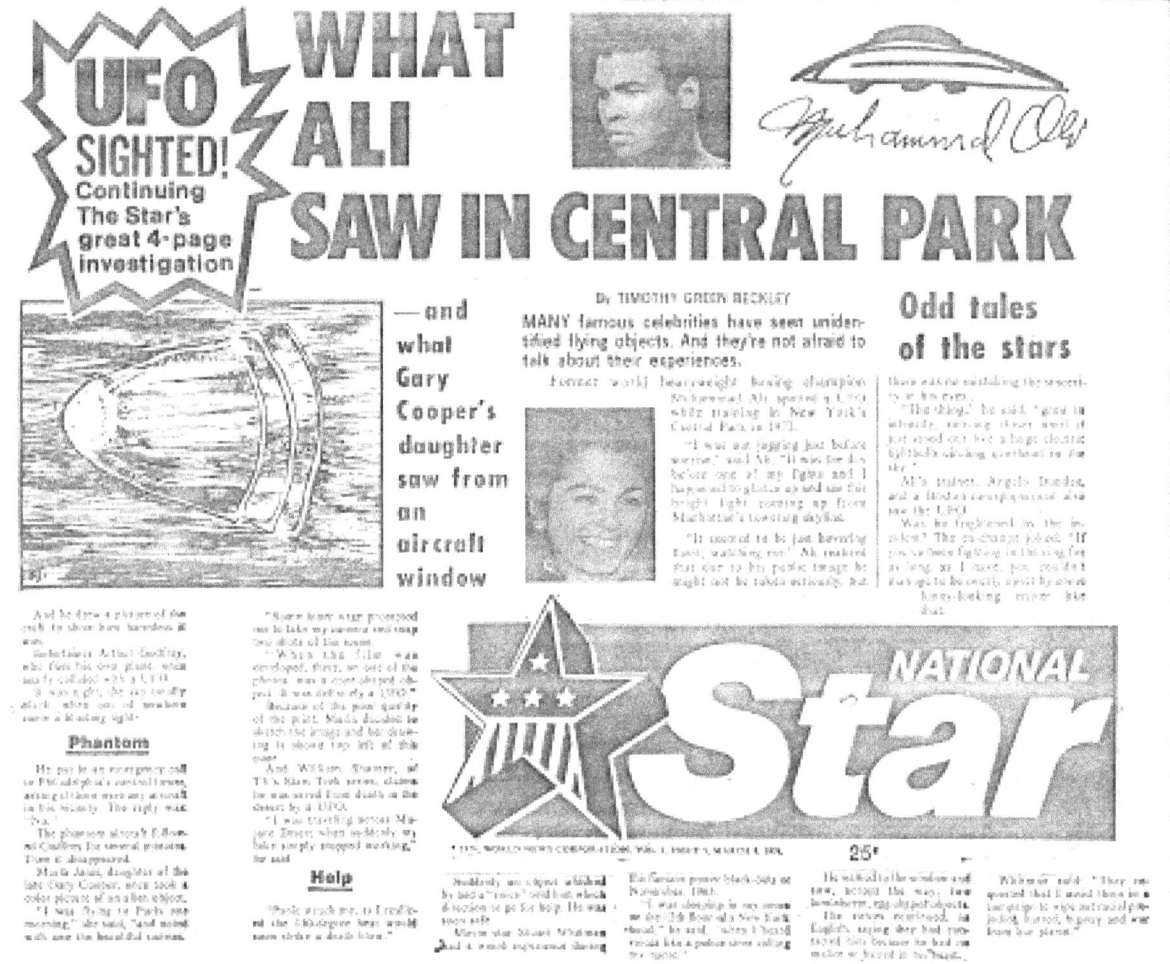

Their front page story in "The National Star" (now a glossy called simply "Star") contained UFO art by several of the celebrities they interviewed.

We also found ourselves writing story after story for the national tabloids. In our first attempt to sell to publications that admittedly had a reputation as being gossip sheets, we sent a query letter off to "The National Enquirer" describing the psychic experiences of three celebrities we had spoken with firsthand. **"The Enquirer"** gobbled up all three stories, and we later got a check for around a thousand dollars. We were pitching UFO and paranormal stories as well as celebrity exclusives to not only **"The Enquirer"** but also to **"The Globe," "The National Tattler," "People"** (a paper out of Chicago), and numerous "pulps," as they were known in those days (i.e., magazines printed on ultra-cheap paper).

It didn't take long before celebrities were calling us to tell us about their psychic experiences as well as their sightings of UFOs. Years later, the son of singer Mel – the "Velvet Fog" – Torme, Tracy Torme, said that his father told him that we had written the most accurate article about him ever, even though it had appeared

# SHIRLEY MACLAINE MEETS THE PLEIADIANS

in *"The National Enquirer,"* which had a bad, but totally undeserved, reputation for sensationalism. The article focused on Mel's sighting of a UFO in Central Park while he was out walking his dog. Of course, son Tracy went on to produce "Fire In The Sky," about the abduction of Travis Walton, so something must have rubbed off subject-wise from father to son, perhaps partially due to our reporting in "The Enquirer."

One of the closest bonds we made with a celebrity was with Muhammad Ali, whose home in Cherry Hill, New Jersey, we visited on several occasions (see group shot elsewhere in the book). We also drooped into his training camp in Deer Park, Pennsylvania, and we bought along none other than Uri Geller to spend the afternoon as the champ prepared for his forthcoming fight. We had first met the world champion heavyweight boxer after a one-column item appeared in "The New York Daily News" regarding Muhammad's sighting of two brightly lit, dangling UFOs that he saw hovering over the New York skyline as he jogged around Central Park preparing for his match with Joe Frazier. Salkin and I chatted with him along the jogging path as Ali slowed his pace to accommodate us. Then we retired to his hotel room, where he showed us some of the paintings he had done predicting the outcome of his title match. Ali fancied himself an artist, and his paintings do sell for a "comfortable" sum at auction.

Though I have no way of coming up with an accurate figure, I would say that we probably interviewed several hundred celebrities, politicians, and astronauts, as well as others among the world's rich and famous. Many of them had had UFO and psychic experiences. Many of our articles were published right away, but some we held onto because the individuals in question did not want their stories circulated until their passing.

Besides writing these stories up for the tabloids, we did a regular feature for the nationally-distributed magazine, *"Saga's UFO Report."* Our column, *"Saucers and Celebrities,"* ran in this publication for several years before the magazine folded. Before its demise, *"UFO Report"* had the largest circulation of any newsstand publication of this genre and remains a collector's item, being praised as probably the most influential enterprises of this type. And – from a writer's point a view – they paid handsomely for articles, whereas today's web publishers bitch poverty.

# SHIRLEY MACLAINE MEETS THE PLEIADIANS

**ENTER SHIRLEY MACLAINE**

One can't help but admire Shirley MacLaine. Her life and career have been so diversified that she can best be described as an overall show business "trouper." Dancing, singing, acting, not to forget her interest in humanitarian endeavors, cooking and, of course, the paranormal, with UFOs right there on top of the heap. Oh, and did we forget to mention writing? Her book, ***"Out on a Limb,"*** was a bestseller from which a TV miniseries was produced. And Shirley has never been without influential friends and acquaintances, from world leaders to the Rat Pack of Frank Sinatra, Dean Martin, Sammy Davis, Jr. and Joey Bishop.

Before going any further, it would seem appropriate to mention that Shirley MacLaine has not endorsed this book nor has she sanctioned its publication. However, it does not profess to be a biography of any sort – official or unofficial – as it only covers a small aspect of her fascinating life and career. That said, I don't believe anyone else affiliated with the paranormal could do such a fair and honest job of summing up her prevailing views on UFOs, the Pleiadians, reincarnation and Karma.

We have more or less followed the same path, though Shirley, I would have to say, is a bit more spiritual and mystical in her paranormal leanings, while I am a "show-me" type of guy who wants to see evidence laid out from A to Z.

Shirley and I both seem to agree that the book ***"A Dweller on Two Planets"*** is one of the most inspiring and important works in this category. It was channeled by a 20,000 year old Tibetan through a young man who lived at the summit of the mysterious and sacred site that is Mount Shasta in Northern California, near the Oregon border.

Shirley says the book nearly flew into her hands while she was combing the stacks of a Parisian bookstore some years ago. Her consumption of the information contained in this book has led her on a spiritual quest like no other. Our own publishing company, Inner Light/Global Communications, has issued forth with

# SHIRLEY MACLAINE MEETS THE PLEIADIANS

its own edition of this amazing work. In our edition, called *"The Secrets of Mount Shasta and a Dweller on Two Planets,"* updated and revised by Sean Casteel, the young author/channel Frederick S. Oliver spins a tale so compelling and so spiritually uplifting that it is doubtful that it was written by him alone as a human being. The reader will immediately see that this book contains such a wealth of detail about Atlantis and the spiritual realms that it could not be conjured from the imagination of an eighteen-year-old farmhand. Oliver worked as a simple fence-mender for his father, who raised cattle near their home along the base of the mysterious and legendary Mount Shasta in Northern California.

Oliver foreshadows much of what would come after him, like the feminist movement of the 20th century and the coming of UFOs with their external, multi-colored, revolving lights and the interiors of the craft lit by some unseen source, details verified repeatedly by modern-day alien abductees and UFO contactees. In fact, many of the illustrations in this book of cigar-shaped craft look remarkably similar to the ships said to have been photographed by George Adamski and others many decades later. Oliver, while in the channeled thrall of an Atlantean and ancient Tibetan soul, also predicts television and cell phones in a time that predated even rudimentary radio.

Furthermore, like myself, Shirley places a great deal of importance and spiritual relevance into synchronicities. My thoughts and experiences on the sub-

Though channeled well over a century ago, the illustrations in "A Dweller on Two Planets" showing a cigar-shaped UFO submerging in a body of water look remarkably similar to many of the craft seen in our skies today.

# SHIRLEY MACLAINE MEETS THE PLEIADIANS

ject are generally known and can be found by Googling my name and the subject matter, which will lead you to several broadcasts on YouTube, including the show "Behind The Paranormal," hosted by Paul and Ben Eno on radio station WOON in Woonsocket, Rhode Island.

Likewise, in an interview conducted by bestselling author Whitley Strieber on his **"Unknown Country"** podcast, Shirley asks the author of **"Communion"** if he had ever heard this rumor: on the night Dr. John Mack (the controversial Harvard psychiatrist who, in two books on the subject, took the claims of alien abduction experiencers quite seriously) was run over and killed in London by a drunk driver, another man with the exact same name met the same unfortunate fate not too far away. Whitley admitted that he hadn't heard the rumor but he obviously saw more than a mere "coincidence" in the passing of Shirley's abduction researcher and Harvard professor friend.

And so we leave you with a book full of UFO stories. Some true, some perhaps like that told by William Shatner, who insists he made up the story to get a reaction out of a journalist like myself, a bit more fictionalized than we care to believe.

And what about the story told by Jackie Gleason about seeing some dead "Martians" in a freezer at Andrews Air Force Base in Florida while in the company of President Nixon? What are we to make of this tale of wonderment?

It's all up to you to decide as you read these remarkable stories of celebrities, pop stars and the world's most influential people.

"Sweet Charity" lobby poster; Shirley MacLaine and Sammy Davis, Jr.

# SHIRLEY MACLAINE MEETS THE PLEIADIANS

## SHIRLEY MACLAINE: A MODERN DAY DWELLER IN TWO WORLDS – FROM ACTRESS TO UFO/NEW AGE ADVOCATE
### By Sean Casteel

There is a famous scene in the 1969 movie *"Easy Rider"* in which the three principals, a pair of drug-dealing, free spirit motorcycle enthusiasts, played by Peter Fonda and Dennis Hopper, and an alcoholic ne'er-do-well lawyer, played by Jack Nicholson, are sitting around a campfire passing the time as they pass a joint. Hopper looks up at the night sky and points at a strange configuration of lights passing over them.

Nicolson's character has a ready explanation for his two companions.

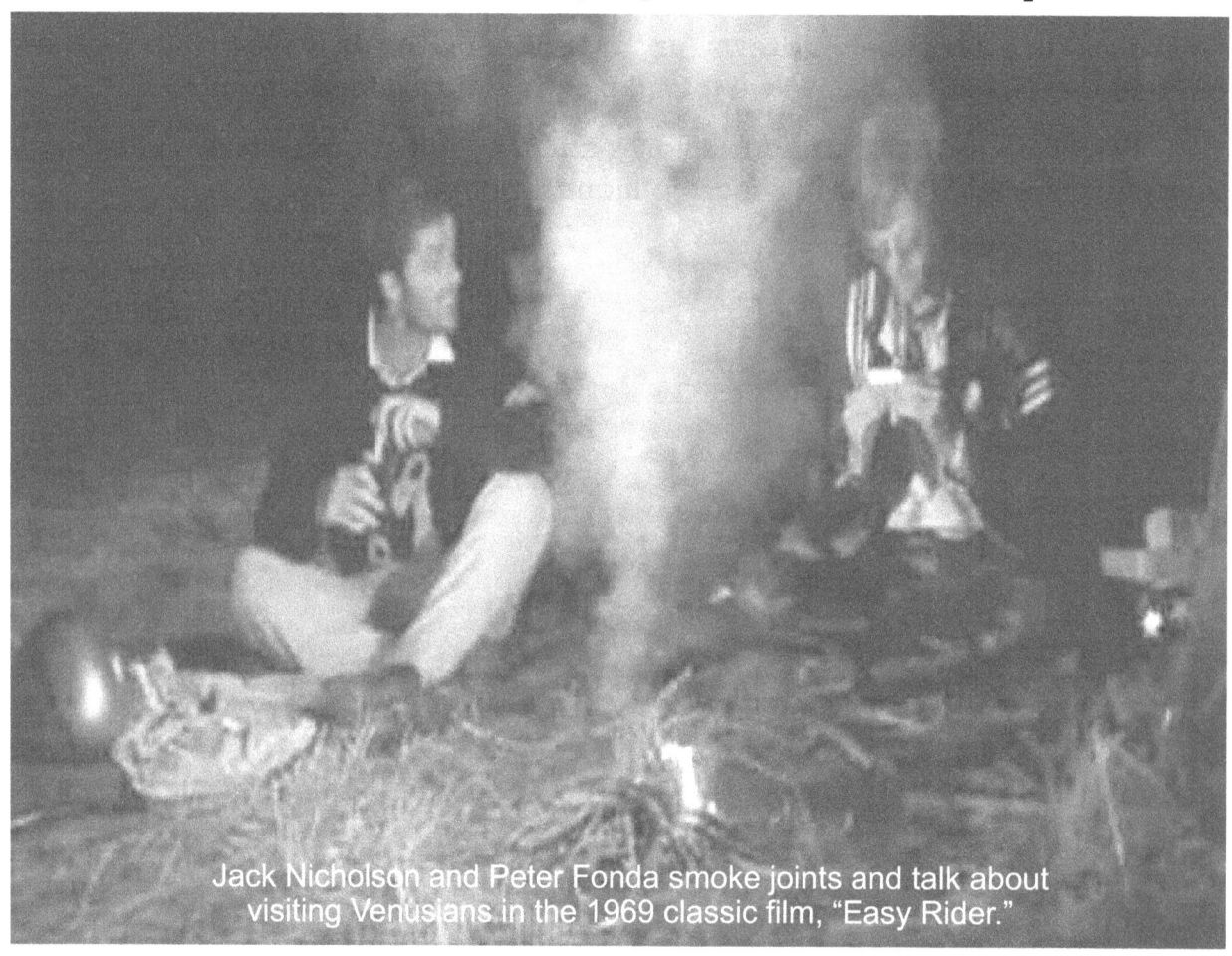
Jack Nicholson and Peter Fonda smoke joints and talk about visiting Venusians in the 1969 classic film, "Easy Rider."

# SHIRLEY MACLAINE MEETS THE PLEIADIANS

"That was a UFO beamin' back at ya," he says. "Me and Eric Heisman was down in Mexico about two weeks ago and we saw 40 of 'em flying in formation. They've got bases all over the world now, you know. They've been coming here ever since 1946 when the scientists first started bouncing radar beams off of the moon. And they have been living and working among us in vast quantities ever since. The government knows all about 'em."

Such cinematic moments in which the reality of UFOs is casually slipped in with a moment of dialogue are nowadays thought to fit into a larger overall pattern of cultural programming intended to prepare the general public for open contact with extraterrestrials. By frequent exposure to the possibility of alien life, we gradually grow more comfortable with the idea and therefore become more likely to accept the inevitable disclosure without mass panic or a societal breakdown.

The American actress, Shirley MacLaine, seems to have long ago crossed over into total and unashamedly public belief in UFOs and may be a small part of that cultural programming whether she is totally conscious of playing such a role or not.

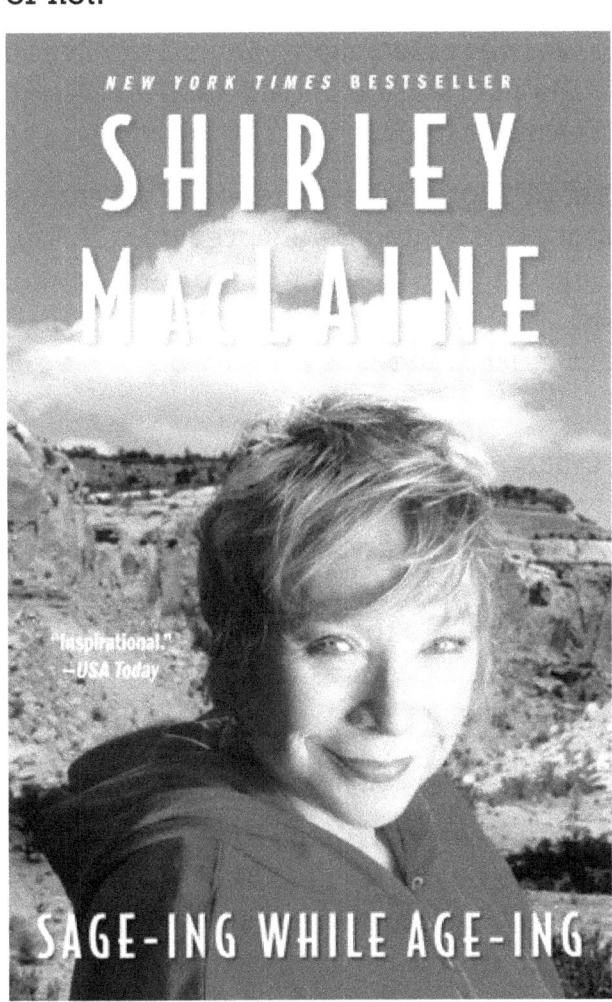

In her 2007 book *"Sage-ing While Age-ing,"* MacLaine wrote about how her interest in UFOs began when she was a young woman in Virginia and heard about the now legendary sighting of flying saucers over the nation's capital.

"It was a Saturday night, in 1952. I know," she writes, "because I recorded it in my diary. A pilot reported seeing UFOs and two Air Force F-94 jets streaked over Washington in hot pursuit. The next morning the banner headline in 'The Washington Post' was 'SAUCER OUTRAN, JET PILOT REVEALS.' *'Life Magazine'* did a cover story called 'There is a Case for Interplanetary Saucers. Have We Visitors from Outer Space?' It reviewed ten recent UFO sightings and concluded that they could not be written off as hallucinations, hoaxes or earthly aircraft. An unnamed officer was quoted as saying, 'The higher

## SHIRLEY MACLAINE MEETS THE PLEIADIANS

you go in the Air Force, the more seriously they take flying saucers.'"

In *"Sage-ing While Age-ing,"* MacLaine also writes about a 1954 encounter between President Dwight D. Eisenhower and the aliens. Allegedly the meeting constituted a formal "First Contact Event."

The Eisenhower/Palm Springs story is pretty familiar history for UFO believers, but MacLaine has a story that most people in the UFO community had not heard until her book came out – the first sighting by future president Ronald Reagan.

It was the 1950s, and Reagan was an actor with his political achievements still many years ahead of him. Reagan was invited to a party that actor William Holden was hosting in Hollywood. Two of those attending, comedian Steve Allen and actress Lucy Ball, both told the story of Reagan's encounter.

Reagan was missing when the party began. He and his wife Nancy arrived nearly an hour late. According to both Allen's and Ball's version of events, Reagan was very excited. He said that he and Nancy had seen a UFO while driving to the party and had stopped to observe it.

But the bombshell part of the story was revealed many years later when Ball told MacLaine that Reagan claimed that the UFO landed and an alien emerged. The alien told Reagan to quit acting and take up politics.

Grant Cameron, a widely respected UFOlogical researcher of all things presidential, writes on his website, "The story of a United States president telling someone that he had talked to and taken advice from an alien is a big story, so I began to check the story. It turned out not to be a British tabloid-gone-wild [story] but actually true. Shirley MacLaine had put most of the story in her book *'Sage-ing While Age-ing.'*"

Cameron quotes MacLaine's book thusly: "Reagan had seen a craft when he was an actor as he and Nancy were driving on Mulholland Drive in Los Angeles. Apparently, the craft landed and an occupant descended who then spoke to him telepathically. He never told me directly, but he did tell a party of people who were waiting for him [at the party]. Lucille Ball told me that he had arrived ashen and confused and told her the story. She told me because, as a Democrat, she wanted me to know that Ronnie must have been crazy."

### FROM MOVIE STAR TO NEW AGE ADVOCATE

Shirley MacLaine's acting career began in 1955 with Alfred Hitchcock's *"The Trouble with Harry,"* a black comedy that earned her a Golden Globe Award for "New Star of the Year – Actress." From that initial flush of success she would go on to appear in numerous feature films side-by-side with A-list stars like Jack Lemmon

# SHIRLEY MACLAINE MEETS THE PLEIADIANS

and Jack Nicholson. MacLaine garnered a Best Actress Oscar for 1983's *"Terms of Endearment."*

In addition to being a close friend of the author for many years, Jim Dilettoso collaborated with UFO researcher Wendelle Stevens to analyse early on the controversial photos of Swiss contactee Billy Meier. Jim has been a special adviser to Shirley MacLaine, who supports the Meier case fully.

< A most alluring beauty, Shirley Maclaine.

Shirley takes a break. Her appearance with Jack Lemmon in "The Apartment" scored another major hit for her.

# SHIRLEY MACLAINE MEETS THE PLEIADIANS

According to Shirley MacLaine, President Reagan had an actual encounter with a UFO being who wanted to make sure he ran for the Oval Office.

Dennis Kucinich's description of the strange object he saw in the sky did not win him a lot of support from ultra-conservative Republicans.

# SHIRLEY MACLAINE MEETS THE PLEIADIANS

But alongside all that Hollywood glitz and glamor, MacLaine was also on a spiritual quest, much of which revolved around reincarnation. She claimed that in a previous life in Atlantis she was the brother to a 35,000-year-old spirit named Ramtha, channeled by American mystic teacher and author J.Z. Knight. Her other past lives were as a medieval warrior, an orphan raised by elephants, a Japanese geisha and a model for post-impressionist painter Toulouse-Lautrec. Even her beloved pet rat terrier, Terry, is a reincarnation of the jackal-headed Egyptian god Anubis.

With the publication in 1983 of her bestselling autobiographical book, **"Out on a Limb,"** MacLaine opened herself to an onslaught of ridicule when she began to express her interest in spirituality and metaphysics to a large reading audience. She was also very frank when discussing UFOs during interviews on CNN, NBC and the Fox News Channel.

In an interview with talk show host Bill O'Reilly about her book **"Sage-ing While Age-ing,"** O'Reilly asked MacLaine, "Do you believe that Bush and Cheney and all these guys know that there are extraterrestrials around? That they personally know it?"

"From talking to Jimmy Carter," MacLaine replied, "and from my contacts with people around Reagan, the presidents are not on a need-to-know basis from military intelligence. So I would say possibly Cheney but I would not say anyone else knows. And from the intelligence point of view, they have no need to know."

She goes on to say the aliens prefer to be called "star beings." O'Reilly then asks if the aliens look like us.

"God, I hope not," MacLaine shot back.

## MACLAINE MEETS AN ABDUCTEE

Before pioneering alien abduction researcher Budd Hopkins died in 2011, he published his memoirs in a book called **"Art, Life and UFOs."** Part of a chapter in the book is devoted to a meeting between MacLaine and abductee "Kathie Davis," a pseudonym. Kathie is the focus of Hopkins' groundbreaking book on her case, "Intruders" (1987), in which he chronicles her traumatic experiences at the hands of her alien abductors, including being made pregnant while still a teenager and a virgin.

Hopkins and Kathie were attending the Mutual UFO Network's annual conference in Washington D.C. that same year of 1987. Kathie, a shy person not accustomed to talking about herself, had agreed to join a Sunday panel of people who had had repeated abduction experiences.

# SHIRLEY MACLAINE MEETS THE PLEIADIANS

"As the banquet speaker droned on," Hopkins writes, "a man I knew as some kind of Hollywood operator came up behind us and whispered, 'Budd, would you like to meet Shirley MacLaine? She's staying in a hotel nearby and she's a friend of mine. I think she'd like to meet you and Kathie.'"

Hopkins intended to decline the invitation because he knew that MacLaine believed the aliens were benevolent Space Brothers intent on helping mankind while his *"Intruders"* presented a much different take on the subject. Hopkins hoped to avoid an unpleasant discussion on the subject of the movie star's New Age beliefs, but Kathie overheard the conversation between Budd and his Hollywood acquaintance and was excited at the prospect of meeting MacLaine.

Upon arriving at MacLaine's hotel, the opulence of which was thrilling for Kathie, they were ushered into a main room where MacLaine sat "as if presiding over a royal court," Hopkins writes. Also present were Congresswoman Bella Abzug – she of the big hats – as well as a Senator and a retired Navy Commander. Kathie and Hopkins were introduced and two chairs were brought out for them, like they were "defendants on trial," according to Hopkins.

MacLaine then asked Kathie to tell the story of her UFO experiences, an extremely complicated endeavor even under normal circumstances. As a shy, intimidated Kathie began to speak, all eyes were fixed on her, seemingly with sympathy. Her telling was interrupted by her tears from time to time as she recounted the still-painful events.

When Kathie was finished, MacLaine came over to her, offering whatever comfort she could, and whispered that she understood what Kathie had been through.

"We stayed only a short time after that," Hopkins writes. "I answered a few questions and then we left."

## A CONGRESSMAN SIGHTS A UFO

Another event recounted in MacLaine's *"Sage-ing While Age-ing"* is the story of Congressman Dennis Kucinich's seeing a UFO while visiting MacLaine at her home in Graham, Washington.

"Dennis found his encounter extremely moving," she writes. "The smell of roses drew him out to my balcony where, when he looked up, he saw a giant triangular craft, silent and

# SHIRLEY MACLAINE MEETS THE PLEIADIANS

observing him. It hovered, soundless, for ten minutes or so and sped away with a speed he couldn't comprehend. He said he felt a connection in his heart and heard directions in his mind."

Leslie Kean, in her widely respected book *"UFOs"* (2010), writes about the aftermath of the sighting for Kucinich.

"The need for a new way of thinking about UFOs was painfully illustrated," Kean writes, "when NBC's Tim Russert popped a surprise question to Ohio congressman Dennis Kucinich during the nationally televised presidential debate in 2007. Russert asked Kucinich whether he had actually seen a UFO, as was

Shirley MacLaine in a scene from "The Other Half of the Sky."

reported in a book by Shirley MacLaine. Snickers from the studio audience became audible as soon as the dreaded 'U-word' was uttered. The poor man replied, accurately, that yes, he had simply seen something unidentified, reiterating that it was 'an unidentified flying object.' Despite the straightforward honesty and clarity of his reply, Kucinich could not escape the laughter that had begun even before he had the chance to speak. He followed his comment with a joke of his own, as a way of saving face."

Kucinich's attempt at face-saving humor went like this: he joked about moving his campaign office to Roswell and said that in public opinion polls the numbers were higher for UFO believers than for then-president George Bush's popularity rating. But the fact remained that Kucinich had essentially been "outed" as a UFO believer by the story in MacLaine's book and his presidential hopes were basically quashed as a result.

# SHIRLEY MACLAINE MEETS THE PLEIADIANS

MacLaine commented in a 2012 article in the UK's *"Daily Mail"* that she was eager to share her knowledge of UFOs with then-Secretary of State Hillary Clinton.

"It's very important that she knows who else is out there looking at her," she said.

MacLaine has become accustomed to people thinking she's crazy, she added.

"I've never had the urge to please anybody," she said. "I'm used to people thinking I'm wacky, so I don't take myself seriously."

Even MacLaine's brother, actor Warren Beatty, thinks she's a bit nuts. She has written bestselling books about mysticism, spirituality, aliens and UFOs, but if she tries to discuss spaceships with Beatty, the conversation goes nowhere.

"Politics – yes. UFOs – no. He changes the subject," she said.

## LEARNING LIFE LESSONS FROM "DAVID"

MacLaine's 1983 book, *"Out on a Limb,"* which was later made into a TV miniseries in 1987, included a character named "David," who she claimed was a composite character.

On a shared visit to Peru recounted in *"Out on a Limb,"* David confesses to having actually met extraterrestrials, a revelation MacLaine finds threatening to her own belief system. Especially troubling is David's belief that he is in telepathic contact with an extraterrestrial woman he had met eight years before on an earlier trip to Peru. The alien female calls herself "the Mayan" and comes from the Pleiades star system; she has chosen David as a vessel to convey psycho-spiritual truths to one special person. David is commissioned to find this person, who will bring out these truths to the world in a book. MacLaine is the person, and what became *"Out on a Limb"* is the book.

Ironically, MacLaine, on first hearing David's ideas, thinks he is crazy. But she slowly acquiesces as David reveals more of the aliens' "truths."

"David talked about the unseen energies that the Pleiadians had learned to work with," she writes. "He called it the divine 'God-intelligence-force' and said the energy of that 'God-intelligence' and the human soul were made up of the same characteristics."

David continued by saying, "Technology without an understanding of God is destructive. Technology with an understanding of God is virtually unlimited. And everybody – each of us – in our own souls, in our own hearts, knows that. Because our heart, our soul, is a reflection of God. The divine force is what the

# SHIRLEY MACLAINE MEETS THE PLEIADIANS

soul is made of."

One component of MacLaine's composite "David" character is assumed to be adventurer and writer Charles A. Silva. It is Silva who journeyed to Peru with MacLaine in July 1977 and acted as her guide throughout.

"It was during this journey," Silva writes, "that she learned firsthand about the extraterrestrial connection."

One stop on their trip was the area around Lake Titicaca, where local folklore alluded to a lot of unusual and unexplained occurrences, like strange underground noises, lights and flying objects.

"Why do you suppose the space people chose this remote place in South America?" Shirley asked.

"Here," Silva replied, "they can fly undisturbed by radar and military aircraft. The natives are so used to it now that it doesn't even cause any excitement anymore."

"That's right," Shirley said, "The existence of flying objects is common knowledge. The people are so used to seeing these things. They laugh at all the scientists, astronomers and tourists who make their way up these mountains to search for UFOs."

Shirley pursued the subject of UFOs relentlessly wherever she and Silva went, talking to people from all walks of life. She encountered the same matter-of-fact attitude toward the UFOs everywhere the two visited. The well-known Inca ruins at Machu Picchu provided another interesting story for MacLaine to absorb, a story told by several people speaking excitedly all at once.

"In a place not too far from Cuzco, maybe thirty miles," an old man began, "there is a lake where several people claim to have seen a flying egg. They say it looked like two half watermelons placed against each other at their wide openings and was green in color."

"And it raised out of the water and came from the egg-like object," interrupted a teenager.

"Five smaller spheres, black in color, emerged," added another witness.

"They hovered for a few minutes and then flew out into space," yelled a tamale vendor.

Silva writes that, as he was translating the locals' story for MacLaine, she seemed to grow more and more mesmerized. It was most likely the moment when MacLaine's belief about the reality of the UFO phenomenon was being etched into the stone of her memory.

# SHIRLEY MACLAINE MEETS THE PLEIADIANS

Silva would go on to write two books. One is called *"Date With the Gods"* and deals with his close encounters with a female ET named Rama in Peru. The other is entitled *"Composite Characters,"* an obvious reference to his partially disguised role in *"Out on a Limb."* The title also reflects a falling out between Silva and MacLaine that happened when Silva wanted to be publicly credited with his role in helping MacLaine discover so many of the metaphysical truths she later wrote about.

## BILLY MEIER MEETS MACLAINE

MacLaine took very seriously the claims of Billy Meier, the Swiss contactee who has produced countless photos of UFOs he calls "beam ships." While the photos remain controversial and have been labeled as forgeries even by people within the UFO community, none of that did anything to faze MacLaine. That Meier was part of the composite character of "David" is a possibility since his story also stresses a belief in an alien race from the Pleiades nearly identical to Silva's as well as regular contact with an alien female.

Writers Lee and Brit Elders researched Meier for many years and in 1979 published a book called *"UFO: Contact from the Pleiades."*

MacLaine would write much later, in her 2007 book *"Sage-ing While Ageing,"* that she found Meier's case to be both credible and fascinating. She journeyed with the Elders to Meier's village of Hinderschmudruti in Switzerland in 1981.

"For about two weeks," she writes, "I listened to his stories about contact with the Pleiades. Billy had UFO contact when he was a child. He was a lonely and isolated child, beaten by his father and ignored by his mother. When he was first contacted out in a field, the craft landed and an older man descended who gave him encouragement and love. Now, as an adult, about twice a month at about 2 A.M. he would go out into the countryside for a craft contact."

MacLaine explained that she and the Elders didn't follow Meier when he went out to meet the craft because the Pleiadians did "mental frequency scans" on anyone who might be accompanying Meir to the meeting place.

"If they found out he was being followed," MacLaine writes, "they wouldn't be there when he arrived. We didn't want to be responsible for terminating a contact. Billy asked us not to follow him, and we respected that."

Meier said he was in regular communication with a Pleiadian woman named Semjase. As in many similar contactee accounts, she was beautiful, blonde and human-looking and delivered the standard warnings and consolations about Earth's future. Semjase told Meier that the human race is the "younger brothers"

# SHIRLEY MACLAINE MEETS THE PLEIADIANS

of the Pleiadians.

With her usual expression of sympathy, MacLaine writes that eventually Meier could no longer take the pressures and betrayals from his fellow human beings that came with the territory of being a contactee. He divorced his wife, who later contributed to a FOX TV documentary that attacked Meier's credibility.

"It was all very disappointing," MacLaine writes, "and a comment on what

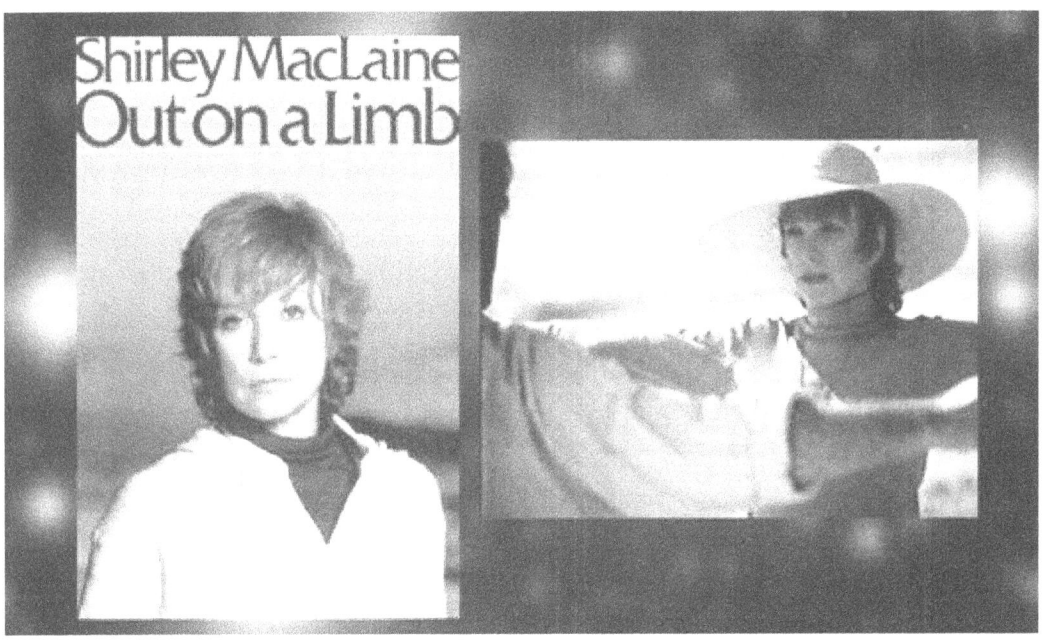

Ms. MacLaine with controversial Swiss "UFO Prophet" "Billy" Eduard Albert Meier.

# SHIRLEY MACLAINE MEETS THE PLEIADIANS

extraterrestrial material had in store for itself where human receptivity is concerned. I feel [Meier's case] is probably the most authentically researched case in modern UFO history."

## THE SYMPATHETIC EAR OF OPRAH WINFREY

In 2011, Oprah Winfrey's website published a summary of an interview with MacLaine in which the Hollywood legend talked frankly about UFOs appearing around her New Mexico property.

"I've seen a mothership here and I've seen them at my ranch," MacLaine said. "One famous day, a friend of mine was sitting in my hot tub out there and three UFOs came over and hovered over the hot tub for about ten minutes."

MacLaine told Winfrey that she believes extraterrestrials are attracted to the many crystals around New Mexico.

"Crystals amplify the consciousness," she explained. "They're attracted to that crystal amplification."

Although she has never seen an alien, she believes they have taught her that the soul does not die. "The soul is everlasting and its learning experience is lifetime after lifetime." For this reason, she never attends funerals, saying, "Nobody's dead, so why am I going to a funeral? You go to another level of understanding until you decide to come back to the schoolroom again – Earth. It could be that you decide to reincarnate on another planet. That's why we're so interested in star nations and extraterrestrials and so forth, because we've probably had experiences there and it's in our memory system."

MacLaine's beliefs about UFOs, aliens and reincarnation have earned her a fair share of critics, but she reiterated that, "I never had the urge to please anybody. I don't know where that came from."

"It comes from a tremendous sense of your own self-worth," Oprah replied supportively.

To which MacLaine answered, "I felt very comfortable being alone. That's why I live alone now. That's why I never had a conventional marriage. That's why I loved to travel alone."

With such a claimed hubbub of alien life around her, one can only wonder what "alone" really means in MacLaine's terms.

# SHIRLEY MACLAINE MEETS THE PLEIADIANS

## DID RUSSELL CROWE PHOTOGRAPH A UFO?

In March 2013, Oscar-winning actor Russell Crowe posted, or "tweeted," possible photos of a UFO taken above the Royal Botanic Gardens in Sydney, Australia.

The pictures were put together in a video uploaded on YouTube and were  originally part of some time-lapse photography Crowe and a friend set up to capture fruit bats. Crowe's agent in Australia told an Australian news website that the photos were actually taken four years prior and he was unsure why Crowe decided to tweet them when he did.

The YouTube video shows a series of three timed exposures with a flat red light moving across the frame. Crowe said the pictures were taken by a camera – a Canon 5D with no flash, to be precise – that was set up on the balcony of his office in the Sydney suburb of Woolloomooloo Bay. (Yes, all those "o's" are the correct spelling.) When the UFO showed up on the film and not the intended fruit bats, Crowe said, "This was a big surprise."

Some commenters quickly speculated that the UFO was nothing more than reflections from a light, perhaps a beacon on a sailboat that was passing through nearby Woolloomooloo Bay. But Crowe defended the images on technical grounds. He argued that "The camera is on a balcony, not behind glass," so the image was not caused by a reflection. He answered another critic by saying that the image "can't be a lens flare because it moves and the camera is fixed."

Crowe says further that the YouTube video was made after the fact utilizing still photos. "It's not [originally] a video, it is three time-lapse photos in 4.5 seconds. I will grant you that at the time the music wasn't playing. Also, yes, we have pushed in on the frame. This is three photos in order, nothing added."

It was speculated that Crowe was attempting a publicity stunt to jumpstart interest in his newest movie at the time, a crime drama called **"Broken City"** that was faring poorly with audiences and critics. What he actually received, however, was the usual ridicule for his efforts in making the UFO photos public. Meanwhile, **"Broken City"** would go on to bomb at the box office, recouping much less than its $35 million dollar production costs.

# SHIRLEY MACLAINE MEETS THE PLEIADIANS

## ROBIN LEACH'S LITTLE KNOWN UFO-RIA

What study of UFOs and celebrities would be complete without mention of Robin Leach of the former long-running television series *"Lifestyles of the Rich and Famous"?* In a November 2011 article from the website of the *"Huffington Post,"* written by Lee Speigel, Leach talks openly about what he still thought of as a taboo topic when it came to the celebrities Leach interviewed.

"UFOs are something that has interested me from way back in England as a newspaper reporter," Leach told Speigel. "And a good friend of mine, Buzz Aldrin, the second man on the moon, has told me stories of astronauts coming back to Earth and reporting UFOs. Now, UFOs doesn't necessarily mean little green men in Martian suits. But there are things that go on in space up there in the sky that cannot be explained."

Speigel makes reference to a rainy night in 1976 when he and Leach went UFO hunting in Maine after hearing stories of local citizens spotting strange nocturnal lights in the sky. They saw nothing in the way of flying saucers, but Speigel reports he had to keep reminding Leach to watch the road and not the sky as Leach drove them through the rain-soaked countryside.

"I think, secretly, we both hoped we'd be abducted," Leach said. "I have met some very strange people and some very strange cats – and I'm not talking about jazz greats. I'm talking about animals that people claim have come from outer space and, boy, they're weird."

But over the decades that Leach has globe-hopped in search of the perfect celebrity interview, he hasn't talked much about his attraction to UFOs.

"I haven't ever really raised the subject with celebrities," he admitted, "probably because they'd think I was weird and mad. But we do know that, over the years, everybody from presidents of the United States to major dignitaries around the world, and, certainly, some of our NASA space boys – they have claimed to have seen and photographed unexplained flying objects or phenomena."

# SHIRLEY MACLAINE MEETS THE PLEIADIANS

## WAS PRESIDENT OBAMA ONLY JOKING?

In March, 2015, when President Barack Obama appeared on the talk show *"Jimmy Kimmel Live,"* Kimmel put some questions to him that elicited what many felt were cryptic responses that could be interpreted as jokes on the one hand but might be "disclosure" of a kind on the other. As he had previously with former President Bill Clinton, Kimmel asked Obama if he had ever looked into Area 51 and UFOs in general.

Kimmel broached the topic to Obama by saying that if he were president, the first thing he would do is immediately look into what the government knows about Area 51 and UFOs in general. Obama replied that this is why Kimmel will never be president. Kimmel then asked if Obama had ever looked into the subject.

"The aliens won't let that happen," Obama said. "You will reveal all their secrets. They exercise strict control over us."

Kimmel warned Obama that people were going to look at his facial expressions and analyze every move as he answered these questions, to which Obama responded, "I can't reveal anything." Kimmel told the president that Clinton has told him Clinton's own investigation had revealed nothing.

Obama answered, "That is what we are instructed to say."

That was the extent of the extraterrestrial discussion. Writing on the *"Open Minds"* website, Alejandro Rojas says that reading the transcript without watch-

## SHIRLEY MACLAINE MEETS THE PLEIADIANS

ing the video makes the conversation sound "somewhat ominous," adding that, "I am sure some people will take this as a confirmation that aliens are controlling the government. However, Kimmel and Obama were smiling and laughing the whole time. Kimmel certainly felt the President was joking and seemed to find his responses quite funny."

Rojas reminds his readers of an earlier moment when Obama seemed to be joking about aliens. A few years prior to the Kimmel appearance, actor Will Smith took his family for a visit to the White House. While in the Situation Room, Smith's son, Jaden, asked the president if aliens were real. Jaden told *"Wonderland Magazine"*: "I talked to President Obama about extraterrestrials. He said he could neither confirm nor deny the existence of aliens, which means they're real. If people think we're the only people that live in this universe, then something is wrong with them."

Obama also cracked a few jokes with MacLaine during the annual Kennedy Honors reception in 2013, making reference to the notorious Area 51 – the Nevada installation where the government is allegedly storing UFOs and alien life.

"Now, when you first become president," Obama said, "one of the questions that people ask you is, 'What's really going on at Area 51?' When I wanted to know, I'd call Shirley MacLaine. I think I just became the first president to ever publicly mention Area 51. How's that, Shirley?"

*"TIME Magazine"* later reported: "The president couldn't resist the opportunity to joke about the decades of conspiracy theories surrounding mysterious lights and aliens at the Nevada installation. The official use for the Nevada Test and Training Range and Groom Lake is far less otherworldly."

# SHIRLEY MACLAINE MEETS THE PLEIADIANS

In still another incident of what might be called "presidential joking," Steven Spielberg was invited to the White House in 1982 to screen his movie *"ET: The Extraterrestrial"* with President Ronald Reagan. Spielberg says that after the movie was shown, Reagan stood up and said, "I wanted to thank you for bringing 'ET' to the White House. We really enjoyed your movie. And there are a number of people in this room who know that everything on that screen is absolutely true."

Spielberg says the room erupted in laughter. When asked whether he thought Reagan was joking or not, Spielberg said, "I'm a little bit of a UFOlogist. I was hoping that there was something more to the joke than met my eye. I'm sorry to say I think he was simply trying to tell a joke."

In that same 2007 presidential debate, referred to earlier in this chapter, in which Dennis Kucinich squeamishly answered Tim Russert's question about the sighting Kucinich had at Shirley MacLaine's house, a similar question was put to Obama. Russert asked the future president if he believed in life on other planets.

Obama, who has always given every indication that he has no interest in UFOs, answered Russert by saying, "You know, I don't know. And I don't presume to know. What I know is there is life here on Earth, and that we're not attending to life here on Earth."

## UFO REFERENCES IN ROCK LYRICS

The man who is generally acknowledged to be the greatest lyricist in the history of rock and roll, Bob Dylan, has never publicly stated that he has sighted a UFO, met any aliens or believes in intelligent life elsewhere. But like so many a pop culture poet, one can find references even to alien abduction in Dylan's lyrics that may not have been "consciously" inspired but were instead a response to abduction experiences that were wiped clean and replaced by what alien abduction researcher Budd Hopkins called "screen memories." Hopkins also called the phenomenon an alien-imposed "merciful amnesia" designed to minimize the trauma of meeting creatures from another world.

One obvious example comes from Dylan's 1965 smash hit, *"Mr. Tambourine Man."* Dylan sings, "Take me on a trip upon your magic, swirling ship. My senses have been stripped, my hands can't feel to grip, my toes too numb to step." The lines seem to eloquently express a willingness to be an abductee, to freely enter the swirling ship that is a UFO, even as the singer experiences the disorientation of his senses being "stripped" and the physical helplessness of his hands that "can't feel to grip."

# SHIRLEY MACLAINE MEETS THE PLEIADIANS

The band The Byrds might have been "Eight Miles High" when they performed "Hey, Mr. Spaceman."

Some musical comrades of Dylan, the folk-rock group The Byrds, conveyed a similar willingness to cooperate with aliens in their song **"Hey, Mr. Spaceman."** "Please take me along," they sing, "I won't do anything wrong. Won't you please take me along for a ride?"

In both instances the writers can be seen as expressing a common emotion among abductees. It is often found that, while most abductees find the experience traumatic to some degree or another, they also develop feelings of attachment for their alien abductors and come to "miss" them when they're gone. This longing for the aliens to return is one facet of the many complex emotions abductees feel as they struggle to come to terms with what is happening to them.

These and other alien-inspired lyrics are another example of celebrity contact with UFOs. And although it is more of an "implied contact" than something more overt, it nevertheless serves the cultural programming intended to prepare the world for more open contact, as was explained at the beginning of this chapter.

# SHIRLEY MACLAINE MEETS THE PLEIADIANS

We get the "coming of the aliens" message from TV, movies and popular culture in general all the time. From Shirley MacLaine to Russell Crowe to a joking President Obama to classic rock lyrics that are now 50 years old, UFOs are indeed maneuvering "among the stars" on many levels. Their message, as delivered by so many celebrities in so many ways, forecasts the inevitable – and inescapable – appearance on the world scene of an alien force who has given us all plenty of fair warning.

# SHIRLEY MACLAINE MEETS THE PLEIADIANS

**SOURCES FOR THIS CHAPTER**

"Mysteries and Haunts of the Mojave Desert – Secrets of Death Valley," the chapter called "The Hollywood Stars Are Big and Bright and So Are ALL the UFOs!" by Timothy Green Beckley.

"Review of Shirley MacLaine's 'Sage-ing While Age-ing,'" by Alan Stanfield.

"Shirley MacLaine Enters 'The No Spin Zone' to Talk with Bill about UFOs," November 19, 2007, Fox News Website.

"The Day You Have Been Waiting For – Disclosure," by Grant Cameron, October 15, 2012, Presidential UFO website.

"Was an ALIEN Responsible for Reagan's Presidency?" The Daily Mail (a UK newspaper), September 18, 2012.

A review of "Out on a Limb," author unknown, May 1, 2003, the website at: www.believersweb.org/view.cfm?ID=659.

"Jim Nichols, UFO Art," the website at: www.thewebmatrix.net/jimnicholsufo/message.html

"Art, Life and UFOs: A Memoir," by Budd Hopkins, Anomalist Books, 2009.

"UFOs: Generals, Pilots and Government Officials Go On the Record," Leslie Kean, Harmony Books, 2010.

"Hollywood Legend Shirley MacLaine," interview with Oprah Winfrey, April 11, 2011, the website at: www.oprah.com/oprahshow/Hollywood-Legend-Shirley-MacLaine

"The Mysteries of Laguna De Huaypo," by Charles A. Silva, the website at: www.unicusmagazine.com/html/15/silva15.htm

"Russell Crowe's UFO Sighting Explained," by Eric Pfeiffer, the Sideshow on Yahoo.com blogs.

"Russell Crowe Tweets UFO Pics from Sydney," by Alejandro Rojas, March 7, 2013, "Open Minds" website at www.openminds.tv

"Russell Crowe Claims He Saw a UFO, Posts Snapshots Online," by Jordan

## SHIRLEY MACLAINE MEETS THE PLEIADIANS

Zakarin, March 6, 2013, "The Hollywood Reporter."

"Russell Crowe's UFO Video Explained," March 6, 2013, "Cosmic Log" at NBC News website.

"Robin Leach on UFO Hunting and 'Lifestyles of the Rich and Famous,'" by Lee Speigel, November 4, 2011, the "Huffington Post" website.

"Obama Talks Area 51, UFOs and Aliens with Jimmy Kimmel," by Alejandro Rojas, March 13, 2015, "Open Minds" website.

"Obama Makes History – Mentions Area 51," by David Jackson, December 9, 2013, the website of "UFO Today."

Shirley MacLaine has a website at www.shirleyMacLaine.com

# SHIRLEY MACLAINE MEETS THE PLEIADIANS

Mike Farrell of "MASH" fame gave UFOs some credence after hosting the nationally syndicated program "UFO Cover-Up...Live." Broadcast from Washington, D.C., the 2-hour telecast from LBS Communications included startling testimony by government officials regarding UFO phenomena and alien contacts, including a live segment from Russia and interviews with those talking about a crash landing of a space ship just outside the town of Roswell, New Mexico.

# SHIRLEY MACLAINE MEETS THE PLEIADIANS

## SIGHTINGS AMONG THE STARS

Not all UFO sightings are made by "ordinary people." Some very famous individuals have seen them and had their lives changed.

Based upon first-hand interviews and casual social contact, the author reveals the often-startling influence these "otherworldly" powers have had on the world's best known celebrities, musicians, sports figures.

If you think that only the whacky and the weird – the "fruit loops" of society – believe in, or see, UFOs, you're sadly mistaken, good friend.

The truth of the matter is that observations of odd and unusual objects that dart and coast about in the sky – as well as hover above our ego-inflated heads – have been made by good folks from all walks of life.

In the course of my investigations as editor of various nationally-distributed UFO publications, pilots, astronauts, doctors, housewives and hobos, who have absolutely nothing else in common, other than that they have been caught up in what can only be classified as a truly OUT OF THIS WORLD fever, have told me their stories.

A good portion of the "weird things" that have been sighted in the sky can hardly be defined as a "craft," as we might make reference to a physical, nuts-and-bolts spaceship. A lot of what people see are dazzling streaks of light, floating and brightly glowing globs, as well as a host of other unexplained phenomena that end up loosely being termed UFOs. But then let's admit it – most of us are not astronomers and it's damn easy to mistake a conventional object seen at times under very unconventional conditions.

Now, on the other hand, if somebody says they've seen a silvery disk land in front of them and creatures get out ... well, the possibility is that they've either hallucinated the whole affair, are among the world's biggest liars, or they may simply be telling the truth pretty much as they perceive it to be.

To be frank, if you're a non-believer (and about fifty percent of the population still is), chances are that nothing I say is going to assure you that aliens are here (other, perhaps, than shaking hands with a web-fingered ET yourself).

# SHIRLEY MACLAINE MEETS THE PLEIADIANS

Likewise, if you're a true believer, I don't have to spend my time trying to convince you of anything, because you probably already know that we were invaded from outer space just about this time last week.

Thus, don't expect me to try and sway your vote one way or another, because under the Constitution, you're entitled to believe just about any damn thing you please. What I wish to do, instead, is take you backstage to hear what the celebrities – those trendsetters whom we love to read about so much – have to say regarding the subject of UFOs and ETs.

As a stringer, off and on over the years, for those ever-sensational "supermarket tabloids," I've had the glorious opportunity to quiz the famous on a variety of matters – and because of my own personal interest in the matter, there has hardly been an occasion when the subject of unidentified flying objects hasn't popped up. Naturally some of these celebrities and pop stars I interviewed thought I was absolutely crazy and quickly changed the subject (or booted me out of their dressing room in extreme cases), while a sizable percentage had a personal sighting or even a close encounter of their very own to reveal.

Most of the stories in this book have been captured firsthand, though a few are based upon secondhand testimony, and are clearly labeled as such.

One last matter:

Just because someone is rich and famous doesn't make them any better or more perceptive than you or me. It simply means that their story carries a bit more weight because of the influence they have. Let's face it, their account is more likely to make the front page of "The Enquirer" than our experience would!

So put on your space gear, strap yourself in and get ready to be put into flying saucer overdrive.

If nothing else, it's likely to be a journey through the universe of stars you'll never forget.

Timothy Green Beckley

# SHIRLEY MACLAINE MEETS THE PLEIADIANS

## ANTHONY HOPKINS PHILOSOPHICALLY PROFESSES:
## "WE ARE NOT ALONE!"

At the time we interviewed Academy Award winner Anthony Hopkins backstage at the Plymouth Theatre on Broadway, he was still being compared to Richard Burton.

Anthony Hopkins looks like he might have seen a ufo...CLOSE UP!

That would obviously be before he was cast as Hannibal Lector. Not only was the then 37-year-old actor born in the same small Welsh town as his talented show business predecessor, but admirers claimed that Hopkins' manner and speech were closely reminiscent of a young Burton. And, in addition, there were several other strange parallels in the two men's careers, including breathtaking performances by both in "Hamlet" and other Shakespeare plays.

But now that Hopkins has walked away with an Oscar for "Silence of the Lambs," there is no reason to compare him to Burton or anyone else as he's more than able – and has been for many years – to stand on his very own two feet in the entertainment arena.

A deeply philosophical person, Hopkins freely admits that he hasn't read that much about UFOs to comment on the possible arrival of spaceships and aliens, but he is smart enough to realize that the universe must be teeming with life in all manner, shape and form. Feeling that a philosophical beginning to this book is necessary (perhaps to counterbalance the sometimes "wild nature" of most UFO claims), we draw upon this celebrity's wisdom to begin our journey into the almost limitless bounds of time and space.

# SHIRLEY MACLAINE MEETS THE PLEIADIANS

"It's really a mathematical certainty that we are not alone," confirms Hopkins. "It would be a fundamental, lonely joke to think that we're the only ones in the universe. The vastness of the universe alone tells us something. By using fundamental logic we can safely and mathematically assume that there must be millions and millions of forms of civilizations – civilized life – and that some of these may be highly advanced. I think it's a high probability – not just a possibility. Otherwise, what the hell is it all about, unless the whole thing is an illusion?"

Expanding on the idea that we create our own reality, Hopkins notes that, "Bertram Russell once said that the stars are in our minds. It's either this is reality or you have to take the non-rationalist dream that life is a total illusion; that what we presume is a fact is but a fiction of life. If we don't accept that this is a total illusion, we then must presume it is for real, that materialism is materialism as we understand it, and that we really are touching this table top.

"Therefore," concludes Hopkins, "we must be surrounded in our galaxy alone with thousands of forms of life."

Going a step further, Hopkins was asked if he personally believed such alien lifeforms might have stopped by for a visit at least sometime in the past. His answer shows a bit of bewilderment as to how such visitations could take place on such a frequent basis. This is a question often posed by hard-nosed UFO skeptics, but one that Hopkins himself manages to answer when he brings up the idea of other realities.

"In my opinion, writers like the fellow who did 'Chariots of the Gods?' are a bit too spectacular in their claims. But, I think it was Einstein who said that it is possible that we have been visited by superhuman beings. We don't know, maybe they exist in a different space-time continuum. Otherwise how could they get here from the nearest other star system that is four and a half light years away?"

Well, Anthony, believe it or not, at least several of your fellow actor friends will have some additional theories and explanations for this "problem" in the pages that are to follow.

# SHIRLEY MACLAINE MEETS THE PLEIADIANS

William Shatner cut a handsome intergalactic figure as Captain Kirk on the original "Star Trek" series.

## WILLIAM SHATNER'S AMAZING COSMIC CONNECTION

A good many of us are beginning to realize that just because something appears in print doesn't necessarily make it true.

Many moons ago, one of the weekly tabloids printed a supposedly first-person interview with William Shatner. They made it sound as if the conversation was a recent one held between the famed movie-stage-TV personality and the head of a local, New York-based UFO club (who shall go nameless since he simply craves recognition and hardly deserves any). In actuality, this interview was "bogus" to the degree that this self-professed UFO "expert" never met the celebrity in question but was simply quoting from one of the few in-depth interviews "The Star" has ever given on the controversial topic of UFOs. It so happens that the conversation was really held with this author backstage at the Ed Sullivan Theater (now the Ritz) in New York, while Shatner was taping a segment of Dick Clark's "Ten Thousand Dollar Pyramid" game show, broadcast daily in those days.

At the time of our chat, I was publishing a now-defunct (it only lasted two issues) science fiction newspaper entitled, appropriately enough, "Tomorrow." I had previously seen a brief clipping dealing with Shatner's UFO encounter and was anxious to obtain all the details I could in what I realized might be the once-

# SHIRLEY MACLAINE MEETS THE PLEIADIANS

in-a-lifetime opportunity to speak personally with one of "Star Trek's" original players.

Though there were many highlights, the big "bombshell" came when Shatner began to unfold a spine-tingling, real-life episode that he has always been rather reluctant to talk about. What he revealed not only placed the actor among the ranks of several million other North American citizens (Shatner is Canadian by birth) who have reported sightings of otherworldly craft, but in this instance possibly even a close contact with extraterrestrial intelligence as well.

Shatner repeatedly emphasized that he has no axe to grind when it comes to UFOs. He made it clear to me that he is not a "flying saucer buff," and he even seemed to go out of his way to play down what happened to him. But, with further questioning, the details gradually emerged, and he was re-enacting his weird brush with death and unearthly powers on the burning sands of California's Mojave Desert.

Shatner first broached the topic upon my bringing up the name of Erich von Daniken, since he had narrated a documentary based on the ancient astronaut theory. The following is a word-for-word transcript of that part of our conversation dealing with UFOs.

SHATNER: Erich von Daniken has definitely caused a great deal of curiosity by speculating that extraterrestrials – or ancient astronauts, as he refers to them – visited our tiny planet in ancient times. I've always tried to disparage this type of thought, although my interest is as intense as anyone else's, because of various factors inherent in the world today. Many of the things Mr. von Daniken writes

## SHIRLEY MACLAINE MEETS THE PLEIADIANS

about are the unexplained mysteries. We don't know, even with our advanced technology, how the pyramids were built or what caused man to suddenly start writing 5,000 years ago. I won't enumerate the puzzles of the universe, for they are almost countless, and they intrigue me as they would any thinking person.

BECKLEY: Reports of UFOs – flying saucers – have continually popped up in the national press. A recent survey conducted by the Gallup Poll showed that fifty-one percent of the American people now believe in the existence of such objects. In fact, some eleven percent – over fifteen million individuals – say they have seen "something" in the heavens that they cannot readily identify. Do you give any credence to these accounts?

SHATNER: I'll tell you a story that happened to me and is open to any kind of interpretation you wish. This experience is the subject of a half-hour film that may or may not eventually be released.

In the late '60s, when "Star Trek" was on, there were a lot of UFOs being sighted in the desert near Palmdale, California. We heard all kinds of stories about these objects, craft, spaceships – call them what you will. There was even one fellow who said he talked with creatures from space.

During this period, I used to drive my motorcycle a great deal and would occasionally head for the wide-open span of sand and sun. With my sense of humor, I'd say to myself, "Well, if I were a little green man in a flying saucer and wanted to get publicity" – which is what they would seem to be seeking – "who would I contact faster than Captain Kirk of the Star Ship Enterprise?" It was kind of a gag I played on myself, but in a half-serious fashion. I would catch myself looking up in the air and wondering if they were capable of picking up such thoughts.

Real or imagined — this is the dirt bike Shatner rode while being stalked by a UFO under the hot desert sun.

BECKLEY: In other words, you're trying to tell us you were sending telepathic messages to UFOs.

# SHIRLEY MACLAINE MEETS THE PLEIADIANS

SHATNER: Remember, you said that – I didn't! I was simply looking into the sky. Okay? One day I was out driving with four other guys, around noon, that's the hottest part of the day in the desert, when I hit a hole and fell from my bike. I must have fainted when the bike collapsed on top of me. When I came to, I estimate that I was unconscious for only about a minute, I couldn't get my motorcycle started. The motor refused to "turn over." To this day, I don't know what caused the problem, but she wouldn't move an inch.

So here I am in the middle of the desert with a metal helmet on, wearing a leather jacket, heavy pants, boots and a machine next to me worth close to five

Shatner has encountered UFOs before — at least while narrating the doc drama "Mystery of the Gods."

thousand dollars. Maybe it was greed – although that's silly, because who's going to steal your bike in the middle of the desert? But in the confusion caused by the heat and the smack on the head, I couldn't make up my mind whether I should leave behind my cycle or not. In addition, I found myself taking my helmet off and putting it back on. I must have done this at least five times. It was a question in my mind of keeping it on and suffering from heat prostration, or removing it and getting sunstroke. You must remember that the temperature out there was well within the range of killing a human being. It was like being in a blazing oven.

This may all seem a bit idiotic now. Sensibly, I should have dropped the bike, taken off my heavy helmet and wrapped the shirt I was wearing over my head to block out the sun's deadly rays. Of course, when you're under this much tension, this much pressure, you don't always draw sane conclusions.

When the bike fell on top of me, it provided my prostrate form with a life-giving shade. As I came to – and this is where the story begins to get crazy – I thought I saw and heard something. After that, I didn't feel as weak and dehydrated any longer.

BECKLEY: What was this "thing" you thought you saw? Can you give us a better description?

SHATNER: Putting this into simple words is not easily done. Basically it was like when you have a nightmare and you feel something crawling over your body or wrestling with you. As you awaken from the dream, it turns out your blanket

# SHIRLEY MACLAINE MEETS THE PLEIADIANS

was the thing crawling over you. In other words, it was more of a sensing – a feeling – a shadowy phantom. All I know, positively, is that I suddenly felt better.

As I said, when I came to I couldn't get the bike to move. No matter what I did it refused to start. Finally, I tried pushing it up a hill, but it wouldn't go in that direction. Then I turned around and decided to go down the hill, but it still wouldn't budge. Nor did it obey my command to turn left. Eventually, I shoved it to the right and it began to move as though it was going someplace on its own. By this time I was doing what I was feeling. One could say I was doing what I was told to, but I was just doing the easiest possible thing.

Fantastic as it may seem, the motorcycle appeared to have a way of going on its own. At this point I thought I saw somebody – another cyclist – in the distance waving me on, and so I continued to struggle with the heavy metal monster until I stumbled upon civilization in the form of a gas station in the middle of the desert, resting at the side of an old paved road.

It was then that, off in the distance, I saw an object glistening in the heavens. I don't know if it was a flying saucer. I can't state for certain it wasn't. Please get this correct. I don't claim that I was led out of the desert by some mysterious force. All I've told you are just the facts.

BECKLEY: One question. Why did your pals – the guys you were riding with – leave you behind? Obviously, they must have realized you weren't riding with them anymore.

SHATNER: This is another eerie part of the episode, something I can't fully account for myself. As a bit of an explanation, we had been riding using the old buddy system, everybody looking out for the guy behind. Somewhere along the way, our cycle pack was joined by a fifth person – a stranger – who had obviously been wandering in the desert alone, something he should never have been doing, as the desert air can be as hostile as the surface of the moon.

So this fellow joins our ranks, pulling into line behind me. I guess when the third cyclist – the rider in front of me – turned and looked back over his shoulder and saw our "friend," he must have figured it was me. To him, four riders meant four riders. It was just not part of his awareness that someone else had linked up with us.

I understand they later looked around and this "stranger" was gone. Finally, someone said, "Where's Shatner?" Well, Shatner was back quite a few miles, burning up from the 110-degree heat and trying, unsuccessfully, to get his vehicle started.

BECKLEY: Do you think this "stranger" who joined the pack and later van-

# SHIRLEY MACLAINE MEETS THE PLEIADIANS

ished is the same fellow you saw off in the distance waving you on in the direction of safety?

SHATNER: I have no evidence that he was. I can't say for certain he wasn't.

BECKLEY: You've hedged a couple of times in telling us this story. Although you don't claim you saw a flying saucer or were guided to civilization by ESP, you are nonetheless leaving this open as a possibility.

SHATNER: It's possible that's what happened – merely one of the explanations. I don't wish to go overboard. Better to understate something of this nature. However, the whole experience was real enough and happened as I've told you. I will let you make the interpretations.

## WILLIAM SHATNER'S "WEIRD OR WHAT?" ASKS ME FOR VERIFICATION OF ALIEN CORPSE

And now we need to teleport ahead 400 light years (OK, let's settle for 4 decades) and a phone call I received from a production company representing "Captain Kirk" and a new TV series he was hosting. They were "longing" for me to go on his "Weird Or What?" show to proclaim a certain "little fellow" caught in a claw trap in Mexico as an extraterrestrial whose life had been snuffed out while visiting here.

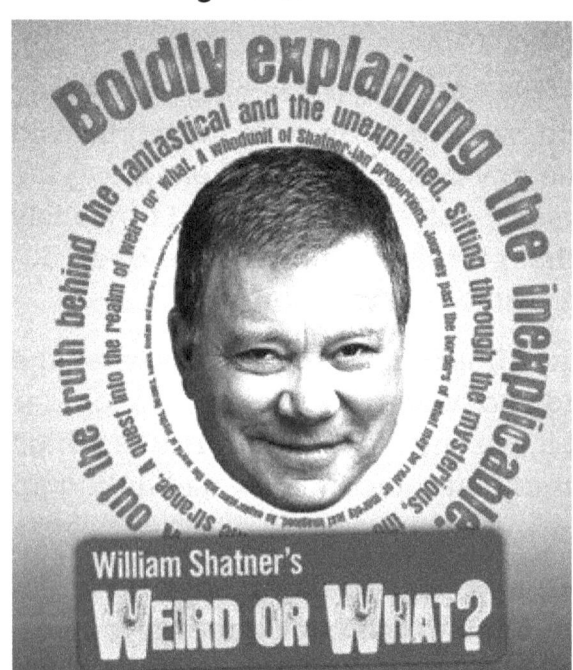

On an episode of "Weird Or What?" author Tim Beckley tried to convince WS that a suspected alien caught in a trap in Mexico was in reality a shape-shifting Djinn.

As far as the "aliens" go, I prefer to identify them as Ultra-Terrestrials because none of us can be certain of their true origins. Yes! Some could be legitimate ETs, but we have no definite way of proving this theory, so it's each to their own when it comes to verification. Regardless of their home stomping ground, we can't deny they have been cunning, cagey and crafty. We can't believe for one minute what they tell us, because they seem to change their modus operandi and personal narrative with every single close encounter. In addition, who can accept as gospel the word of any being that can shape-shift in front of our eyes? From an alien to a gnome in less than sixty seconds does not built up confidence. In the course of my UFOlogical career I have seen and heard just about everything.

# SHIRLEY MACLAINE MEETS THE PLEIADIANS

I am never amazed anymore at the bizarre claims that I have to deal with. They come to me either directly from those involved or from what I consider to be credible sources. As editor of such publications as "UFO Review" and "UFO Universe," there has been such a continuous stream of raw data that I now possess file cabinet after file cabinet crammed with all sorts of information of varying quality.

Today there is a multitude of postings on the Internet pertaining to UFOs, but as far as I am concerned there is no way of checking on the validity of these incidents. In the "old days," we relied a lot on the mass media – both local and international – for information. And usually as much effort as possible was put into authenticating the story before it was printed. You at least knew the individuals mentioned in the clippings were not a figment of the imagination of some editor over at "The Weekly World News," a tabloid that regularly lampooned the subject even if some gullible readers didn't realize they were being put on.

Caught in a trap – Djinn or alien? Shatner tries to sort out the facts in an episode of "Weird Or What?" featuring Tim Beckley.

Even if I say so myself, "THE AUTHENTIC BOOK OF ULTRA-TERRESTRIAL CONTACT" contains some of the best reports and encounters that fascinate me the most. They are as spine-tingling to me now as they were when they originally appeared in print. They were clipped out of newspapers most of us have never heard of and sent to me by a legion of associates worldwide. Very few other researchers possessed the network of freelance stringers that I did. Though it's gotten more difficult to verify some stories because of the unanimity of the World Wide Web, I do my best to maintain a certain standard before I will say I absolutely believe in something. Reiterating, I received a call from a Toronto-based production company. CINEFLIX is the outfit behind "William Shatner's Weird Or What?," a paranormal "fact or fiction" show that was in its third season, originally only airing on the History Channel Canada before landing a slot on the U.S. side of the border.

As I've already said, initially I met Shatner backstage at Dick Clark's "$10,000 Pyramid" game show sometime in the 1970s. William Alan Shatner is a Canadian actor, musician, recording artist, author and film director whom just about everyone adores. He has a charming sense of humor and a down-to-earth,

# SHIRLEY MACLAINE MEETS THE PLEIADIANS

charismatic personality. Over the years, Bill and I have shared a mutual friendship and I even spent an hour in jail due to a misunderstanding of the hilarious kind. The unprovoked incident took place while Shatner was performing with a philharmonic orchestra inside in the world famous Madison Square Garden arena. The circumstances that surround this story are too complex to go into right now and are not relevant to the matter at hand anyway. But it still causes a chuckle or two whenever I relate the circumstances around this "misdemeanor" – at the time – not so uproarious episode. I can say this much for sure – Bill loves a challenge. He is not above doing almost anything to cause a stir and to draw attention to his performance art, even if it might seem a bit hokey or silly to some. "Captain Kirk" is as fascinating in real life as he obviously was to millions of adoring fans who remember him from the "Star Trek" days of his career. He always has been hard-pressed to say "no" to any opportunity presented to him, even if it requires him to recite poetry or to record a selection of his favorite songs, including "Rocket Man" and "Bohemian Rhapsody." In order to set the stage for my recent invitation to appear on "William Shatner's Weird Or What?" I have to turn back the clock to our initial meeting. I was working at the time as a freelancer for several of the national tabloids including the "Enquirer," the "Star" and the somewhat seamier scandal sheet known as "Midnight." This was in the days before having to stalk a celebrity to get a good story was required by such publications. I met dozens of well-known personalities and on a more or less equal basis. Some of them wanted to hear all about UFOs and the paranormal as much as I wanted to hear about their careers.

The "Star Trek" stalwart, as noted, wanted to tell me about his UFO experience as a means, I suspect, of trying to break out of the Trekkie rut as far as speaking with a journalist goes. And so we arranged to meet in the heart of Manhattan, just off of Hell's Kitchen.

Shatner began his now famous UFO narrative "I'll tell you a story that happened to me, and is open to any kind of interpretation you wish," Shatner began. The story he told me was to become his often-quoted epic encounter with a spaceship that he felt at the time had nothing to do with his having been a character in a weekly televised science fiction series.

The rest of the story is a part of history. People have asked me for years if I thought Bill was talking about a legit encounter or was he making the entire episode up? And if so, why did I fall for it so easily? I've always explained to those who will kindly remove the wax from their ears that it was a celebrity story and was not meant to be a high-profile, peer-reviewed paper. No lie detector tests were administered, no documentation was sought. End of case.

Though I apparently was Shatner's prime target to relate this experience

## SHIRLEY MACLAINE MEETS THE PLEIADIANS

to, because he knew it was going to appear before the "Enquirer's" almost three million readers in those days, I know he repeated this extraordinary tale numerous times to other interested parties.

Some critics may say that Shatner created this account for the sake of publicity. If Bill says it's so now, no reason to doubt him. Publicity is good when you're an actor on a TV series that has been yanked off the air and are looking to expand your horizons.

I got chastised numerous times for accepting his story at face value. I was always quick to point out that I was not on assignment to seek testimony from a pilot or a police officer, nor was it necessary to conduct a polygraph examination. This was more or less an entertainment piece, not a scientific inquiry, and so I let it go at that. Did his potentially lifesaving UFO experience really happen, or can we put it down as an urban legend of the Mojave Desert told by one of the most entertaining actors of our time?

Shatner intimated during a TV interview that he had concocted the entire incident, I would surmise – as stated – to get some non-"Star Trek" media attention, as all celebrities must garner some form of publicity if they are to stay at the top of their game. I have been asked if I am offended that Shatner "took advantage" of the situation and used me in effect as a patsy to grab the limelight and possibly boost his "ratings" among UFO fans, who are not usually all that thrilled by "Star Trek" and science fiction in general? Not at all! It was a wonderful story and it paid my overdue electric bill at the time, I am sure. Like I say, there was no call for a close scrutiny of the events Bill Shatner related. But it seemed to be a well thought out story; still, Bill is an actor and that's what good actors do best – create believable stories that will live on (like Shakespeare?).

### DEAD MICRO MINI "ALIEN" CAUGHT IN TRAP BY MEXICAN FARMER – "WEIRD OR WHAT?" WILLIAM SHATNER WANTS TO KNOW

But now let's speed up and time travel ahead to the present day. Somehow CINEFLIX got wind of what they thought would be a great story to dramatize as part of Shatner's series for the Canadian counterpart of the History Channel. The Canadian cable outlet airs some of the same shows that the History Channel in the U.S. does, but they also have original programming of their own which CINEFLIX produces a great deal of, and very adequately, I might add. I spent three days in Toronto as we went over every minute detail of what we were going to film. If it were Major Donald Keyhoe, he might have flipped out (like he did on "The Armstrong Circle Theater") because, though the show was not "scripted," we did have certain parameters to work within. It was my old friend, Joshua P. Warren, host of "Speaking of Strange" – broadcast every Saturday night out of Ashville, N.C. – who originally hooked me up with the Toronto production company that

# SHIRLEY MACLAINE MEETS THE PLEIADIANS

was looking for "someone in authority" to confirm the legitimacy of a tiny creature caught by a Mexican farmer in a large animal trap that had been dubbed "an alien space baby" by the easily excited and emotional press in that country. I remembered that Josh had talked about this "remarkable" finding on the "Dark 30 Hour" portion of his show and had posted a picture of the alien baby on his website www.SpeakingOfStrange.com. Josh is a real character, a true showman, and so it's hard to define "real" in his world. Josh is a filmmaker, like myself, and we share a lot in common, including a pint of brew from time to time. We met at a horror film fest and didn't realize that each of us was an expert in the paranormal. Josh is a certified ghost hunter supreme and probably the world's leading expert on the mysterious Brown Mountain Lights seen in the dense forest and mountains around Morgantown. Hundreds have gotten up close and personal with these lights and Joshua has even videotaped one (and this is for real!) creature and a video or two

What I told the CINEFLIX staff was that there was no way I could go on "William Shatner's Weird or What?" and declare this a true extraterrestrial. However, upon closer examination, I wasn't ready to write the little tike off completely. Minus its skin layer, the sinister looking carcass did appear strange and unusual – I know Shatner would prefer the word "Weird" in there somewhere – and I was willing to go that far. The legend goes that the farmer Marao Lopez had captured the creature, shown it to a few of his farmhands, and, when it squawked and lunged for them (what would you do if you were tangled up in a nasty trap?) they did the only thing that came to mind . . . they dipped the creature into a vat of acid, which peeled off his skin and killed him. Greetings to you, Mr. Tee.

The men eventually took their possession to a university in Mexico and they were told that it was like nothing born of this earth, though it did have some components that appeared human (like a hybrid?) The scientists said the creature could not have been a mutant of any time as it had no DNA and all living things should have DNA. Tests revealed a creature that is unknown to scientists – its skeleton has characteristics of a lizard, its teeth do not have any roots like humans and it can stay underwater for a long time (well, if it's dead, that last statement has no meaning).

We hear on good authority that the farmer who caught the creature in the trap (there was said to be a second one who escaped) died shortly after all this attention when he was in a bad car accident and burned to a crisp. A case of the Ultra-Terrestrials seeking revenge? My notion was, and this was what I told Shatner's producers, that the creature could not have been a space being. First off, it was too tiny and fragile to wheel itself about at the speed of light. And where was the craft that it arrived on Earth in? And what about the lack of breathing apparatus? And how could a super smart alien (it had an enlarged brain, the examining scientists had said) get himself caught in such a primitive trap? It didn't add up, as far as I was concerned, to something extraterrestrial, that's for damn sure. But what of another possible explanation? In the book "Round Trip to Hell in a Flying Saucer," we dealt with the existence of the Djinn, a shadowy race of demonic creatures known in the Islamic faith as living in another dimension and, for the most part, cursing humans and committing dastardly deeds. They often appear as smoke and possess people just like the devil would do in our Western culture. And the thing is, if you compared a picture or illustration of the Djinn, they offer up a reasonable resemblance to the alien baby of Mexico.

And so exactly what is a Djinn (often spelled Jinn)?

Well, we know about the genie in the bottle from "A Thousand and One Arabian Nights," but otherwise most of us who are not of the Islamic religion don't really know the story/nature of the Djinn and who they really are. Easily put into the category of Ultra-Terrestrials, they are not the nicest of entities.

The following is the definition that seems most prevalent...

The word "Djinn" translates as anything that is concealed or invisible. The Djinn are a race that has no defined physical form of their own, so they are therefore invisible to the naked eye. However, they are shape-shifters who can take on the physical form of just about anything they want. Many say that they walk among us every day. You will often see smoke when a Djinn appears, not because the smoke IS the Djinn, but because it accompanies him/her. It is simply a sign that your Djinn is nearby and ready to communicate, and signifies the presence of energy. Djinn can also appear with orbs, streaks of light, mists or other kinds of phenomena. It can be a big, awe-inspiring appearance, or a subtle, almost-not-noticed kind of appearance. With Djinn, like people, no two are exactly alike and there are countless ways they may manifest. Some Djinn will never manifest in any kind of physical form, but that doesn't mean that they aren't there and watching you. These Djinn will generally communicate with you only during dreams or meditation. They aren't any more or less powerful than other Djinn, they just choose to present themselves differently. So I took a shot and took the train to Toronto where I lauded my theory of the Djinn. I am sure this is the first time the subject of aliens versus the Djinn has been discussed on a widely-viewed television program. Of course, my statements were broken up into brief sound bites, but I do believe I got the message across to Shatner, as well as his very obliging producers and crew, that all strange-looking beings do not have to come from a place far, far away in another galaxy, but might be here living right alongside us. We could almost reach out and touch them... and possibly some of us have. The world of Ultra-Terrestrials is a mystifying one, and there is a lot to learn about those that seem flesh and blood one moment but can metamorphose, can alter their shape,

# SHIRLEY MACLAINE MEETS THE PLEIADIANS

size and appearance as well as their density.

I can't say for certain that Shatner took me at my word about the Djinn, but, just like in the interview I did with him way back before time machines were all that much in vogue, I presented my case as convincingly as possible that all ETs do not necessarily come from outer there, but could be camped out much closer.

SUGGESTED READING – BOOKS BY TIMOTHY BECKLEY AVAILABLE FROM AMAZON.COM

The Authentic Book of Ultra-Terrestrial Contacts: From the Secret Alien Files of Timothy Green Beckley

Round Trip to Hell in a Flying Saucer: UFO Parasites - Alien Soul Suckers - Invaders from Demonic Realms

UFOs – Wicked This Way Comes

*"Flying Saucers Are Real...*
*The Air Force Doesn't Exist!"*
—Gabriel Green, Candidate for President, 1964

# SHIRLEY MACLAINE MEETS THE PLEIADIANS

## ED ASNER REPORTS ON THE FORT MONMOUTH UFO COVER-UP

Seen here as journalist Lou Grant, in real life actor Ed Asner was involved in UFO sightings over the military instillation that is Fort Monmouth in New Jersey.

Like a lot of folks in the "ordinary world," veteran actor Ed Asner, who became popular as Lou Grant, a slow-burning newsroom chief on "The Mary Tyler Moore Show," has every reason to believe that Uncle Sam is failing to tell us all it knows about UFOs and their occupants.

Not one to rely on second-hand information or hearsay, Asner knows from personal experience

that the military has gone out of its way to silence UFO witnesses. In a telephone conversation from his home, the 1971 and '72 winner of an Emmy for "Outstanding Actor in a Supporting Comedy Role" says he was caught up in an extensive UFO scare that rocked the top brass of a military installation where he was stationed.

# SHIRLEY MACLAINE MEETS THE PLEIADIANS

The incident took place in the summer of 1952, while the actor was on duty at Fort Monmouth, New Jersey. Asner insists that many of his Army buddies in the Signal Corps were seeing UFOs on a regular basis almost every day. In addition to the visual observations, the unknowns were also being picked up on radar.

"I remember one particular sunny afternoon, just after 12 o'clock, the base was in an uproar. One of the enlisted men had come running in and started telling everyone that there was a formation of flying saucers overhead. At first they thought he was crazy, but finally a number of the company engineers went outside and, sure enough, there they were! The men were kept busy for several days tracking these strange discs through binoculars and calculating their speeds – which I was told were astronomical – with sophisticated scientific instrumentation."

At the height of the UFO flap, Asner says, an emergency call was placed by a high-ranking officer at Fort Monmouth to a nearby Air Force base. "A request was made that pursuit planes be sent to chase the objects. I don't believe they were ever able to get very close. The UFOs apparently outdistanced them with ease."

It was at this point that the enlisted personnel at the base were told to keep quiet. "Things were getting pretty hairy," Asner recalled. "Just about everyone had seen them, when one day all the men, during class, were formally told, 'If you went home yesterday and told your wife that you saw a UFO, you will go home today and tell her that you didn't!' The implication of such a statement was made perfectly clear. I guess they didn't want us to know too much. After all, we were just a bunch of Army slobs – privates – and probably weren't supposed to be kept abreast of such matters. It wasn't our business!"

# SHIRLEY MACLAINE MEETS THE PLEIADIANS

## CHARLES BRONSON'S "INTRUDER"

It was a blazing hot, very humid afternoon in mid-August 1971 when the "intruder" arrived on the grounds of the plush Bel Air estate owned by "Death Wish" star Charles Bronson. The uninvited visitor was, needless to say a UFO. And while the king of movie "tough guys" was away on location, the object was sighted firsthand by Bronson's charming actress wife, the late Jill Ireland.

A firm believer in metaphysics and the personal growth field, Jill was open to talk about what happened, probably realizing full well the existence of alternative realities and a superior intelligence at work in the universe. Although we never met in person, via telephone she admitted that "the episode stuck in my mind."

A leading lady in her own right, Jill, who appeared beside her husband in "Breakout Pass" and "Hard Times," declared: "My youngest girl was only three months old at the time. I remember it was about five in the afternoon when we had the sighting. I was sitting on the veranda, holding the baby in my arms. Our child's nurse, Zizi, was standing around talking to me when my eyes suddenly drifted

Jill Ireland and Leonard Nimoy in the 1967 Star Trek series episode: "This Side Of Paradise."

# SHIRLEY MACLAINE MEETS THE PLEIADIANS

to a bright blue patch of sky. Something up there – which had been reflecting the rays of the sun – caught my attention."

Though the harshness of the glare made it difficult to ascertain the exact shape and dimensions of the object, Jill imagines it was "round" with "perhaps a dome or tower on top." She feels that she would have gotten a much clearer view if the sphere had shown up on a slightly more overcast day. "It was really hard to pick out any specific features," Jill notes, "since the sun was striking the body of the craft as if it were a mirror."

Initially, Jill thought the object might be a balloon sent aloft by the weather bureau to take atmospheric measurements and readings, but she ruled out this explanation when the UFO began to rapidly rise higher and higher, traveling against the wind. "It just went up and up, and very fast," Jill explained, "and shortly it simply vanished from sight."

Jill was never sure what it was she saw. "The possibility exists that it could have been a secret craft manufactured by the government," Jill speculated, "or it truly might have been a space traveler paying our home a brief visit."

Whatever the explanation, Jill was so impressed by her sighting that she told husband Charles Bronson about it the moment he arrived home.

When asked his opinion, Charles willingly backed up his wife all the way. "There's got to be something to it. If Jill says there was something strange in the sky, I see no reason not to take her at her word. I remember she talked about it for quite a while afterwards, and, besides, I know she wouldn't make the whole thing up! Why would she?"

Jill Dorothy Ireland (April 24, 1936 – May 18, 1990)

Charles Bronson (born Charles Kasimir Buchinsky; November 3, 1921 – August 30, 2003)

# SHIRLEY MACLAINE MEETS THE PLEIADIANS

## CLIFF ROBERTSON'S "BIG PUZZLE"

Actor Cliff Robertson took pen in hand, and though he readily admits he's not even half an artist, he drew a sketch of the object in the sky that remains a puzzle to this very day.

"I have no idea what it could have been," Robertson began, but he does know it "made a believer out of me."

"Before my sighting, you would have had to classify me as a skeptic," he confesses. "But I know I saw something truly unusual in the sky that afternoon and I can no longer discount the theory that UFOs might be traveling to Earth from somewhere out there in the vastness of space.

The star of numerous motion pictures (including "Charly," for which he won the Academy Award), Robertson sighted the UFO in July 1963, while living in a house that overlooks the ocean in Pacifica Park, California. This is how Robertson describes his experience:

"It was a crystal clear day, around 3:00 PM, with not a cloud visible in the sky. I was standing out on an observation deck that overlooks the sea, watching the gulls fly by, and taking a bit of fresh air. Suddenly, my eyes were diverted toward an object high in the sky. Whatever it was, was traveling from south to north and sparkling like a diamond as it reflected the rays of the mid-afternoon sun.

"At first, I didn't pay it any attention, thinking it probably was just a passing airplane. But I quickly dismissed this idea when I realized it was traveling much too slowly to be a commercial airliner, and a helicopter would have absolutely no reason to be that far away from land.

"Next, I thought, it has to be a balloon of some sort. This, too, I eventually ruled out, when the object began to hover in one spot. I'm absolutely convinced that the prevailing trade winds that whip along the coast would have sent any lighter-than-air device rapidly off in the opposite direction."

Completely stumped as to what he was viewing, Robertson picked up a pair of binoculars and focused on the object. He was certain that by magnifying the image he would be able to make a positive identification. He was in for the shock of his life!

"By no means was I prepared for what I saw through the binoculars. Instead of supplying me with a rational explanation, it only convinced me that no identification was possible.

"I've been a pilot for years," the actor explained, "and I have to be honest and say that never before have I encountered anything remotely like this during my experience as an aviator. There, in front of me, was a weird, alien contraption, a cylindrical-shaped craft made of highly polished metal."

Robertson says the UFO hovered motionless for more than 10 minutes before it finally shot straight up and disappeared from sight.

"It just hovered out there, high up over the water, then – boom! – all of a sudden it was gone. It disappeared in the twinkling of an eye, blasting off straight up at a tremendous velocity. I was able to follow it for 15 or 20 seconds and I would say it was really traveling!"

Having seen rockets blast off before, Robertson was doubly confused by the fact that the UFO left no contrail. "The sky was empty, totally empty. One moment it was there, and the next it was gone."

Cliff says that, since that day, he has reflected on his sighting many times and still finds there is no logical explanation for what he saw. "It was definitely a UFO like so many other people have seen around the world. I was awed by its sleek design, its trim appearance, and the fact that one minute it could hover on a dime and the next blast off into space at a fantastic speed. I don't know of anything built on this planet that could maneuver in such a fashion."

Prior to his UFO observation, Cliff hadn't thought too much about life in outer space but now he's certain that extraterrestrial beings do exist. "Years later, I played Buzz Aldrin, the astronaut, on a television special, and because of my own sightings I could appreciate much more what it must have felt like for Buzz to be out there in the cosmos with all those stars and planets passing by and what a thrill it must have been for him. The vastness of space boggles my mind. There has to be life out yonder!"

Clifford Parker "Cliff" Robertson III (September 9, 1923 – September 10, 2011)

# SHIRLEY MACLAINE MEETS THE PLEIADIANS

Mainly known for his roles as an all American cowboy, Glenn Ford also served as the leading man opposite such sex symbols as Rita Hayworth.

## GLENN FORD'S
## HALF HOUR ENCOUNTER

UFOs are nothing to scoff at, according to actor Glen Ford. "Millions of Americans have sighted them," the well-known actor pointed out during the course of an interview, "and it's a well-established fact that some twenty per cent of such observations remain unexplainable."

Ford maintains that there must be something to the matter since he too has seen a UFO. While in Great Britain, "I was trying to relax, taking it easy, and so I decided to spend a few hours alone on a beach near Oxnard, England."

What Ford says he saw shocked him greatly. "All around me, as far as I could see, was nothing but a beautiful blue expanse of sky and water. Suddenly my attention was attracted to an object skipping across the heavens. Looking closer, I saw what definitely was a disc-shaped object. What they call a UFO or flying saucer.

"I watched it for a good half hour as it darted about back and forth right in front of my eyes. There is no way anyone can convince me what I saw wasn't some sort of intelligently controlled craft. This 'thing,'" Ford went on, "made sharp right angle turns that our fastest and most advanced military jets could not accomplish at the time."

Ford admits that he is not one to discredit the many reports constantly coming in from all parts of the globe. "I see absolutely no reason why our planet cannot be receiving visitors from outer space. Scientific evidence now exists that proves that thousands of inhabited worlds can thrive throughout the cosmos. I'm positive that there are other worlds nearby that contain lifeforms of one type or

# SHIRLEY MACLAINE MEETS THE PLEIADIANS

another."

Taken aback by what he saw, Ford says he reported his observation to some friends in the military because he felt it was his duty.

"Unfortunately, they would not take me seriously. In fact, they acted as if I were a bit crazy" he acknowledges.

A captain in the U.S. Naval Reserve himself, Glenn Ford believes UFOs are probably friendly and piloted by creatures coming to Earth "simply out of curiosity."

Glenn Ford (May 1, 1916 – August 30, 2006)

## RUTH WARRICK: THE "WALK-INS HAVE ARRIVED!"

Now that we've heard from a half dozen or so rough-and-tumble Hollywood types, let's give a few charming ladies their say on the matter of UFOs. I knew Ruth fairly well at the peak of her soap opera career and she was one of our closest comrades in the world of UFO celebrities.

Over the course of her extensive career, actress Ruth Warrick has won many awards and honors. A native Missourian, she has appeared in more than a dozen motion pictures, including "Citizen Kane," "Journey Into Fear," "Song of the South," "China Sky," "The Corsican Brothers," "The Iron Major" and "The Great Bank Robbery." She is, however, probably best known for her role on TV's popular soap, "All My Children," in which she appeared regularly as the meddlesome matriarch, Phoebe Tyler up until her passing in January 2005.

Ruth was a long-time believer in the entire spectrum of the paranormal and had had her share of ESP and other psychic experiences, starting with precognitive dreams when she was a little girl, and, later, a vision that President Kennedy was going to be assassinated.

During the years, I had invited Ruth to several UFO events, including the showing of some very amazing movie footage of a strange craft coasting in and

# SHIRLEY MACLAINE MEETS THE PLEIADIANS

out of view over Christ Church, New Zealand (she attended the press conference I put together in New York to obtain media coverage for this historic color film). Another time, Ruth showed up at a sky-watch I helped organize on the penthouse roof of a Manhattan apartment during the height of a UFO flap right in the middle of the Big Apple. It would seem from our various discussions over the years that the reason for Ruth Warrick's personal interest in the subject lay fairly close to home, as she revealed the somewhat remarkable story of her son and his claim that he was in contact with space beings and may even have been a "Walk-In."

"My son is very mystical – always has been," she told me. "He's attuned to space and the possibilities that exist outside of the normal realm of experience. Fifteen years ago, I crossed the Atlantic on the Ile de France (ocean liner), and, on impulse, after arriving in New York, called this woman psychic who was a friend of mine. I had been thinking about doing theatre and live TV work.

"As I walked through the door to her apartment, she said, 'You're going to do it, and it will lead to something that will work out very well for you.'

"Without seeing my son, the psychic described him as perfectly as if she'd lived next door. She said she saw him crawling under two grand pianos, which we did have in a small room at home.

# SHIRLEY MACLAINE MEETS THE PLEIADIANS

"She went on: 'You're totally comparable, but this little soul was following you around for years; he had chosen you for his mother . . . Your son knows his mission here on Earth!'

"He is aware of other planetary beings," the veteran actress calmly stated. "My son says he is in touch with them. Any other mother would have trouble accepting this. It's like a recollection he has of previous lives on some other planet."

Ruth says he once told her: "We have put our faith in institutions – government, politics, religion, science – and they don't seem to work. It's a matter of collective consciousness, and institutions are lacking in this.

"I think an experiment is going on, here on this planet. When this planet was created, we had everything going for us. The history of Earth has been one of total greed, and we are incredibly unaware and unappreciative!"

As to whether or not we are entering what has been termed "The Last Days," Ruth's son said that while things do not look good on a cosmic scale, "human thought is capable of changing anything," and that "we still have a better-than-even chance."

Ruth Warrick didn't know what to make of all this, but she was convinced something is going on. After all, her own psychic experiences have taught her not to scoff at things that seem unlikely, because nothing is!

Ruth Elizabeth Warrick (June 29, 1916 – January 15, 2005)

# SHIRLEY MACLAINE MEETS THE PLEIADIANS

## MARIA JANIS – FROM OUT OF THE WILD BLUE YONDER

From the living room of her apartment in New York's Upper East Side, Maria Janis – daughter of the late Gary Cooper and wife of the internationally-acclaimed pianist Byron Janis – came out and revealed her belief in the existence of UFOs and the extraterrestrials operating them.

For a long while she has felt almost certain there were inhabited worlds in outer space and freely admits that "for years I have been fascinated with the many accounts of strange ships flying about in our atmosphere."

Maria does not try to hide the fact that one of her closest friends is super psychic Uri Geller. "He's been to our place many times and he always manages to amaze us with his abilities." On one occasion, Geller transported – or maybe teleported is a better word – a heavy stone object into the room they were in from the home of an associate who was living upstate. It has long been rumored that Geller is in contact with space entities who are behind his amazing, almost otherworldly, powers.

Stepping into a reality far beyond conjecture, Maria told about a particular incident that made her personal faith in UFOs stronger than it had ever been before.

Maria Janus and Uri Geller

# SHIRLEY MACLAINE MEETS THE PLEIADIANS

"I was flying to Paris one morning and noted with awe the beautiful sunrise spread out before me over the clear sky. Some inner urge prompted me to take my camera and snap two or three shots of the delightful, sun-drenched clouds. And, sure enough, when the film was developed, there, on one of the pictures, was a cone-shaped object. It was definitely a craft, a commonly observed type of UFO."

Even years later, Maria had to admit she could not offer any explanation for what the camera caught on film, not having the necessary technical know-how as to why the sensitive camera lens might have picked up something she was unable to see. She did, however, express a theory that certain UFOs operate on a different vibrational level, making them invisible to the human eye, but allow them by some force to be caught with the fast shutter movement of a camera, showing up quite easily on film as a mere streak of light.

Because of the poor reproductive quality inherent in such a faint print – and probably because it was her only copy – Maria decided to sketch out the impressions she had of the UFO and I am happy to be able to reproduce it here for all to see.

Sketch made by Marie Janis of the object that flew by the window on her way to Paris.

# SHIRLEY MACLAINE MEETS THE PLEIADIANS

## CHARO: IT WAS NO MEXICAN JUMPING BEAN!

Though the Latin bombshell may not talk about the subject often, she did let her hair down backstage at what used to be the Ed Sullivan Theater, located just off Broadway on 54th Street in Manhattan. We met while she was taping "Saturday Night Live," and, in between chatting with fans and producers, she managed to get across the details of her sighting.

Waving her arms frantically in the air, Charo tried to conjure up the image of what she saw. "I was in Murzia, Spain – that's my hometown – many years ago. I was still a little girl. One evening, while I was out in back of the house, I happened to look up at the sky, and there, passing overheard, was this shiny object. It was really big, bigger than a star. Holy Chihuahua, I thought, what is this?"

Although it was traveling high in the sky, Charo insists it wasn't a satellite. "It hopped about the sky like a Mexican jumping bean. I was very impressed. So much so that I have never forgotten what happened."

Charo is not certain when the UFOnauts will make themselves known to the

general public. "Maybe they won't do this right away. Maybe they are afraid of us, no?" However, she does think the day will eventually arrive when we will have the opportunity to meet with beings from beyond the stars. "Who's to say when this will happen? Maybe tomorrow. Maybe 200 years from now!"

# SHIRLEY MACLAINE MEETS THE PLEIADIANS

# SHIRLEY MACLAINE MEETS THE PLEIADIANS

### LILLIAN ROTH: "IT WAS AS LARGE AS THE HINDENBURG DIRIGIBLE!"

Perhaps Lillian Roth won't be an easily recognizable name for those "youngsters" out there, but those readers who (pardon the expression!) "go back a few years" will remember her from the all-time motion picture classic story of her life, "I'll Cry Tomorrow," in which she is portrayed by Susan Hayward. Now deceased for a number of years, Lillian was a child celebrity at the age of five and the toast of Broadway and Hollywood before she was twenty. Her cinema credits are lengthy and include a leading role in the Marx Brothers film, "Animal Crackers."

I met Lillian several times in her West Side digs, where she lived with her

# SHIRLEY MACLAINE MEETS THE PLEIADIANS

six or eight dogs (can't remember the exact number, but they were running around all over the place, especially between my feet). Actually, she was a lot closer with my associate Harold Salkin, who was working as a sort of non-paid publicist trying to get her back into the gossip columns after several years of "laying low" from the entertainment business. It was actually Harold who turned me on to Lillian's UFO sightings and, after pressing me repeatedly to do an interview, I finally consented.

As it turned out, Lillian Roth had encountered UFOs on two occasions, though she had refrained from speaking about them to others simply because "I doubt if anyone else would take me seriously. After all," she wanted to know, "how do you prevent people from laughing out loud when you tell them you've sighted a space ship that was as large as the Hindenburg dirigible?"

She related that her initial confrontation with aerial phantoms occurred in April of 1951. At the time, Lillian was traveling cross-country from New York to California with her third husband, Burt McGuire, Jr. On the evening in question, they had decided to stay overnight in an out-of-the-way motel located in the Arizona desert.

Lillian Roth compiled these notes and sketches pertaining to the twin sightings of UFOs.

"I was out walking my three pet dogs around 7:00 PM when I caught a glimpse of something that rocked my senses. There, as if suspended from some invisible thread, was a tremendous object, shaped kind of like a child's toy top. It was huge, perhaps 150 feet in diameter. Standing perfectly still, it remained in one position, hovering at what would be the height of a 15-story apartment building."

Lillian told me she was fearful that it was going to land nearby. "When it got directly overhead, I remember thinking, 'Is this thing going to fall on me?'"

Lillian Roth compiled these notes and sketche[s]

# SHIRLEY MACLAINE MEETS THE PLEIADIANS

Composing herself as much as possible, she shouted for her husband to come take a look.

"The UFO had a metallic body, similar to aluminum. All around the hull were small portholes or windows, which were lit up with different colored lights."

The effect, she says, was like the lights on a Christmas tree. "They were red, white, green, blue, and orange, each shining forth with its own sparkling brilliance, adding to the total effect of dazzling and beautiful color."

After hovering for about five minutes, the craft shot upward at fantastic speed. "It rose very high in the sky, appearing as a small speck in the deep blue above."

As quickly as it rose, it returned – scooting downward to the same location directly overhead. "It remained stationary another two minutes, then it began moving away at a gradual angle upward, toward the east. This time it went slowly, but steadily, with no sound ever being heard. Soon it was out of sight in the twilight sky."

Less than one year later, Lillian insists that she was "spied on" from above, this time while appearing in a night club in Fort Lauderdale, Florida.

"One night in March, 1952, Burt and I were driving north on the main highway, heading from Fort Lauderdale toward Palm Beach, a distance of 50 miles. It was a nice clear evening. Actually, it was shortly after sunset when this event happened. We were in an open stretch of road, with unobstructed views in all directions."

Without warning, there suddenly appeared – "as if from nowhere," she maintains – a huge, cigar-shaped vessel, hanging a little above the horizon and directly down the highway in front of their automobile. Lillian said that the object was "a strange pinkish color, as if covered with a pink, velour-like velvet."

According to her account, the "cigar" stretched straight across much of the horizon.

"I would say, just as a guess, that it could easily have been as large as the famed dirigible, the Hindenburg. Of course, it was much slimmer than a dirigible. Actually, the sides were parallel, just like a cigar."

Pulling to the side of the road, Lillian and her husband gazed in awe at the spectacle before them. "I remember commenting to Burt, 'Nobody will believe this!' Not only had I seen an oval-shaped flying saucer, but now a cigar-shaped one. According to published reports, these are the two most commonly sighted types of spacecraft. Apparently the larger ones, known as 'mother ships,' carry

# SHIRLEY MACLAINE MEETS THE PLEIADIANS

the smaller 'scouts' inside. They are then released in the Earth's atmosphere."

As they observed the object, they were able to make out a grayish smoke or "haze" trailing above and below the UFO, almost surrounding it. "This effect was not, I'm positive, caused by clouds, as the sky was almost totally clear in this area. Rather, the 'haze' seemed to be emanating from the UFO itself, forming a delicate, filmy aura that played gently about the pinkish expanse of the ship's surface. We saw it there for two or three minutes and then started driving again. As we watched, the great ship suddenly faded away – just simply vanished into nothingness – hard as it may be to believe!"

As amazing as the scene may have been, the events of the night were not yet over. "About 11:30 PM, we were returning from my club appearance. We were driving south on the same highway, going quite fast, and were approaching the same stretch of road where we had the twilight sighting. Then – again it happened! The same – or an identical – UFO loomed up above the horizon, reaching out majestically with its pinkish velour body gleaming softly in the heavens."

Lillian said, "I remember exclaiming to my husband, 'Well, they're just trying to prove to us that they're really out there!' Burt just smiled and said nothing. This time he didn't stop the car but continued to drive as if nothing unusual were taking place. You might say we were very well-adjusted people. We increased our speed to see if we could get closer to it. After about five minutes, as we roared along, it suddenly began to move off to our left, toward the ocean, and slowly drifted out to sea."

A warm smile crossing her face, Lillian explained how the second episode alleviated her previous fears and put her at ease. "I don't know why I should have been worried. Anyone who could construct such marvelous flying machines must be more advanced than we meager Earthlings. I think, if they're developed to this stage of technology, they must have – somewhere along the line – managed to do away with wars and fighting on their planet. What a surprise for all of us if they would land! I would certainly welcome them. I really would enjoy talking to whoever is onboard these beautiful ships."

Asked why she waited so long to reveal the details of her two sightings, Lillian reported that "people seem a lot more open-minded toward visitors from outer space and UFOs than ever before."

Lillian Roth (December 13, 1910 – May 12, 1980)

# SHIRLEY MACLAINE MEETS THE PLEIADIANS

Sammy with Michael Jackson

## SAMMY DAVIS, JR.: "I'M NOT AFRAID!"

There was a secret side to the late Sammy Davis, Jr., that probably only his best friends knew about. For, in addition to singing, dancing and acting, the late "Sandman" held a lively belief in UFOs – having made four observations that were "positively out of this world."

"I was never afraid of aliens or whatever it is that pilots these UFOs," Sammy declared, admitting that he had seen a number of times what were often referred to in those "early" days as flying saucers.

"My most impressive sighting was just outside of Palm Springs, California. There were a lot of sightings around 1952-53, and I wasn't to be left out."

Sammy says he was with a group of people when they spotted the discs as they literally "floated overhead." He was amazed at how they could accelerate from a dead stop to almost fantastic speeds. "First they would stand still and then they would take off and stop again, before finally shooting away in a flash."

Though I wish I could have been in the same room with Sammy as he told his story, I had to be content to carry on a long distance telephone conversation while he was performing in his favorite city, Las Vegas.

Drummer Buddy Rich had arranged the interview after discovering that my interest in UFOs was not just a "passing fancy."

"Another time," Sammy continued, "I had just appeared onstage in the Boston area and was driving back to the hotel where I was staying with some mem-

# SHIRLEY MACLAINE MEETS THE PLEIADIANS

bers of my band when we caught sight of something bewildering just up ahead."

From the description that Sammy gave me, it sounded like he had witnessed a typical dome-shaped UFO. "I know from reading books since then that others have seen craft like this. It was immense and glowed brilliantly from the lights that surrounded it. Actually the object was so bright that I had a hard time keeping my eyes on it."

Sammy says he and his friends watched in awe as the object hovered quite close. "Some of the guys with me were afraid that the object was going to come after us. They felt it might attack us, but I didn't have any such fear, as I felt quite strongly that if they wanted to harm the human race, they could have done so a long while ago."

Over the years before his passing, Sammy met with other celebrities who shared his interest in the topic, and he says that he even met with an astronomer associated with the Air Force's investigation of UFOs. Probably he was referring to Dr. J. Allen Hynek, who worked with the now-defunct Project Blue Book.

Sammy Davis Jr. never told me just what his best friend, the "Chairman of the Board," Frank Sinatra, thought of his interest in the strange goings-on in our skies.

Samuel George "Sammy" Davis, Jr. (December 8, 1925 – May 16, 1990)

# SHIRLEY MACLAINE MEETS THE PLEIADIANS

## STUART WHITMAN: UFOs AND "THE GREAT BLACKOUT"

No doubt the most incredible story ever related to me by any actor has to be the account given by veteran actor Stuart Whitman, who was involved in an "incredible incident" on the night of the great blackout of November, 1965.

The blackout caused more than 15 million homes and businesses to be without electricity. Indeed, if there is any hint of intelligent reasoning behind the UFOs' seemingly repeated attempts to be seen by, and to communicate with, well-known celebrities, the episode recalled by this Hollywood actor seems to hold at least a partial clue to the UFOnauts' alien thinking pattern.

While Stuart Whitman has no regrets for being best recognized for his adventurous appearances in such screen epics as "The Sound And The Fury" and "The Comancheros" (in which he co-starred with John Wayne), the actor has welcomed disclosure of his encounter with UFOs and the prophetic message he was told to spread far and wide, "to all those with ears that will hear."

From his Hollywood residence, Whitman recounted freely an experience that occurred during the far-sweeping blackout of November, 1965:

"I was sleeping in my room on the twelfth floor of a New York hotel when I heard a loud buzzing sound akin to the noise made by a police siren. Then I heard my name being called. 'WHITMAN, WHITMAN!' It was as though the voice was being projected over a loud-speaker not far from where I was resting."

Drawn to the window by some unseen force, the actor said he looked out and saw positioned across the way two luminescent, egg-shaped objects which were clouded in a haze, making it almost impossible for him to make out any specific details. "I could tell that one was bright orange in color, the other a phosphorescent blue."

# SHIRLEY MACLAINE MEETS THE PLEIADIANS

The voices continued, always speaking in English, saying that the reason they had contacted Whitman in particular was because he had no malice or hatred in his heart. "They were concerned about our continued use of uncontrolled nuclear weapons and about the chaos and lack of morality now in existence on our planet," the Californian went on.

Pressed for more details about the meaning of his experience, the actor said the blackout was apparently only a small demonstration of the power that the aliens possessed to stop us from annihilating our civilization and the nearby inhabited worlds.

"We are dealing with unknown quantities that we do not fully understand or comprehend, and the 'space people' are trying to prevent us from harming ourselves. They informed me that they will definitely interfere if we go too far in our war-like attitudes. They claimed that they are able to stop all electrical apparatus from functioning and could put a halt to our normal everyday activities any time they wanted to!"

His experience was confirmed, Whitman says, by an identical blackout that occurred on December 2, 1965, when four key military bases, and a population of at least a million, were plunged into darkness in New Mexico and Texas. "If I had any doubts left in my mind at the time, it was cleared up after this second episode," Whitman said.

As for the validity of other stories focused on contact with saucer pilots, Whitman says the voices told him that they had indeed contacted other individuals and wanted help in spreading the word of their concern for our welfare. "They requested that I attempt to assist, in any possible manner, their campaign to wipe out racial prejudice, hatred, bigotry and war from our planet."

When asked if he was disturbed by what he had seen and heard, Stu's reply was typical of most saucer witnesses. "I was not frightened, but strangely elated," he replied. "I had no fear, as I somehow knew they would do me no harm."

Stuart Whitman is so convinced that he was destined to be in touch with these UFOnauts again that on frequent trips alone at night in the desert, he finds himself looking at the star-streaked heavens, wondering if and when they will reappear to him.

# SHIRLEY MACLAINE MEETS THE PLEIADIANS

**"GREAT BALLS OF FIRE"**

*"There are those among us who live in rooms of experience that you or I can never enter."*

John Steinbeck

In the context of this book, one almost begins to wonder what Jerry Lee Lewis was referring to when he said, "You shake my nerves and you rattle my brain." Well, on a conscious level, he probably wasn't talking about a UFO experience, but maybe somewhere in the dark recesses of the "Killer's" mind there lurks yet another "silent contactee."

Frankly speaking, I've always been close to the "music scene." Weaned on the likes of Little Richard, Elvis and Chuck Berry, it was perhaps only natural that with my entrepreneurial skills I would want to be a rock promoter. In the early 1970s I put together several fairly "happening" concerts at which luminaries such as John Lennon and Andy Warhol showed up to party.

These concerts were reported on in "Rolling Stone" and "The New York Times." And though it was not my destiny to score big in this area of entertainment, I always managed to retain the respect of those whom the colored spotlights struck more directly. Truthfully, I even wrote a couple of long-out-of-print books on rock music, and, at one point in my varied editing career, I was probably writing 30 articles a month on whoever was the big rock band or teen favorite at the moment.

The majority of the experiences related in this chapter were told to me personally, but a few may have come "through the grapevine."

Some of the musicians I spoke with on the subject are dead serious about UFOs, while others take these things "more lightly." Regardless of this, UFOs – for me anyway – have always been a door opener to the inner sanctum and have led to some fairly lively conversations and some damn exciting nights out on the town!

# SHIRLEY MACLAINE MEETS THE PLEIADIANS

## JIMI HENDRIX: THE SPACE WIZARD

I can't say in all honesty that I really knew Jimi Hendrix, but I did see him give a number of really good performances, some of them in the small New York nightclubs where his career began several decades ago. One of the most stunning shows was an outdoor festival held on Randall's Island. It was one of those post-Woodstock concerts where the promoter had disappeared with all the funds (or maybe there just weren't any!) and everyone was getting in for free and wandering around totally spaced out.

Somehow – as usual – I managed to wind my way backstage, where things were really in an uproar. Nobody knew what they were doing, much less who was

# SHIRLEY MACLAINE MEETS THE PLEIADIANS

going to walk out on stage next. As I recall, Dr. John the Night Tripper was putting on his voodoo makeup and garb, while Jimi Hendrix was leaning up against a wall of amps and speakers. As I walked past him, we both just kind of nodded as if we recognized each other, and to this day I can swear I heard him ask me, "And what planet are you from, pal?"

Jimi was, of course, one of the most legendary figures of the "Aquarian Era." A star at Woodstock, his songs as well as his virtuoso guitar playing made him an immensely popular folk hero, especially with young people.

At the same time, a large percentage of the adults found his "message," his manner of dress and his lifestyle very confusing. What they did not know was that the young black man from Washington State probably felt totally out of place and alienated simply because there is a good chance that he really did not belong here – that he had come from "somewhere else" and stepped into an earthly body. Jimi Hendrix fits perfectly some of the characteristics often representative of "Walk-Ins."

World traveler Bill Cox has investigated any number of cases involving those beings who have come here from other worlds and, with the permission of a human, transplanted their spirits inside one of us (usually at the moment of death, just after an accident). Often, Bill says, the original earthly individual is not able to withstand the change in vibrations. He explains it in the chapter, "Life Isn't Easy For Space Emissaries," in his book, "Unseen Kingdoms."

"There are emissaries among us who know who they are. They know they are quite different from average men. They may even be misfits in the physical world . . . I find that, among this group, some become excessively involved with alcohol, drugs and sex; anything to try and escape from this – our world."

Jimi Hendrix could easily be placed into this category; nobody would deny that.

But what is not generally realized is that Jimi expressed a great interest in matters of an extraterrestrial nature, had admitted seeing UFOs, and once told a reporter from "The New York Times" that he was really from Mars.

# SHIRLEY MACLAINE MEETS THE PLEIADIANS

And he wasn't kidding either. David Henderson, in his book "The Life of Jimi Hendrix" (Bantam), quotes Jimi's feelings about life on other planets: "There are other people in the solar system, you know, and they have the same feelings, too. Not necessarily bad feelings, but see, it upsets their way of living for instance – and they are a whole lot heavier than we are.

"And it's no war games, because they all keep the same place. But, like, the solar system is going through a change soon and it's going to affect the Earth in about 30 years."

On several occasions during his career, UFOs just "happened" to show up while Jimi was giving a concert. During the last days of his life, he performed on the rim of an extinct volcano in Maui.

"Jimi played three 45-minute sets," says Henderson in his bestseller. "After each set, he retired to a special sacred Hopi Indian tent.

"Later, witnesses in Maui testified that they heard musical tones emanating from rocks and stones. UFOs were also sighted over the volcano by people who called in to a local radio show. A cameraman on the set said that he fell from his

# SHIRLEY MACLAINE MEETS THE PLEIADIANS

perch after seeing a UFO through his lens."

And in the film "Rainbow Bridge," Hendrix rattles on for several minutes about astral projection and the philosophy of the Space Brothers. He also tried to master the art of psychic healing through color and sound.

Recently, I had the honor to speak with one of Jimi's best friends. Fellow musician and songwriter Curtis Knight had befriended Jimi early in his career and teamed up with the long-haired guitar player, performing any number of gigs in various dimly lit Greenwich Village night clubs that were popular back in the early 1960s, before Hendrix became a star.

Curtis knew all about the episode involving the UFO in Maui. "It was an odd-looking craft that glittered in the bright sunlight.

Jimi felt certain the UFO had come down to put its spiritual stamp of approval on the show. He told me that he'd been emotionally and physically recharged by the experience."

During the course of our conversation, Curtis also revealed the fascinating details of the time a UFO landed in front of them and actually saved their lives.

The event took place on a cold winter's night near Woodstock, New York, in 1965. According to Curtis, if it hadn't been for the occupants of this metallic stranger, Jimi and his fellow musicians might have frozen to death.

# SHIRLEY MACLAINE MEETS THE PLEIADIANS

Jimi (left) with the Curtis Knight band (center) before he struck out on his own.

"We were in upstate New York," Knight began. "It was four o'clock in the morning, and we were trying to make it back to Manhattan – a drive of more than 100 miles – through the worst blizzard I can recall. The wind was whipping the snow around our van so fiercely that we missed the turnoff leading to the state highway that would put us in the direction of home. The next thing I remember is getting stuck in a drift that reached the hood of our vehicle. Soon it got so cold. The windows were rolled up tight, and we had the heater on full blast to protect us from the rawness of the elements. I had my doubts about seeing the light of day. We could have turned to human icicles very easily. That's how bitter it was!"

Curtis says the road in front of them suddenly lit up, as a bright phosphorescent object – "cone-shaped, like a space capsule" – landed in the snow about 100 feet up ahead. It stood on tripod landing gear and gave the appearance of being something right out of science fiction. "At first we thought it was an apparition caused by the cold and our confused state of mind. I mean, we just couldn't believe our eyes."

Prodding Jimi with his elbow, Curtis asked if his imagination was playing tricks on him or whether the future rock star saw it too. "Jimi didn't answer, but sort of smiled. He seemed to be staring out into the night, his eyes riveted on this thing resting within a stone's throw."

The veteran musician was also unable to get a response from the other occupants of the van. "Three other members of the band were sleeping curled up beneath blankets in the back of the truck. I tried to wake them, but they wouldn't budge. I was afraid that carbon monoxide, caused by the exhaust fumes and the rolled-up windows, might be getting into their lungs."

At this point, Curtis admits he was overcome with fright. Before he could make a move of any kind, a door opened on the side of the craft and an entity came forth. "He stood eight foot tall, his skin was yellowish, and instead of eyes, the creature had slits. His forehead came to a point, and his head ran straight into his chest, leaving the impression that he had no neck."

The being proceeded to float to the ground and glided toward the trapped occupants of the van. It was then that Curtis noticed the snow was melting in the wake of the creature.

"His body generated tremendous heat, so much so that, as it came across a small rise, the snow disappeared around in all directions. In a matter of what seemed like seconds, the being came over to the right-hand side of the van where Jimi was seated and looked right through the window. Jimi seemed to be communicating telepathically with it."

Curtis relates that immediately the interior of their vehicle began to heat up. "Suddenly, I was roasting! One moment it had been bitter cold, and the next moment we might as well have been in Haiti." The heat coming from the UFOnaut evaporated the snow enough to free their imprisoned van.

"As it glided behind our truck, I saw that the drift had completely vanished. Turning on the ignition, I gunned the motor and got the hell out of there. As I looked back through the rear view window, I could see the road filling in with snow again. The object – the strange craft – was at the same instant lifting off like a rocket from a launching pad."

A miracle had transpired. Curtis Knight to this day believes his life and that of his friend Jimi Hendrix were saved by a UFO. "Jimi never did talk much about what happened. He sort of let me know that the cool thing to do was not to bring up the subject. It was to be our little secret. However, from what he did say, I sort of suspect that the object arrived to save our necks chiefly because Jimi had been practicing trying to communicate by ESP with the beings onboard. I know this may be hard to believe, but I'm putting it straight, just like it happened, you hear?"

Reviewing the incident, Curtis admits he is unable to produce additional witnesses. "The boys from the group who were with us remember nothing. They were out cold in the back. As we got into the main road, they revived. It's as if they had been placed under a spell – you know, hypnotized."

A capsule review of Jimi's songs shows that he incorporated some of his interplanetary ties in with his music. The lyrics of many of his songs contain veiled references to UFOs. His album, "Axis – Bold As Love," opens with an announcer talking about flying saucers, with the cut following being a catchy tune called "Up From The Stars."

Though he has passed from this plane, it wouldn't be hard to imagine that, somewhere "out there," Jimi is watching over Earth and smiling. And we certainly do miss this vibrant star child who was once in our midst.

Jimi Hendrix (born Johnny Allen Hendrix; November 27, 1942 – September 18, 1970)

# SHIRLEY MACLAINE MEETS THE PLEIADIANS

A "more mature" Bowie who has given up the flashy, glittery space suits in recent decades.

## DAVID BOWIE: "STARMAN"

I first met David Bowie during his original tour of the United States when he had adopted the stage persona of "Ziggy Stardust," a sort of lost-in-space androgynous alien, complete with cosmic makeup and a painted lightning bolt zigzagging across his face down to his naked chest.

Before venturing across the pond, Bowie had caused quite a sensation in the British press not only because of his outlandish – to some – image of a rock and roller from Mars, but also because of his independent and very liberal sexual lifestyle.

Bowie was introduced to me at the RCA studios in Manhattan by Walli Elmlark, a bedazzling young lady who wrote a regular column for "Circus Magazine." "Circus" was a sort of heavy metal version of "Rolling Stone" that was printed on glossy paper with color photos of pop star favorites who were emerging on the then-burgeoning glam and glitter rock scenes.

As usual, at the time I was wearing several hats. I was promoting a number of local rock bands who never quite "made it," editing the widely distributed "UFO Review" (the world's only official flying saucer newspaper), and running the New

# SHIRLEY MACLAINE MEETS THE PLEIADIANS

The gorgeous poet and entertainer, Cherry Vanilla, promoted David Bowie in the early days of his career and was responsible for relating the story of a UFO that crashed in the desert which Bowie heard and was impressed with.

York School Of Occult Arts and Sciences, among the first metaphysical centers in the country where you could take classes in anything from astral projection to hypnosis to witchcraft. Which is how I came to be acquainted with Walli Elmlark. As I originally wrote in "UFOs Among The Stars – Close Encounters of The Famous" (Global Communications), Walli was known widely as the White Witch Of New York. Because of her contacts in the music industry, she had established quite an eclectic clientele for whom she would offer spiritual guidance and occasional good luck or love spells, but always of a positive nature. She didn't dabble in black magick or even gris gris (a New Orleans form of "gray magick" that incorporates poppets and the use of talismans kept in a personal mojo bag). Walli was lively, imaginative, energetic, well spoken, and quite attractive in her flowing white garments complete with fashionable silver moon adornments. Oh did I forget to mention long black hair, complete with dyed green streak highlights? Indeed, Wallie made a very bold fashion and occult statement wherever she went.

## BOWIE - THE MAN WHO FELL TO EARTH

Early in life, Bowie had established his interest in all matters extraterrestrial. As a Brit teenager, David had helped edit a flying saucer newsletter. He admitted to me that he loved science fiction and was fascinated with life in space and the possibility that quite a few cosmic visitors had ended up on our earthly shores.

During a conversation, Bowie had gone out on a limb revealing that he had once had a close encounter. In the book "Laugh Gnostic," author Peter Koening paraphrases what Bowie said: "A friend and I were traveling in the English countryside when we both noticed a strange object hovering above a field. From then on, I have come to take this phenomenon seriously. I believe that what I saw was not the actual object but a projection of my own mind trying to make sense of this quantum topological doorway into dimensions beyond our own. It's as if our dimension is but one among an infinite number of others."

In the February 1975 issue of the long defunct "CREEM Magazine," Bowie seems to admit to a reporter that he might have an implant or metal inside his

# SHIRLEY MACLAINE MEETS THE PLEIADIANS

Bowie as the alien in "The Man Who Fell To Earth."

body. It's hard to define his exact feeling on this, but this is the quote attributed to him by Bruno Stein, the writer who conducted the interview:

"Well, it turned out David was in luck. If he went to a little town in Missouri at a certain time, he would be able to see in a seemingly empty field a fully equipped flying saucer repair shop at work.

"It was one of those fascinating things you learn at a Bowie soiree. This evening the gathering was rather intimate. There was Corinne, David's charming personal secretary, who ducked out early due to exhaustion (although another participant gossiped that she had someone interesting waiting for her in her hotel room). "I used to work for two guys who put out a UFO magazine in England," he told the flying saucer man. "About six years ago. And I made sightings six, seven times a night for about a year when I was in the observatory. We had regular cruises that came over. We knew the 6.15 was coming in and would meet up with another one. And they would be stationary for about half an hour, and then after verifying what they'd been doing that day, they'd shoot off.

David Bowie in his persona of Ziggy Stardust, the ET that helped propel his career to fame and fortune.

"But, I mean, it's what you do with the information. We never used to tell anybody. It was beautifully dissipated when it got to the media. Media control is still based in the main on cultural manipulation. It's just so easy to do. When you set up one set of objectives toward the

80

# SHIRLEY MACLAINE MEETS THE PLEIADIANS

public and you've given them a certain definition for each code word, you hit them with the various code words and they're not going to believe anything if you don't want them to..."

From his performances, you could tell that nothing was too "non-establishment" for David. He incorporated time machines and space capsules into his act and wrote "A Space Oddity" and talked about how a "Starman" would like to come and visit us, "but he thinks he'd blow our minds." His appeared in the motion picture "The Man Who Fell To Earth," which has become a classic. In concert, Bowie was radiant and his fans were floating on a cloud, but behind the scenes an ominous specter was forming from which the master of time and space would quickly need some righteous assistance in order to escape a wall of paranoia that was building around him.

## AND ALONG COMES MR. SCRATCH

Like many rockers before and after, David had taken a liking to the good life. You know the old adage: sex, drugs and rock and roll. Well, on top of this, add a heap of consciousness expansion and an interest in the occult and you will have the prevalent influences on what might have seemed like Bowie's immortal being.

But paranoia soon struck in the form of the ole nemesis "nose candy," commonly known as cocaine. With the help of Bowie himself and some close associates at the time, Marc Spitz details in "Bowie: A Biography" (Crown) how David was living in L.A. just a few houses away from the estate where Charlie Manson's gang had terribly mutilated Sharon Tate and her friends in a ritualistic murder. Bowie had taken to doing blow regularly and was getting more and more desperate and paranoid with each passing day.

In a number of shocking revelations, biographer Marc Spitz explains precisely what was transpiring in the pop singer's troubled life: "While planning the follow-up to 'Young Americans,' Bowie would sit in the house with a pile of high-quality cocaine atop the glass coffee table, a sketch pad and a stack of books. 'Psychic Self Defense' (Dion Fortune) was his favorite. Its author describes the book as a 'safeguard for protecting yourself against paranormal malevolence.'

# SHIRLEY MACLAINE MEETS THE PLEIADIANS

"Using this and more arcane books on witchcraft, white magic and its malevolent counterpart, black magic, as rough guides to his own rapidly fragmenting psyche, Bowie began drawing protective pentagrams on every surface."

Bowie told the author, "I'd stay up for weeks. Even people like Keith Richards were floored by it. And there were pieces of me all over the floor. I paid with the worst manic depression of my life. My psyche went through the roof; it just fractured into pieces. I was hallucinating 24 hours a day."

Spitz adds, "Increasingly Bowie was convinced there were witches after his semen. They were intent on using it to make a child to sacrifice to the devil, essentially the plot to Roman Polanski's 1968 supernatural classic 'Rosemary's Baby.'"

Seeing that he was in desperate need, poet and songwriter Cherry Vanilla hooked Bowie up with Walli Elmlark, who Spitz describes as a "Manhattan-based intellectual...who taught classes at the New York School of Occult Arts and Sciences, then located on Fourteenth Street, just north of Greenwich Village." (As mentioned previously, I was the director of the school, which began in the mid-1960s and thrived for more than a decade promoting lectures and classes by the who's who of paranormal and UFO experts of that era, including Cleve Backster, Stanley Krippner, Jim Moseley, John Keel – and, of course, Walli Elmlark, the White Witch of New York.)

As added confirmation of the madness David was trying to cope with, ex-wife Angie Bowie reveals even more details of his fascination and dabbling into the occult in her own personal remembrance, "Backstage Passes: Life on the Wild Side With David Bowie."

"There was a beautiful Art Deco house on six acres, an exquisite site property and a terrific value at just $300,000, but he took one look at a detail I hadn't noticed, a hexagram painted on the floor of a circular room by the previous owner, Gypsy Rose Lee.

"A great deal of coddling and reassurance got us through that crisis, and I went and found the Doheny Drive house. Built in the late fifties or early sixties, it was a white cube surrounding an indoor swimming pool. David liked the place, but I thought it was too small to meet our needs for very long, and I wasn't crazy about the pool. In my experience, indoor pools are always a problem.

"This one was no exception, albeit not in any of the usual ways. Its drawback was one I hadn't encountered before and haven't seen or heard of since: Satan lived in it. With his own eyes, David said, he'd seen HIM rising up out of the water one night."

Feeling demonic forces moving in, David felt strongly that he needed an

# SHIRLEY MACLAINE MEETS THE PLEIADIANS

exorcism and asked that his newfound friend, white witch Walli Elmlark, be called upon to lend her assistance to remove the evil from his surroundings.

"A Greek Orthodox Church in L.A. would have done it for us (there was a priest available for such a service, the people had told me), but David wouldn't have it. No strangers allowed, he said. So there we stood, with just Walli's instructions and a few hundred dollars' worth of books, talismans, and assorted items from Hollywood's comprehensive selection of fine occult emporia.

"There he (David Bowie) was, then, primed and ready. The proper books and doodads were arranged on a big old-fashioned lectern. The incantation began, and although I had no idea what was being said or what language it was being said in, I couldn't stop a weird cold feeling rising up in me as David droned on and on.

"There's no easy or elegant way to say this, so I'll just say it straight. At a certain point in the ritual, the pool began to bubble. It bubbled vigorously (perhaps 'thrashed' is a better term) in a manner inconsistent with any explanation involving air filters or the like."

The rock and roll couple watched in amazement. Angie says she tried to be flippant – "'Well, dear, aren't you clever? It seems to be working. Something's making a move, don't you think?' – but I couldn't keep it up. It was very, very strange; even after my recent experiences I was having trouble accepting what my eyes were seeing."

Angie said that she would peek through the glass doors which lead to the pool every so often and was dumbfounded by what she saw.

83

# SHIRLEY MACLAINE MEETS THE PLEIADIANS

"On the bottom of the pool was a large shadow, or stain, which had not been there before the ritual began. It was in the shape of a beast of the underworld; it reminded me of those twisted, tormented gargoyles screaming silently from the spires of medieval cathedrals. It was ugly, shocking, malevolent; it frightened me.

"I backed away from it, feeling very strange, went through the doorway, and told David what I'd seen, trying to be nonchalant but not doing very well. He turned white but eventually became revived enough to spend the rest of the night doing coke. He wouldn't go near the pool, though.

"I still don't know what to think about that night. It runs directly counter to my pragmatism and my everyday faith in the integrity of the 'normal' world, and it confuses me greatly. What troubles me the most is that if you were to call that stain the mark of Satan, I don't see how I could argue with you.

"David, of course, insisted that we move from the house as quickly as possible, and we did that, but I've heard from reliable sources (Michael Lipman for one, the property's real estate agent) that subsequent tenants haven't been able to remove the shadow. Even though the pool has been painted over a number of times, the shadow has always come back."

Several years went by and Walli met an untimely passing. She could not remove the demons in her own life, even though she had a dramatic and positive impact on almost everyone she came in contact with. Besides teaching at the School Of Occult Arts And Sciences, Walli teamed up with the likes of T. Rex's Marc Bolan (whom she nicknamed the Wizzard) and King Crimson's guitarist, Robert Fripp. The trio went off to merry old England to record a spoken word album.

The White Witch of New York, Walli Elmlark, was convinced that Marc Bolan came from another place and time to help in our cosmic evolution. (Photo copyright Helen Hovey).

# SHIRLEY MACLAINE MEETS THE PLEIADIANS

Although "The Cosmic Children" has never been released, the soundtrack was years ahead of its time, centering on those special souls who Walli believed had reincarnated on Earth from "elsewhere" at a very important time in the human evolutionary process to pass on the light to others who were destined to change the world through music, literature and an emerging New Age philosophy. The recording is out there somewhere – perhaps safely in the vault of Robert Fripp – who, hopefully, if he reads this, will contact me and allow us to do a limited pressing for those who would truly find this effort transformational.

Walli and I worked for a number of years on several projects and even co-authored a book together. Out of print for decades, once in a while I still run across a copy of "Rock Raps of the Seventies" offered on e-bay or elsewhere at an exorbitant price.

Somehow, I can't deny the possibility that Walli looks down from time to time and perhaps sings along with David Bowie as he performs all over the world in concert. Long recovered from drugs and the dark aspects of occultism, he is now raising a family and going on with his chosen task. And perhaps, before you know it, his "Starman" song may take on a reality all its own if the predicted disclosure about UFOs and extraterrestrials ever comes about in our lifetime.

Over the years we had heard unsubstantiated rumors that Bowie was intrigued by an incident where a UFO was said to have crashed in the desert. We were never able to pin anything down about this incident until we found out that it was actually scribed by Bowie's original publicist and a longtime friend of ours, Cherry Vanilla, who was in his hotel suite when the story came over the TV. Writing under Bowie's name, this is what the fiery redhead is quoting as having been said under Bowie's name in "Mirabelle," a sort of diary published by Bowie's camp.

"I heard the most incredible thing the other day that I must tell you about, and I promise every single word of it is true! I was in Detroit, where I was due to do a concert, and before the show I was sitting in my hotel room listening to the radio.

"Suddenly, the newsman interrupted the regular program with the news that a spaceship had been found in the desert – an alien spaceship about six feet wide and thirty feet long – and inside were three alien beings. The three creatures were killed on impact when the spaceship plummeted to Earth, but they were taken to a hospital to be examined anyway. These people looked like human beings but were much smaller and, when they were examined, it was discovered that their vital organs were like human beings too! The catch is that their brains were found to be much farther advanced! Wow!

# SHIRLEY MACLAINE MEETS THE PLEIADIANS

"As soon as the newscast was over, I got all the band and my back-up singers together and had them ring up radio and TV stations all over the country to see if they had all got the report. About half the stations said they had and half denied it. So, it really is quite a mystery. No one knows what's happened to the spaceship or the spacemen at this point, and it seems that someone is trying to cover up the whole matter completely!"

And so it goes. And while Bowie has given up his Ziggy Stardust roots he does not seem to have abandoned his interest in UFOs and the Star People which have been such an influence on his career.

# SHIRLEY MACLAINE MEETS THE PLEIADIANS

Marc Bolan — looking very much the wizzard.

## MARC BOLAN (T. REX): INSIDE THE MIND OF A "WIZZARD"

### FOR MARC BOLAN

We are pioneering in an age that's just begun.
In a time of thought continuum and space beyond the sun.
Where some acknowledge there is a spirit that is free
But most of the world are planes below and therefore cannot see
To speak at them of Priestesses and places just past Mars
Is only wasting energies, so speak to them of cars.
Speak to them of mortgages and tax rises
While teaching them of mind power in your "Pop Star" now disguise.

—Walli Elmlark

# SHIRLEY MACLAINE MEETS THE PLEIADIANS

Walli Elmlark was known widely as the White Witch of New York. Because of her contacts in the music industry – which were established while writing a column for "Circus," a popular heavy metal magazine that had a sizeable distribution in its heyday in the Seventies – she had established quite an eclectic clientele for whom she would offer spiritual guidance and occasional good luck or love spells, but always of a positive nature.

During the time that I was running the New York School of Occult Arts and Sciences, Walli would hold court in our 14th Street loft lecturing on Wicca, the afterlife and anything that fit into the niche concept of the paranormal.

One of the things Walli was convinced of is that many of the popular rock stars so admired among the youth were being reincarnated – or located – here on Earth at this specific time in history in order to bring about a beneficial change in our cultural attitudes.

Robert Fripp, leader of the British band King Crimson, David Bowie, Eno and Marc Bolan, lead singer of T. Rex (who died in a car crash just when his career was starting to peak in the States) were amazed by Walli's work in the spiritual community and decided a spoken word album that they could get behind might propel her teachings to a mass audience.

At some point, Walli headed off to the UK to work on the album. The album was to be called "The Cosmic Children" and is best described by Sid Smith, a King Crimson biographer:

In June 1972, Fripp finished recording an album with a Wiccan journalist called Walli Elmlark. The album was called "The Cosmic Children." Side one consists of Fripp and Elmlark in conversation where she outlines her experiences and commitment to Wicca. On side two, she talks to DJ Jeff Dexter about cosmic children – spirits from other places who take physical forms such as Hendrix, Bolan, Bowie and Mike Gibbons, drummer with Badfinger. Talking to NME's Simon Stable, Fripp stated: "The function of the album is to reach out to the children like the drummer from Badfinger. I want to say: 'You're not nutty, you're not a freak because you can't relate to what's around you.'"

Fripp and Elmlark were supposed to hook up with Bowie and Bolan in UK. We don't know whether they ever did or not because the spoken word tapes – with musical interludes by these famous artists – have never surfaced and are believed to have been destroyed.

# SHIRLEY MACLAINE MEETS THE PLEIADIANS

I know Walli used to be particularly enthralled with the "cosmic charm" of Marc Bolan, who many knew as the "Wizzard." Said the white witch about this glam artist who sang and played guitar with the band T. Rex: "I have had to meet hundreds of 'pop' stars, but it is a rare name that I can't wait to meet. Marc Bolan was one. I had gotten a very definite impression of what Marc's thinking would be like from listening to his lyrics. They are filled with allusions to wizards, priestesses, planet queens and other varied cosmic complexities."

Countless T. Rex songs written by Marc Bolan refer to flying saucers and outer space, including "The Visit," "Ballrooms of Mars," "Space Boss," "Galaxy" and "Interstellar Soul."

Years later I had the opportunity to speak with record producer Tony Visconti, whose greatest success was "Electric Warrior," the album that made T. Rex front man Marc Bolan a superstar and cemented Visconti's producing prowess. Visconti did nine T. Rex albums and also produced for David Bowie. I was hoping that perhaps Visconti knew the whereabouts of the master tapes to this very unusual record, or could at least clue me in on some of Marc Bolan's cosmic wisdom. And was it true that he was a sort of "Walk-In," a child of the cosmos?

"I can tell you for a fact that Marc wasn't into any of this magical stuff at all,"

Photographer Helen Hovey captured this image of Marc Bolan as he performed with his band T. Rex at the Academy of Music.

© Helen Hovey

## SHIRLEY MACLAINE MEETS THE PLEIADIANS

Bolan was a wizzard, a warlock and a true electric warrior.

Visconti said. He floored me with his comments, which were totally contradictory to what Walli would have had me believe.

Tony pooh-poohed the entire the idea of a musical metaphysical metaphor. He shrugged off the entire concept, and I could see he just didn't want to be bothered with answering questions about UFOs, witchcraft, magic and the like. He could have at least mentioned that John Lennon's sighting of a UFO over the NYC skyline had taken place in the company of May Pang, Tony's one-time wife, who of course was standing near the former Beatle when the craft started to close in on their position on a balcony, sans clothing and with pizza in hand.

Strange remarks indeed in view of the story Walli told about meeting Marc in his hotel room. Walli became convinced that "there was a side of Marc that millions never had seen because it is outside of the realm of general understanding. The concept is so tremendous that it will take a great deal of time before the world is ready, but, right now, all around you are the teachers, the forerunners, the guides that have already begun their work.

"Jimi Hendrix is a prime example," Walli continued. "It is amazing how each of these cosmic teachers at one point had an encounter with Jimi. It was almost as if he travelled the planet hand-picking his people before he returned to that place in time somewhere beyond Mars from which he came."

A very wacky concept in the mid-1970s that has caught on with many New Agers today.

For a while, after seeing a live performance, Walli began to lose faith. Maybe

# SHIRLEY MACLAINE MEETS THE PLEIADIANS

Marc was not such a wizzard after all as his monitors blew up and the sound system went haywire. But she had a meeting set up with Bolan in a couple of days and she wasn't about the cancel it!

Marc was late showing up for the interview, but, when he did return to his room after a whirlwind series of interviews set up with journalists all around the city, he flew into the place like a fireball.

"We went into a back room and I sat on the floor next to him," Wallie recalled. "I listened to him try to explain to a large woman that none of us ever really die (naturally, we believe in reincarnation). He spoke of cosmic awareness, mind power, the fact that he spends a lot of time with gypsies 'because while they are not into formal schooling. They KNOW!'

"Our last five sentences came about when my photographer interrupted long enough to catch the last few leap-year day rays of light for pictures. 'I wish I could go insane or die at times,' I said. 'But I'm not allowed.'" [Walli did die by her own hand, tragically.]

"Of course you're not," Marc consoled her. "You are one of the children, you know that. We know we are all lonely, we must be. We live in a different place, but there is nothing to be done for it."

"Marc, there is a song on your album. It's the shortest song in there, but it gives me such strength. The words came at me like cryptic messages, a few days ago, when I really needed help to go on. I needed a sign that all we know is true, for at times we all wonder if we're just not totally mad. The song is 'Life's a Gas.' I had just thrown a whole group of people out of my life. They hadn't learned, and they were draining me. I hated to get rid of them, but I knew I had to and it would be all right. But I was very down. One hour later, I put on your record and heard, 'It doesn't really matter at all, no it really doesn't matter at all, life's a gas.' And I felt my strength returning. Was I right?"

Marc's eyes lit up and the magic poured through with its blinding brilliance.

"But of course! That's what the whole song's about! It doesn't matter at all. You must not let things matter. Things happen for a reason, and we can make them happen. There is nothing about my career that is an accident."

"We looked at each other and the understanding was total.

# SHIRLEY MACLAINE MEETS THE PLEIADIANS

"My photographer kept saying, 'Look into the camera, Marc. Walli, please, look into the camera.' It was difficult. We are big on eyes. That is where the spirit, soul and heart come through. So much can be said when no words can be spoken. When we left, it was almost like a physical loss. There had been so little time. Yet, at the same time, I felt a tremendous gain. We had been together as if we were two people making love."

There were never to be any future meetings as Marc died prematurely on a winding road, perhaps traveling out of the body back to where Walli believed he came from. Our photographer Helen Hovey's onstage picture of Bolan can be found on his main fan page.
http://nataliemcdonald.com/bolan.htm

Marc Bolan (September 30, 1947 – September 16, 1977)

# SHIRLEY MACLAINE MEETS THE PLEIADIANS

## ROCKER SAMMY HAGAR: A LIFELONG ABDUCTEE?

### (This section on Sammy Hagar written by Sean Casteel)

In 2011, classic rocker Sammy Hagar added his name to the list of celebrities who have spoken publicly about UFO and alien abduction encounters. While it was easy to anticipate the ridicule that would ensue regarding how the rock and roll lifestyle can easily lead to hallucinations and half-remembered dreams, the debunkers are not necessarily going to be right in this case.

Hagar made his remarks about alien abduction in an interview posted on MTV's Hive website, and the story was quickly picked up by other news outlets. Hagar was doing the interview as part of a publicity campaign to promote his new autobiography, "Red: My Uncensored Life in Rock," some of which was excerpted in the March 17, 2011, edition of "Rolling Stone." The autobiography is the typical "tell all" account of excessive substance abuse and wildly out of control egos clashing with one another.

Hagar had previously been a member of the 70s band Montrose and had a fairly successful solo career before he was asked to replace David Lee Roth as the lead singer for Van Halen in 1985. Hagar's description of guitar legend Eddie Van Halen as a monument to drug abuse and alcoholism would be almost poignant if it weren't so frighteningly unpleasant to imagine. The guitarist's descent into total ineptitude on stage as he battled his demons during a 2004 reunion tour was also

## SHIRLEY MACLAINE MEETS THE PLEIADIANS

not easy to read about and was extremely painful for Hagar to witness. The two haven't spoken for many years now.

But getting back to Hagar's interview with MTV's Hive and his comments about the aliens: After the obligatory discussion of groupies and some gossipy talk about the unfriendly attitude evinced by David Lee Roth toward Hagar, the interviewer asks:

"Before reading 'Red,' I didn't realize you had an interest in mysticism. You've apparently consulted with psychics and studied numerology and had crazy dreams about UFOs. Why haven't we seen more mystical themes in your music?"

To which Hagar replies, "I didn't write about it much in Van Halen, but I have done a few songs that have sci-fi themes. There's 'Space Station #5' on the first Montrose album, and then on the second album there's 'Space Age Sacrifice.' My first solo album, there's 'Silver Lights' and 'Hot Rocks,' which are about UFOs coming and taking people away."

It seems Hagar's sci-fi mysticism was "hidden in plain sight" and was a theme of his writing from very early on. His next solo album included "Little Star" and "Someone Out There," which are about how humankind is not alone in the universe. Sample lyrics go like this: "I feel so scared and lonely to think we're the only ones, when I know there's someone out there and someday they'll come."

"People say there's no other life in the universe," Hagar said by way of explanation. "But you know how big the universe is? It's freaking huge! If we're really the only ones out there, that's scarier to me than thinking there are aliens. So my whole career I've been writing about these kinda things. But they've never been the hits. They've only been underground songs. If anything in the book has been played down, it's my mystical side, because I don't want to sound like I'm crazy."

The fear of seeming crazy Hagar complains of is one of the most frequent emotions felt when one first begins to assimilate the fact that one has experienced contact with aliens. When an abductee finally makes the brave decision to speak about his encounters, he must do so in spite of the possibility of being rejected by family and friends as a new and strange reality begins to take hold.

But it is a reality that Hagar seems to inhabit a little more comfortably at times.

"My opinions about the UFO stuff," he enthused, "well, I could write a whole book just devoted to that. I love it, man. I'm into it deep."

The MTV interviewer finally asks, point blank, "Okay, let's just cut to the chase. I'm just going to come out and ask it. Have you ever been abducted by

# SHIRLEY MACLAINE MEETS THE PLEIADIANS

aliens?"

"I think I have," Hagar said.

"What? Really? I was kidding. You seriously believe that?"

Hagar laughed and said, "Now you're making me sound like a crazy person."

"How is that crazy? I wasn't there. I don't know what happened to you."

"Remember the story in the book," Hagar said, "where I have a dream about being contacted by aliens in the foothills above Fontana?"

The MTV interviewer answers, "Yeah, yeah, I've got the page right here."

The interviewer then reads aloud, "I saw a ship and two creatures inside of this ship. And they were connected to me, tapped into my mind through some kind of mysterious wireless connection."

He then asks, "You're telling me that wasn't a dream?"

"That's right," Hagar responds. "It was real. Aliens were plugged into me. It was a download situation. This was long before computers or any kind of wireless. There weren't even wireless telephones. Looking back now, it was like, 'F***, they downloaded something into me!' Or they uploaded something from my brain, like an experiment. 'See what this guy knows.'"

Hagar's decision to call the experience a dream when he wrote about it in his book is typical of abductees in many ways. The abduction experience, when it is recalled consciously and without resorting to hypnotic regression, is often thought of as being a "dreamlike" experience in spite of the fact that it is happening in physical terms. Another familiar aspect of what Hagar is talking about is the need for the UFO contactee to continue to keep the experience filed away as an "unknown," to preserve a sense of "unreality" in his memories of the event. Crossing over to total belief is a dangerous thing for the mind to attempt and is fraught with more complications than the mind can easily deal with. The abductee must be content to let the memories waver in some netherworld of "real/unreal" that he can never totally resolve.

The fact that the aliens "downloaded" information into his brain and also "uploaded" information out of it is often seen in abduction accounts. There is nearly always an exchange of information and data between the abductors and the abductee, though this exchange takes several different forms, occurring frequently as telepathic conversation.

After again affirming the truth of the story he told, Hagar moves on to re-

# SHIRLEY MACLAINE MEETS THE PLEIADIANS

count another experience, this time from his childhood.

"Another thing happened when I was about four," Hagar said, "that I didn't put in the book. One time I saw what I considered to be, well, at the time I thought it was a car with no wheels. We lived out in the country and I saw this thing floating across a field, creating this big dust storm. I threw rocks at it and s***. And I don't know what happened after that."

"You blacked out?" the interviewer asked.

"I guess," Hagar answered. "I just have no memory of it. And that wasn't a dream. It was during daylight."

At that point, the interviewer sympathetically says that he understand Hagar's reluctance to talk about his experiences, acknowledging that alien abduction is a "tough sell."

"Especially back a few decades ago," Hagar said, "when this stuff happened to me. I couldn't talk about it because I didn't know how to explain it. I didn't understand the technology. But now I'm pretty sure it was a wireless situation. Either a download or an upload. They were tapped into my brain and the knowledge was transferred back and forth. I could see them and everything while it was happening. There was a visual involved, almost like . . . I don't know. (Laughs.) Don't get me going!"

Which seems to imply that Hagar has a lot more to talk about, to the right audience and at the right time. If an interviewer more steeped in the literature and everyday manifestations of UFOs and the alien presence were given the opportunity to interview Hagar in more detail, one can only wonder what other revelations would be brought forth. We might even learn why the occasional celebrity becomes a "Chosen One" along with the mere mortals we more often hear about.

One can even ask if rock and roll is an alien invention altogether, the electrified siren's song from the great unknown leading us to new levels of evolutionary development. Stranger things have happened, right? Or maybe not.

# SHIRLEY MACLAINE MEETS THE PLEIADIANS

## MICK TAYLOR: A "ROLLING STONE" AND A WANDERING UFO

God knows just how many gold records the Rolling Stones have to their credit. And while the band hasn't been overly active in recent times, just about everyone from five to fifty knows of Mick Jagger and the rest of the Stones.

What they might not know, however, is that on one particular cold Sunday morning in January of 1970, ex-Rolling Stone guitarist Mick Taylor crunched his way through two feet of snow to get a better view of a glowing UFO.

The place was Warminster, England, the scene of reported UFO activity for approximately 15 years and very close to the area where those mysterious crop circles have been showing up imprinted in the landscape as of late. Back then, ghostly forms and mysterious "whooshing" noises in the dead of night were being reported on almost a daily basis from the mid-1960s on, and just about everyone who ventured into the countryside had a sighting or two of their own to talk about, including this writer. I had actually "communicated" with a glowing disc by way of Morse code sent via a powerful flashlight.

On this dark, eventful morning, Arthur Shuttlewood, editor of the local daily newspaper, "The Warminster Journal," followed Taylor and several American friends of the Rolling Stones around Warminster's dense crops. Taylor, who had been with the Stones since their "Sticky Fingers" album and several subsequent records before going on to a solo career, observed the pulsating glare of the UFO as it positioned itself overhead. "It was so bright," recalls Shuttlewood, "that we all could actually distinguish were the sheep on a nearby hillside huddling together for warmth."

Off in the distance, those present could make out two additional UFOs "wandering about."

"I recall the Rolling Stone mulling over what was happening and wondering if his eyes weren't playing tricks on him. But he eventually had to conclude that the UFOs were quite real as all seven in the sky-watch party had seen the same identical thing."

# SHIRLEY MACLAINE MEETS THE PLEIADIANS

## ACE FREHLEY: KISSED BY A UFO

Few people actually know how I got the nickname, "Mr. UFO." They assume it has something to do with the fact that I've written all those UFO books or edited a half dozen saucer magazines (in about twice as many years). Or they think it's an honorary title bestowed on me because of the hundreds of radio and TV appearances I've made trying to popularize – some say by sensationalizing – the subject.

Well, in actuality the honor really has to go to Ace Frehley, the guitar-wielding member of the phenomenally popular rock band known as KISS. A favorite among the young set – and we older heavy-metallers – the group consisted in those days of four guys who came onstage in heavy makeup, each disguising themselves as a different character from the realm of fantasy, horror and science fiction. They had all kinds of gimmicks as well, including fireworks and a million-dollar stage show to excite their audience. For three years I followed KISS around – Gene Simmons, Peter Criss, Paul Stanley and Ace Frehley (the original members of the group) –asking all kinds of stupid questions in order to fill one magazine article after another.

At this point, there was always an entire troupe of journalists and photographers following them around backstage, trying to get the next scoop. With all these people around, it's a wonder they knew who anybody was. Ace used to refer to me as "Mr. UFO," since I had once printed a short item about his sighting in a UFO magazine.

"It was very strange," Ace was the first to admit. "We were flying from Los Angeles to New York. This happened some time before the end of July 1974, following the recording of our second album.

"The flight had been delayed six hours, and, by the time we boarded, it was

# SHIRLEY MACLAINE MEETS THE PLEIADIANS

well after midnight. I took a seat in the rear section of the 747, isolating myself from the rest of the group and the few passengers who were traveling this late at night. An eerie feeling overwhelmed me as I tried to stretch out and get some sleep since the plane was only partially full and the overhead lights around me had been turned off. As I was about to shut my eyes, I noticed a bright ball of light out the window to my right. I blinked once or twice to make certain it wasn't some sort of illusion, but sure enough this 'thing' was still there. I couldn't make out any great detail. It looked like an enormous baseball and its actions were completely erratic, moving from side to side. The UFO remained in view for a brief period, and then darted off, traveling quite rapidly. I know it wasn't a satellite or another plane. We were pretty high up when it appeared, leaving me to conclude it was a UFO."

When asked how he felt about his sighting, Frehley remarked that he was sort of elated by it. "I've always wanted to see a flying saucer."

Recent photo of Ace Frehley taken by Diane Regine as solo performer (minus Kiss spaceman persona). Copyright Dina Regine.

Early photo of Ace Frehley in his Kiss makeup taken by celebrity photographer Dina Regine at the Hotel Diplomat in New York's Time Square. Copyright Diane Regine

# SHIRLEY MACLAINE MEETS THE PLEIADIANS

## HELEN WHEELS: EXAMINED BY ALIENS!

Helen and Peter on family vacation in the early Sixties. Photo: Allan Robbins

Onstage, Helen Wheels gives a totally "no nonsense" performance; her antics as part of the New York punk rock scene are most legendary. I understand she used to open beer bottles with her teeth, and probably her closest ally remains her pet snake, Lilith, a 95-pound Colombian boa who used to wrap itself around Helen's neck as the band blasted out some fairly heavy numbers behind her.

Helen Wheels was probably best known in the music industry for the songs she composed for the popular Seventies group Blue Oyster Cult. "Sinful Love" and "Tattoo Vampires" went platinum, and several gold records for her writing accomplishments hung proudly in the entranceway to her Manhattan apartment.

And while Helen was spending the bulk of her time putting the finishing touches on a book project with the working title, "We Took Dawn for Granted" (done in conjunction with photographer Maria Agular), the Queen of Heavy Metal was never too busy to discuss her various UFO abduction experiences... at least with the right person.

"I had just turned twelve in May of 1961, and this all happened about a month later," Helen recalled as we passed the Chinese food and attempted to take big mouthfuls of Chicken Chow Fun in between catching up on the latest UFO and rock 'n' roll gossip. "Back then, I was living with my parents and my brother, Peter, in Rockville Centre, Long Island, and on this particular day I remember it being rather warm and hardly a cloud in the sky.

"As my brother and I stood chatting in front of our house, we noticed five faint 'spots' in the sky. Before we had a chance to figure out what they might be,

# SHIRLEY MACLAINE MEETS THE PLEIADIANS

they had zoomed up real fast and were now within a relatively close distance."

The "spots," Helen was positive, were disc-shaped UFOs, "not real shiny, but definitely metallic." She says the craft were so low down in the sky that they could see windows in the ships, and later, under hypnosis, she recalled a shadow passing in front of one of these portholes.

Drawing rendered by Helen Wheels of the sighting and abduction.

"It must have been a Saturday at around noon as I don't remember us being in school that day," she said, attempting to fill in the gaps as we went along and remembering as best she could an experience that was to have a tremendous impact on her life in years to come. "We were literally frozen in one spot as the discs took up a V-formation before our eyes. Neither Peter nor I had been into science fiction and we hardly knew how to relate to these things. Suddenly my brother went to run into the house to tell our mother what was going on, but he didn't get very far because from the lower left-hand object came a brilliant blue ray that hit Peter and halted him in his tracks."

The very next thing Helen remembered was seeing this "huge, cigar-shaped, windowless, silver 'mothership' bigger than any blimp. It just sort of appeared and as it moved along, it more-or-less 'absorbed' the five discs. We didn't see them actually go into the ship or being swallowed up by it, but they were gone. Finally, this 'cigar'-shaped ship moves four blocks away from us, tilts to a

# SHIRLEY MACLAINE MEETS THE PLEIADIANS

45-degree angle and rapidly takes off straight up."

At this point, Peter was lying unconscious in front of Helen, but she knew not to try and disturb him. "It's hard to explain, but I was in telepathic contact with my brother at this time. I asked him if he were dead and he 'said,' without speaking any words, 'No, but I don't want to have to talk about any of this.' So I stepped over his body, went up to my room and proceeded to look out the window till suppertime."

Upon regaining his composure, Peter shook the cobwebs out of his head and proceeded to the library to take out a stack of books on UFOs. "We looked through these books all night, but never spoke about the subject for the next 13 years," Helen revealed, as odd as it may seem.

It was many years before brother and sister would begin the lengthy process of jointly confronting what had happened to them.

"Peter was first to undergo hypnosis, and I followed two years later when I agreed to see a private UFO researcher. Pete Mazzola, in addition to being head of an organization called the Scientific Bureau of Investigation, was a police officer with the New York Police Department and was trained in investigative procedures. Together Peter and I passed voice stress tests administered by Mazzola at the John Jay Police Academy, and later I was placed under hypnosis by 'Missing Time' author Budd Hopkins."

While in a hypnotically-induced state, Helen recalled far greater details than her conscious mind was able to drag up.

"While standing on the lawn, I was hit by a white beam of light and actually 'vacuumed up' into the disc that had struck my brother with the blue ray. I was in a small, round, dark area and a tall being came and got me. For some reason, I wasn't really afraid of him, as he kept reassuring me through messages

One of the greats as captured by one of the greats: Helen Wheels performing at CBGBS as photographed by Kate Simon, 1976.

# SHIRLEY MACLAINE MEETS THE PLEIADIANS

in my mind. The only problem was that the 'audio' – if you want to call it that – was turned up so high that I felt like my head was going to explode.

"Taking my hand, he led me into a control room in which there were all sorts of dials, meters and lights – kind of like a cockpit. Gently he put me into a reclining chair and, leaning back, I could see nothing but an expanse of black space and stars that were not twinkling."

From this Helen surmised that she was taken outside the Earth's atmosphere, though she is unable to prove it. "As for the alien who ushered me around, he was approximately six feet tall, had a huge head, but a very slender body.

He wore a one-piece jumpsuit that was a blue-metallic color with no snaps, buttons or zippers visible anywhere.

"He had light gray skin, huge wrap-around dark eyes, dots for a nose and a slit for a mouth, and when he moved he didn't walk but appeared to float. During all the time I was in his company, we never spoke, but he was able to 'reach me' through my brain."

This being acted like he was some kind of "cosmic tour guide," while the entities she was to meet next had Helen wishing all the UFO people were as friendly as this first alien appeared to be.

Helen at CBGBS, early Eighties. Photo: Mariah Aguiar

"Next I found myself in another compartment with eight or nine tiny guys and a floating table. I felt really frightened in their company, particularly since they did not keep reassuring me like the 'big fellow' had. Suddenly I was on this examining table and they were looking down at me with those large bulging eyes of theirs. Something very painful was shoved up my nostril to the extent that it put a hole in my nose and blood poured out. Later, my mother took me to the doctor for this, so I do have some proof this was not a dream or a hallucination."

Thinking back on what happened, Helen said this experience in the examination room reminded

# SHIRLEY MACLAINE MEETS THE PLEIADIANS

her of a well-run dentist's office, where you really didn't want to be, but where the doctor knew what he was doing, regardless of your personal comfort. "I felt totally violated, as if they had proceeded against my will, and for this reason I do not know if I can ever completely trust them."

After the examination was completed, Helen found herself being transported back down the beam of white light to her Rockville, Long Island, home, "where I'm back on the front stairs and I'm stepping over my brother's unconscious body."

Since the day she underwent hypnotic regression, the talented singer and composer said she had recalled yet other experiences at the hands of what can best be called "aliens," for lack of a better term. "I've had a couple of additional sightings – some in the company of others," Helen noted. "As for the large alien, who I refer to as the 'Grown Up,' he's made his presence known other times as well. I can remember as a child him holding me in my room. On several occasions, he had what I call the 'Dough Boys' with him. These are the little grays who look so much alike that they could be clones. Usually they just stand there and do nothing. The big fellow normally has a large box that he carries with him that has a red light on top.

Helen Wheels Band performance flier, 1976.

"When he first appears, he is fairly tiny and then he begins to grow. The box he carries may have something to do with his ability to transform into our reality."

And while Helen said "they" haven't been around her for a while, things were still not fully as they should be. "For a long time I had the power of 'dream control,' where I could wander off anywhere and be in any circumstances I wanted to be in my dreams. This lasted for three years and it was really eerie. Even now objects will appear and disappear by themselves. For example, just recently I was looking for a folio of songs done by the New York band,

# SHIRLEY MACLAINE MEETS THE PLEIADIANS

The Dictators, and it was nowhere to be found. Then, just the other day, I sat down to work on some of my own songs, and there it was, right in front of me."

Even Peter Robbins, her brother, found his life totally changed after their childhood experience. In addition to appearing at conferences and seminars to discuss his own abduction experiences, the talented stage manager and writer was working on a book dealing with a case in England known as the "Bentwaters Affair" (see "From Out Of The Blue," by Jenny Randles, Inner Light Publications) in which the military actually established contact with the occupants of a UFO that landed on the outskirts of two NATO bases. Peter based his research of this startling affair on the work he had accomplished with former Airman First Class Larry Warren, who was present at this historic encounter and whose own firsthand meeting with funnyman Jackie Gleason is featured elsewhere in this volume. Interestingly enough, on one of the nights Larry Warren was visiting the apartment Peter shared with his sister, a 3-D sculpture that depicts a UFO landing in front of a building made a 180-degree turn while everyone was out of the room.

Helen and friend. Photo: Dana Greene

But Helen Wheels admitted that, as strange as that may seem, we hadn't heard anything yet. "Probably the wildest thing that happened is the time that Lilith, my snake that is all of ten feet long, managed to get out of his glass-enclosed living quarters without anyone going near him. The sliding door to his tank was still shut tight and there were no cracks big enough for even a worm, much less for a 95-pound snake to crawl through. And yet there he was in the middle of the living room."

Were UFOs responsible? One can harbor a guess, I suppose, but it was pretty apparent that when you put together flying saucers and rock 'n' roller Helen Wheels, something really weird would inevitably happen – as it has for many of the celebrities I've spoken with!

Helen Wheels (born Helen Robbins; May 6, 1949 – January 17, 2000)

# SHIRLEY MACLAINE MEETS THE PLEIADIANS

**JEFFERSON STARSHIP ASKS: "HAVE YOU SEEN THE SAUCERS?"**

They sang it at Woodstock – it was said to be one of their favorite songs – yet as far as I know, the tune "Have You Seen The Saucers?" was only released as the flipside of an early Jefferson Airplane 45 and never included on any of their albums. This seems particularly strange since for several years meetings were held at the group's large mansion in California for the express purpose of attempting to contact the "Space Brothers," whom the band glorified with its music on occasion.

In fact, the album "Jefferson Starship" was one of the most important vinyl discs of 1970-71, dealing with the hijacking of a spaceship and taking it to another planet. One of the members of the group even went so far as to have his home built in the shape of a pyramid . . . supposedly to pick up on all those good "cosmic vibes."

# SHIRLEY MACLAINE MEETS THE PLEIADIANS

## THE BYRDS GO FOR A RIDE!

"Hey, Mr. Spaceman" was a top 40 hit recorded "way back when" by The Byrds. Roger McGuinn, leader of the hottest folk-rock group of the late Sixties and early Seventies, acknowledged his interest in UFOs many times. In fact, the group once – undoubtedly as a publicity stunt more than anything else – insured themselves for $10,000 should they be kidnapped by aliens. McGuinn is utterly fascinated by reports that these craft can travel at fantastic speeds, make right angle turns and then stop on a dime. "This is something we can't do. Even our government can't explain what's going on," says the lead singer, who has since successfully gone out on his own and is probably still looking over his shoulder.

## ROBERT FRIPP'S BALL OF LIGHT

Among classical rock fans, British born Robert Fripp is considered to be the best guitarist in the world. Back when he was with the group King Crimson, Fripp and the rest of the band were known for laying down some really incredibly eerie tracks, such as their primary hits, "Court of the Crimson King" and "Twentieth Century Schizoid Man."

Though his onstage appearance was that of a "long-haired" rocker, in real life, Robert Fripp is quite down to earth. There is a very "serious" side to him that includes a profound interest in philosophy and things metaphysical.

I met Fripp backstage eons ago at a concert at the Academy of Music in New York, where I handed him a dayglow poster of the "Water Bearer" taken from a deck of New Age Tarot cards I had helped to create at the time.

Through my friend, witch Walli Elmlark, I knew of Fripp's fascination with such matters. We ran into each other numerous times over the years, and he once

# SHIRLEY MACLAINE MEETS THE PLEIADIANS

recounted how he had parked his van not too far from Stonehenge and was "moving some equipment around in the back" when he happened to look out the rear window and saw this "brilliant ball of light go streaking across the starry sky."

"It's hard to believe there isn't life on other planets and that they haven't visited here from time to time," he reminded me in his native British accent, which many of the ladies found so charming. "I've always been fascinated with the concept of UFOs and would like to get a good look at one someday soon."

Fripp almost had his wish granted when he joined me on a UFO sky-watch and we peered at the heavens through binoculars, waiting for the "flying saucers" to appear. Unfortunately, his sighting of the brilliant ball of light near Stonehenge may be the only thing he has to fall back upon as far as UFOs go, though I haven't spoken to him too recently and often wonder if anything "more dramatic" had taken place to expand his horizons even more.

# SHIRLEY MACLAINE MEETS THE PLEIADIANS

**JOHN LENNON'S "BIG APPLE" UFO**

Though we'll never know for sure, we hope the aliens onboard the craft that buzzed John Lennon's 53rd Street penthouse apartment weren't shy. For, according to the late Beatle's ex-girlfriend, the famed "mod rocker" was standing on the balcony in his "birthday suit" enjoying the view when his quiet evening at home was interrupted by the likes of a vehicle from another world.

May Pang is one of the warmest people you'd ever want to meet. She's quick to smile and bring you into her confidence. Unlike many others in the "rock and roll business," who can sometimes take themselves way too seriously, May is happy to share her remembrances about one of the greatest musical legends of our time.

An American-born young lady of Chinese ancestry, May worked for Lennon as his assistant for almost three years, living with the Beatle during the time he was separated from Yoko Ono. Seated in her spacious apartment, May doesn't mind talking about the "old days" and sharing her wisdom and knowledge with those who are truly fascinated with Lennon's contribution to the culture of the Sixties and Seventies before he was cut down by a madman's bullet.

"John was always fascinated with the unusual," May explained, handing me his once-treasured copy of the "I Ching" that she still has on her library shelf. "He was always caught up in his fate, his destiny. He was, it seems, trying to understand his greatness and the impact he had on millions growing up in a very confused, almost lost generation." In an interview, Lennon had once admitted that he held a particular fascination with psychic phenomena since he was a kid. "I used to literally trance out into the alpha," he noted. "I didn't know what it was called then. I found out years later that there is a name for those conditions. But I would find myself seeing hallucinatory images of my face changing and becoming cosmic and complete. It caused me to always be a rebel."

My own inkling that John was truly fascinated with the paranormal came while I was doing an article on a faith healer by the name of Dean Kraft, who it was said had the remarkable ability to move objects across the floor or a tabletop without touching them. It had been reported that Lennon had befriended the gifted sensitive and had invited Kraft over to his apartment in the historic Dakota building across from Central Park. "Yes!" confirmed Lennon in a phone conversation. "Dean apparently does have these powers. One night recently Yoko and I watched as he made some hard candies still wrapped in cellophane just jump out of a candy dish and move across the tabletop until they landed on the floor.

"At no time," insisted Lennon, "did he touch them."

Unfortunately, with the exception of a concert I gave at which his personal backup band Elephants Memory appeared, I never really got to speak with John again. However, May Pang was more than willing to give me the scoop on John's Big Apple UFO encounter because – as it turned out – she was right there at his side during the incident.

"We had just ordered up some pizza and, since it was such a warm evening, we decided to step out on the terrace. There were no windows directly facing us from across the street, so John just stepped outside with nothing on in order to catch a cool breeze that was coming in right off the East River. I remember I was just inside the bedroom getting dressed when John started shouting for me to come out onto the terrace.

"I yelled back that I would be right there, but he kept screaming for me to join him that instant. As I walked out onto the terrace, my eye caught this large, circular object coming towards us. It was shaped like a flattened cone, and on top was a large, brilliant red light, not pulsating as on any of the aircraft we'd see heading for a landing at Newark Airport."

May says she and John stood there mesmerized, unable to believe what they were in the process of observing. "When it came a little closer, we could make out a row or circle of white lights that ran around the entire rim of the craft. These were also flashing on and off. There were so many of these lights that it was dazzling to the mind."

Spellbound, the couple watched the UFO move directly over the building next to where they resided. "It was, I would estimate, about the size of a Lear jet and it was so close that if we had something to throw at it we probably would have

# SHIRLEY MACLAINE MEETS THE PLEIADIANS

hit it quite easily."

During the time that it was almost directly overhead, May says that she didn't hear any noise. "We often had helicopters flying above us, but this was as silent as the night, seventeen stories up above street level."

Finally the object passed from view, leaving John and May feeling that the excitement was over for the evening. But, as it turned out, the UFO returned, and they managed to set up a telescope and view it that way. "The light was so brilliant coming from the craft," May recalls, "that no additional details could be seen. We did take a couple of pictures, but they turned out overexposed."

Immediately, John and May telephoned "The Daily News" and were told that at least seven other reports had been received. "We even called the police – that's how excited we were – and they told us to keep calm, that others had seen it too."

According to May, all night long, John kept saying, "I can't believe it . . . I can't believe it . . . I've seen a flying saucer."

As confirmation of his sighting, John wrote down what he saw and used it as part of the cover art on his "Walls and Bridges" album.

"John had always had an interest in UFOs," May Pang points out. "He even used to subscribe to a British UFO magazine, 'The Flying Saucer Review.' But after seeing what we saw that night, he became even more fanatical, bringing up the subject all the time."

John Winston Lennon (October 9, 1940 – December 8, 1980)

# SHIRLEY MACLAINE MEETS THE PLEIADIANS

**THE MOODY BLUES: PRINTS ON A PANE**

Can't help but like the Moody Blues. As a hard core rocker, their music sticks to your ribs and leaves you craving to devour more. And you have to know there is something "special" about this band when you consider that our longtime UFOlogical buddy, Jim Dilettoso, received a gold album for his work on the album "Long Distance Voyager." Dilettoso has been involved with the concert management business for decades and in the UFO community is well recognized for his association with the Phoenix Lights, for which he did a complete photographic analysis. He also scrutinized the Billy Meier photos for Wendelle Stevens, a well-known UFO researcher who went to Switzerland to visit the one-armed farmer turned major league contactee. J.D. was also one of the original organizers of the International UFO Congress. In the 1970s and 80s, Mr. Dilettoso produced major music and sports events. For a long time, Jim has recognized that the Moody Blues were deeply engulfed in the lore of what used to be called flying saucers.

Few other rock bands outside of the Beatles have had a more lengthy history or track record of successful hits than the Moody Blues, another British rock group that "invaded" the States years ago and then continued to make enduring music. As with many rock and rollers, it was not unusual to be up late at night returning from a show. And so it was that the Moody Blues were just outside of London when they noticed something following their car. Band members Denny Laine, Mike Pinder, Ray Thomas and Clint Warwick were onboard, but it was drummer Graeme Edge who seems to have become most transformed by the sighting.

"At first, I was convinced it was an aircraft," he relates. "However, it acted most peculiarly. What was really strange was that when this thing passed nearby there was no traffic on the road in either direction, and there were none of the usual nocturnal animal or bird noises."

From what Graeme told his friends, it felt like they were "mesmerized as if in a dream." To the Moody's, the object looked like "a fat cigar with a low protrusion on top, with seven dull red lights on it." They told Peter Willsher, who relayed the story to "The British Flying Saucer Review," that, "The upper half of the object appeared metallic, whereas the lower half was red and pulsed from left to right." Eventually the group decided to leave, as they were overcome with a feeling of "dread and panic."

Sometime later, Graeme Edge was asked to make a sketch of what he thought the aliens onboard might look like, and, lo and behold, he drew what has recently become known as the typical ET-type creature, even though very few renderings of such entities had been made at the time. This leads some to believe that the Moody's might have been abducted onboard the craft that night.

According to Jim Dilettoso of Phoenix, who has worked closely with the group over the years as a special effects and lighting consultant, one of the band's hits written by John Lodge, called "Slide Zone," is in honor of their sighting. "Also," Dilettoso recently told me, "Ray Thomas, the flute player, has had at least one close encounter with aliens who visited his recording studio and left smudge prints on the plate glass window as evidence of the incident."

Interestingly enough, famed keyboard player Patrick Moraz, who toured with the band for many years, has more than a passing interest in the subject. In

# SHIRLEY MACLAINE MEETS THE PLEIADIANS

fact, he performed some great cosmic music at the National UFO and Alien Agenda Conference that I sponsored in 1991 in Phoenix, Arizona. Much of Patrick's music has reflected his being caught up in otherworldly matters.

Those who are into "mellower sounds" will be anxious to know that several of their all-time favorites have professed a solid belief in UFOs – usually because of a sighting or experience of their own.

Indeed, not only have "head bangers," punk rockers and heavy metallers experienced the "light," but such reputable musicians as the late Buddy Rich, Mel Torme, Dick Haymes, Neal Sedaka, Vic Damone, and, yes, even Tiny Tim must be placed into the category of those famous individuals who have glimpsed the Unknown first hand. Their stories follow – and they are quite exciting ones!

Concert producer, lighting technician and ace UFO photo analyst Jim Dilettoso received a gold record for his work on the Moody Blues Long Distance Voyager album.

# SHIRLEY MACLAINE MEETS THE PLEIADIANS

## IN A SLIGHTLY DIFFERENT KEY

## NEIL SEDAKA: SLOW AND STEADY MOVEMENT

Regardless of any generation gap, music lovers of all ages quickly recognize the name Neil Sedaka. One of America's foremost singer-songwriters, Neil has penned so many tunes that it would probably take several pages to list them all. Who can't remember humming at one time or another such memorable hits as "Breaking Up Is Hard To Do," "Happy Birthday Sweet 16," and "Calendar Girl"?

In the midst of talking about his career and future plans, the popular vocalist took time out to relate his only observation of a flying saucer. Neil does not make a "big deal" out of what he saw. To him, the idea of life on other planets and extraterrestrial voyagers is taken pretty much for granted.

"It happened a few summers ago," Sedaka began. "I have a home in the Catskill Mountains in upstate New York. One Sunday I was spending the early evening hours playing with my son. We were fooling around outdoors, when we both happened to glance toward the horizon. There, moving slowly but steadily across the sky, was what appeared to me at first to be nothing more than a shooting star. However, its subsequent action convinced me this object was not a shooting star, nor was it an ordinary aircraft."

Sedaka says the object moved rapidly and then proceeded to slow down. He's certain it was controlled by an intelligent – most likely alien – force.

"My second reaction was that the object must be some sort of satellite placed in orbit either by the U.S. or Russia. I ruled this out almost immediately, because the behavior – movement – of the UFO was erratic."

Neil says that the object remained in view for quite a few minutes. "We eventually lost interest in it and finally went inside to eat supper."

Up until our conversation, Sedaka said he wasn't overly interested in telling anyone outside of his immediate circle about his sighting.

"Some people are still prone to laugh, though the number of skeptics are getting to be fewer and fewer in number," he correctly concluded.

## DRUMMER BUDDY RICH: UFO "SUPER BUFF"

Next to Jackie Gleason, big band drummer Buddy Rich would be what you would call a true "UFO enthusiast." Not only did he have several sightings, but he even became a member of the Center for UFO Studies, which included a friendship with Dr. J. Allen Hynek, the group's director.

I spoke to Buddy on two occasions, and he openly admitted his interest in UFOs, a fascination that went back several decades to the first time he saw an unidentified flying object in 1954. In fact, Buddy had a reputation for talking about the subject whenever he could.

He told me he had often swapped UFO stories with Sammy Davis, Jr., and tried several times to get his friend Johnny Carson to describe what he had apparently seen while looking at the stars late one night.

Relaxing between sets in the dressing room of Buddy's Place, a supper club he had opened in New York, the world-renowned musician took time out from his hectic performance schedule to relate the details of his initial observation.

# SHIRLEY MACLAINE MEETS THE PLEIADIANS

"It was back in the summer of 1954. At the time, I was appearing with my band in Atlanta, Georgia. My brother was right beside me in the front seat of our sports car. We were driving along, on the way to do a show, when I happened to glance through the windshield of the auto and saw two brightly illuminated objects coming out from behind the dark side of the moon.

"We stopped the car in the parking lot of the club to get a better look. The objects were now doing figure-eights in front of our bulging eyes. It was as though they were playing tag, engaging each other in a game of cat-and-mouse. They made incredible turns, at highly accelerated speeds. Under normal circumstances, the resulting G-forces should have crushed whoever was onboard."

Within minutes, Buddy and his brother were joined by the members of his band and 200 patrons of the club who had heard about the aerial ballet and had ventured outside to witness the phenomenon.

"The objects remained in view for a few more minutes. Then they shot straight up, disappearing in the star-studded sky."

About 20 miles from where he was performing, Buddy learned, there was an Air Force Base. He was anxious to report his sighting to the proper authorities, feeling certain that they would be able to offer an explanation of some type for what everyone had seen. "An official at the installation told me that they had received well over 500 phone calls, but that their radar indicated nothing was flying in the area at the time. Since then, I've come to learn that this is a typical military cop-out!"

On a clear autumn night in 1966, Buddy Rich and his wife, Marie, were nearly driven off the road by a gigantic saucer-shaped craft. Their harrowing experience convinced the popular entertainer that our planet is under constant surveillance by extraterrestrial beings.

"We were half-way between Los Angeles and Las Vegas, driving across the desert at about three in the morning. Suddenly I received the jolt of my life! There, zooming down out of the heavens, was this 'thing.' It was 40 feet in diameter and shaped like a disc with a slight dome on top. The outside rim was glowing, sort of pulsating red-blue-white. There was nothing to indicate portholes. Nor could we see any light coming from inside the ship."

Buddy says that the UFO made three direct passes at the car before rising straight into the sky and disappearing.

"It wasn't going terribly fast – maybe 400 miles per hour. When it first appeared, the object came from directly in front of us. Then it banked slightly until it took up a position 200 yards away on the passenger side of the car.

"Next, it made a 160-degree turn and dove at us a second time. Then it disappeared totally, only to return several minutes later. On this occasion, the UFO passed extremely close to the car's roof. Finally, it went up like a bullet, and was out of sight in a matter of seconds."

Though shaken, Buddy and his wife quickly pulled themselves together. Immediately they realized that they had been buzzed at close range by a flying saucer. "There is no other logical explanation for what we saw. There was nothing to indicate it was an airplane. No jet trail, no sound, no nothing! A satellite, falling star or balloon is completely out of the question."

Buddy was positive he saw a visitor from another world in space. "I would estimate that it was big enough to comfortably carry a four-man crew," he added matter-of-factly.

Unable to shake the incident from his mind, Buddy began reading everything he could on the subject. He started collecting books, news clippings and photographs of these elusive discs. By keeping his eyes and ears open, the entertainer was able to amass a sizeable file of information. He willingly shared his findings with several well-known experts.

"Dr. J. Allen Hynek, the astronomer and former consultant to the Air Force on UFOs, was a close friend of mine. We swapped information frequently. I've even met John Fuller, the popular author who wrote a bestseller about a New England couple who were taken onboard a spaceship and given a physical examination by slant-eyed creatures." ["The Interrupted Journey"]

Buddy always wanted to see a full-scale, governmental investigation. "I believe that there's a lot more to all this than the government has told us. I resent the fact that the Air Force and the Pentagon are trying to keep the truth from the public. I believe we are adult enough to accept the consequences. That there are things beyond our knowledge and culture, we should not dispute. We are intelligent enough to accept these things. There is a good chance that the beings piloting these craft are here not to harm us but to help us!"

As part of his crusading efforts, Buddy attempted to convince other celebrities that flying saucers exist. Though his efforts have, on occasion, been in vain,

# SHIRLEY MACLAINE MEETS THE PLEIADIANS

many nationally prominent personalities have openly admitted that they have had unexplained sightings of their own. Among these individuals is Johnny Carson, who just finished a 30-year run of his late night television program.

"Whenever I tried to discuss the subject with Johnny, he'd pretend he wasn't interested. Then one morning, several years ago, at around 6:00 AM, he telephoned me at my hotel. We were both in Vegas at the time. I was at the Tropicana; he was at the Sahara. 'Buddy, I just saw one,' he stammered. 'Saw what?' I asked. 'A UFO! It was real bright,' he continued. 'I was standing on the diving board, ready to plunge into the pool, when this brilliant light passed overhead traveling at outrageous speed.'

"Johnny tried to estimate its size to me and the speed at which it was moving. He told me it was the first time he had thought seriously about UFOs. The object was only in view for roughly 40 seconds, but that was enough time to convince him something strange was up there."

Buddy acknowledged the fact that Carson was always reluctant to talk about his experience on the air. "Whatever he may say about UFOs, it is probably half in jest. But one thing he doesn't do is make fun of the fact that he's into astronomy. He knows quite a lot about the stars. He even owns a powerful telescope."

Among the other celebrities he spoke with was Sammy Davis, Jr. "Sammy often discuss with me how he believed in the existence of flying saucers. He had sightings of his own. No doubt these observations left a firm imprint in his mind. I think most people who have seen them never forget the experience. I know I haven't!"

Buddy Rich (September 30, 1917 – April 2, 1987)

Johnny Carson (October 23, 1925 – January 23, 2005)

# SHIRLEY MACLAINE MEETS THE PLEIADIANS

## MEL TORME: LIKE FATHER, LIKE SON

The expression, "Like Father, Like Son," is appropriate to Mel Torme's UFO sighting. Over the years, Mel must have implanted the seeds of belief in his son, Tracy, concerning an event that had puzzled the elder Torme for many years.

Although it was back in the early 1950s that this famous crooner had his only UFO sighting, his son has shown a continuing interest in the subject. As a successful Hollywood scriptwriter, the younger Torme was involved in writing and producing the CBS-TV special, "Intruders," as well as writing the screenplay for "Fire In the Sky," a movie based on the Travis Walton abduction story.

As Mel Torme tells it, it was late one night in 1953 while he was out walking his dog that a UFO put on a heavenly show for him. "At the time I was still married to my first wife, and we had a lovely little springer spaniel named Spooky that I used to take for walks at night.

"As well as I can recall, it was around 2:00 AM and I was standing in the courtyard of my apartment building on York Avenue and 61st Street in midtown Manhattan. The night was pleasant and, from the center of a grassy knoll, I was offered a full view of the sky. As Spooky went about his duty, I happened to see this red light in the sky over the East River, and it appeared to be moving around quite differently than an airplane would. At first it was only a very small red light and I thought to myself it might be a balloon with a light attached to it. But then it moved horizontal, faster than my eyes could follow it, before stopping dead in its path as though it had hit a barrier. Then it did lazy loops almost like a figure eight.

# SHIRLEY MACLAINE MEETS THE PLEIADIANS

Next it made a few more circles and then noiselessly it went zap again to another part of the sky."

Next, for a brief while, the UFO just hovered there. "Against the pitch blackness of the sky the object resembled the typical description of a 'flying saucer.' Eventually, after three or four minutes, it zipped off faster than my eye could follow. As God is my witness, Spooky just looked up at it and remained rooted still. Now, on many occasions the dog has seen airplanes go overhead, but this time he was totally transfixed and it actually looked like he was shaking."

After all those years, Torme said he could still recall the sighting vividly. "My guess is that the UFO was up around 5,000 feet, just looking down at me. In back of this never-ending 'glow,' I could see a strange saucer-shaped craft of unknown dimensions. To be totally honest, it was difficult to tell precisely what kind of configuration l was gazing upon, because of the steady stream of light this object transmitted. However, if it had come down just a bit closer, I'm almost positive I could have made out windows."

Because of its ability to make miraculous turns, Mel came to the conclusion that the UFO was piloted by superhuman beings. "The UFO started doing 'figure eights,' and 'loops.' It put on a real show for me and Spooky, darting back and forth. I am not aware of any aircraft built on this planet that could do these things, especially in 1953. It defied the laws of aerodynamics. Whoever was onboard must have had flesh made out of steel!"

As it turns out, Torme has a pilot's license and therefore has become accustomed to seeing just about every known type of aircraft.

"Nothing matches the description of this thing that I can think of – not then or now! I can't say for certain that it was extraterrestrial. Maybe there are vehicles that the government is experimenting with, but this was no bloody kite. Nor was it a toy like a model airplane. There was a suggestion of great bulk behind the light. Nothing I know of that we have could move about so quickly and yet make absolutely no sound whatsoever."

That remains true even today!

Mel Torme (September 13, 1925 – June 5, 1999)

# SHIRLEY MACLAINE MEETS THE PLEIADIANS

## A "STRANGE PATH" FOR VIC DAMONE

Vic Damone was born Vito Farinola, the only son of a close-knit, musical family. At 16, Vic went to his first audition and was declared winner of Arthur Godfrey's "Talent Scout" show.

Milton Berle, who was backstage, was so enthusiastic about this young singer that he arranged for Vic to appear at the Le Martinique night club for an eleven-week stand. In a short time, Damone, known as the "King of the Baritones," had appeared in ten motion pictures, including "Hell to Eternity" (1960, with Jeffery Hunter and David Janssen) and in his own TV series, "The Lively Ones," which ran during the 1962-63 season.

It was while stationed in the Army at Fort Sam Houston in 1953 that Damone had a chilling UFO encounter that made him queasy for decades afterward.

"I was seated in a drive-in theater and the movie as I recall was rather dull, so my friends and I, we started looking up at the stars and it was just so beautiful out," recalled the singer, who recorded such tunes as "On The Street Where You Live," and "You Are Only Fooling."

"Sometime later, something caught my eye that chilled me to the bone," Vic went on, shedding more light on the subject. "There was this peculiar glowing thing in the sky. I just knew it didn't belong there. You know when you see a comet or a falling star, it just goes 'swish' across the sky and then it disappears right away, leaving no trail or anything else in its aftermath. Well, here was an object that stayed overhead for six or seven minutes, and, when it did disappear, left a trail that could be seen for quite some time later."

Asked how he was certain it couldn't have been a satellite or some other conventional object, Damone was quick to point out that in 1953 "neither the Russians nor the U.S. had any space ships or hardware in orbit." Though not a trained astronomer, the singer insisted that it couldn't have been any type of meteorite because it was "just too bright and lasted too long."

# SHIRLEY MACLAINE MEETS THE PLEIADIANS

## TINY TIM: MAN OF THE FUTURE

Offbeat entertainer Tiny Tim has had more ups and downs in his career than just about anyone else you could name in show business. His hit "Tip Toe Through The Tulips" sold God knows how many records, and his wedding to Ms. Vickie was seen by one of the largest television audiences ever as part of the Johnny Carson Show.

Tiny is the first to admit that his onstage image may preclude people from taking seriously what he has to say about UFOs and related matters. Which, actually, is somewhat of a shame, since his opinions and thinking on the futuristic subject are more far-reaching than many of the other celebrities spoken with.

Actually, Tim has been floating around UFO circles (at least he doesn't cause them that I know of) for quite some time. Years back, before he became a "headliner," he used to perform regularly at several New Jersey nightclubs, where he no doubt ran into UFO veteran James W. Moseley, past publisher of "Saucer News." Tim went to several of Jim's private parties in Fort Lee, where he often listened in on the flying saucer conversations of such experts as Gray Barker (author of "They Knew Too Much About Flying Saucers"), UFO shutterbug August C. Roberts and contactee Dominick C. Lucchesi.

I can't tell you how much Tiny Tim added to the conversation in those days because I didn't meet him till sometime later backstage at a well-attended concert in Central Park. But I do know that when the topic came up in later years, the ukulele-strumming entertainer has been known to get rather hyper defending certain aspects of his beliefs.

"I've always wanted to travel in outer space, go to the moon," he confessed in a matter of fact tone. "I think we live in a very wonderful age, the space age. I definitely believe in life on different planets. I have always believed that the universe is teeming with life. I even believe there's some sort of life on the moon. I don't see thousands and thousands of miles filled with rocks and dirt. I believe that the next generation will see visitors coming to Earth from other planets."

Unfortunately, Tiny Tim didn't think all UFOs are piloted by the good guys. "There are bad and good people everywhere. I believe that there will come a time when Earth people will be captured by them," and, if he was referring to the recent wave of abductions by aliens, he managed to hit the nail right on the head. "Also, around a hundred to two hundred years from now, we'll have nightclubs on the moon and we'll have nightclubs on Mars and Venus. If you want to get somewhere, say California, you can go into your own mail chutes in your own home and, by pressing a button, you will be wherever you want to go – sort of instantaneous teleportation." (Fans of the "Star Trek" TV shows and movies will be familiar with this concept.)

In the popular press, Tiny Tim said he'd seen quite a number of drawings depicting a variety of space beings. "They could all be real," he readily confessed. "It seems very feasible that some of these aliens could be extremely gentle, while others might be outlaws from another planet. It's possible we could become the slaves of these beings. They might keep us in cages. They could be eight to ten feet tall and have superhuman strength."

Tiny Tim said that one of the big problems he saw in any form of interplanetary relations is everyone accepting the same God. "They might have different beliefs than ours. It's possible they could even spread the message of the antichrist." In these "Latter Days," which Tiny Tim saw as being associated with the Biblical Book of Revelation, he thought there may be great calamities striking the Earth, in particular a very destructive earthquake in California that many have foreseen.

"I can't tell when this is going to happen. I'm not psychic like that," Tiny Tim went on. "But every time I'm out there I say to myself, 'For God's sake stop making those tall buildings.' I see celebrities and all of them going under the sea. New York can't be excluded either. Some years ago I saw people working in taller and taller glass buildings and I know they will be demolished. We should have more plants and more apples in order to turn back the tide of pollution. Either that or we

# SHIRLEY MACLAINE MEETS THE PLEIADIANS

will have to go into outer space to find new lands. Eventually, we will have to slow down our pace and stop drilling oil in Alaska and start to store up food because there's a good possibility there won't be any tomorrow."

As far as Tiny Tim could tell, God seemed to be "dissatisfied with Earth right now. Our religious leaders have gone against Him as they beg for money and let the poor starve in the streets." And while he was not betting that UFOs will be around to save us, he didn't entirely discount the possibility that a mass landing of space ships could come calling to save our cosmic necks in the very nick of time.

On a personal note, Tiny Tim had had several psychic experiences that closely relate to the UFO phenomenon. "Back in the early 1960s, we sent a rocket ship to the moon that was supposed to send back information as to what the moon's surface was composed of. I can still remember watching television late into the evening, and I was particularly anxious to know what the results of the lunar tests would be. That night I had a dream in which I saw myself on the moon actually touching the surface. To me, it felt very much like sawdust. Imagine my shock when I discovered later that some of the particles analyzed by our space scientists indicated that they were similar in content to sawdust that could be found on Earth. How did I know? Someone or something, I'm convinced, sent me this information."

On another occasion, Tiny Tim was watching the Rev. Schuller's "Hour of Power" on TV when the image of a strange creature came into his mind. "I picked up a pen and drew what I thought was a Martian," he revealed. "It looked really odd, but later I saw that same alien image in a UFO book!"

Tiny Tim (April 12, 1932 – November 30, 1996)

# SHIRLEY MACLAINE MEETS THE PLEIADIANS

## TIMOTHY GOOD'S
## TELEPATHIC ENCOUNTERS

A professional violinist who has traveled abroad as well as in his own native England with the British Symphonic Orchestra claims to have had several UFO sightings as well as having established mental contact with individuals who might be associated with these otherworldly craft. Good made an extensive personal study of UFOs. His interest began in 1961. The tall, slender violinist is convinced that Earth is under constant surveillance by advanced alien races.

Born in London, Timothy Good completed his formal education at The King's School, Canterbury. As a violinist he gained a scholarship to the Royal Academy of Music, where he won prizes for solo, chamber and orchestral playing. His professional career began in 1963 with the Royal Philharmonic Orchestra. He played for fourteen years with the London Symphony Orchestra and has freelanced with the English Chamber Orchestra, London Philharmonic Orchestra, Mantovani Orchestra and Philharmonia Orchestra, among others. Composers he has played for include Leonard Bernstein, Benjamin Britten, Igor Stravinsky and William Walton. He has also freelanced as a session player for television dramas, commercials, feature films, and recordings with pop musicians. Among those he has recorded for are Phil Collins, Depeche Mode, George Harrison, Elton John, Paul McCartney, Rod Stewart, and U2.

Good was in New York to perform at Carnegie Hall when he first telephoned me, years before he wrote his many articles and books on the subject. Yet, despite the bizarre nature of his experiences, he was more than willing to discuss his findings with me.

"I had read the books by UFO contactee George Adamski and other literature written by those claiming close encounters. Though I don't believe I am the gullible type, I did find some food for thought. Suppose, I reasoned, they were right, and superior beings were traveling here from other planets? What a marvelous discovery this would be for each and every one of us!"

In 1963, Good was traveling by bus with the famed London-based orches-

# SHIRLEY MACLAINE MEETS THE PLEIADIANS

tra. They were touring the Southwest at the time of his first telepathic communication with what he sincerely believes might have been an alien.

"We had stopped off for coffee in a small town near Phoenix. While standing in line in a local cafeteria, I saw this woman who I thought looked kind of peculiar. I don't really know how to express the feeling but I was momentarily overcome with the thought that she was not 'one of us.' Recalling what I had read in the contactee literature, I decided to try and establish some sort of psychic rapport with her. I pushed my way through the line and got directly in back of her. Then I beamed the message that if she were truly from another planet, she should give me a sign."

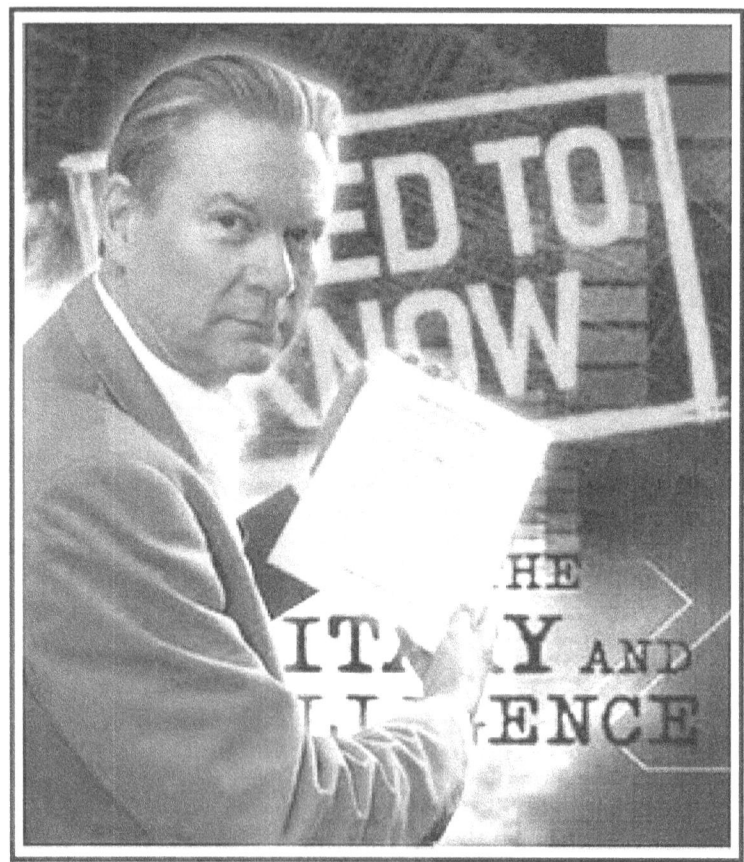

The woman did not respond immediately but went about paying for her lunch. "As I took my seat at a nearby table, the unexpected happened. This woman, whom I suspected of being a stranger here on Earth, walked over to where I had placed my tray, stood directly in front of me and bowed at the waist in a sign of recognition. My heart did a flip-flop!"

Years later, in 1967, Good was staying at the Park Sheraton in Manhattan. "I was beginning to be disillusioned about flying saucers. I hadn't had a sighting in a long while. I wanted definite proof then and there. In order to prove my point (that telepathic contact was possible), I decided to take up a position in the lobby of the hotel. For more than an hour I concentrated as hard as I could. 'If there are any space people around, let your presence be known,' I demanded. Finally, as I was about to give up, a very healthy-looking man, about 5'10", came over, sat down beside me and took out a copy of 'The New York Times' from his attache case. Flipping through the pages nonchalantly, he finally folded the paper back up and put it away. Mentally, I projected: 'If you're a spaceman, touch your finger to your nose.' Without once looking directly at me, he did exactly as I had requested in my silent message!" Timothy Good was so dumbfounded that he was unable to do anything further. "I let this man get away without saying a word to him. There was so much I wanted to ask."

Though he is the first to admit other explanations are possible, in these cases Good is a definite believer that contact via ESP can be made with UFOnauts. "I became convinced 100% shortly thereafter, when I found myself in the home of Madeline Rodeffer, a contactee who worked closely with George Adamski. She lives in Silver Springs, Maryland, and has sighted and even taken motion pictures of UFOs. We were chatting away late into the night when suddenly she got up and walked over to the window. Madeline beckoned to me to follow. 'We're going to see one!" she assured me. Just as the words came out, above the horizon we saw this craft moving along, emitting a shower of sparks. It was in view for almost a full minute, and then disappeared, leaving a trail behind."

A member of the British UFO Research Association and author of the best-selling "Above Top Secret," Good gathers material wherever he goes. "I've visited every continent but Africa. Every place my travels take me, I find people are really seeking answers about the flying saucer mystery."

Loads of questions, indeed!

# SHIRLEY MACLAINE MEETS THE PLEIADIANS

## UFO BUZZES AIRLINER DICK HAYMES IS PASSENGER ON

Don't try to tell Dick Haymes that UFOs aren't friendly! The reason just happens to be that the renowned singer – who was once with the Tommy Dorsey orchestra – was traveling on an airliner that was "buzzed by a 'metallic bullet.'" Furthermore, Haymes believes that "someone" on board that craft tried to communicate with him, convincing Dick that aliens are coming to Earth to assist us in "growing up."

"It was in the summer of 1971," he recalled. "I was flying on a 747 en route from New York to Spain. We were at 38,000 feet – it was just before daybreak – approaching the runway at the airport in Madrid. I was gazing out at the beautiful blue expanse of sky from a port window when my attention was drawn to an oblong object like a bullet which seemed to be flying parallel to our course."

As he watched the shimmering craft basking in the light of dawn, Dick Haymes placed a pair of binoculars to his eyes in order to scrutinize the UFO more carefully.

"The field glasses helped to bring the object into focus and enabled me to get a much clearer detailed view of its surface. It was gigantic – almost twice the size of our jet! I've never seen anything like it.

"It was completely streamlined. No wings, no tail and no markings of any kind visible on the light gray body."

Dick says the UFO stayed "right there with us" for approximately ten minutes. Then, as he watched it, the UFO shot away "faster than any rocket" and was gone!

Luckily, the romantic song stylist was not alone in his observation, as almost all of the other passengers who were awake at this early hour had seen the unidentified escort.

# SHIRLEY MACLAINE MEETS THE PLEIADIANS

"A stewardess came down the aisle and I stopped her. 'Did you see it?' I asked nervously. She nodded. I told her to go up front and check to see whether or not the crew also had it in sight. Minutes later, the young lady returned and told me that the captain as well as the co-pilot had been watching the object as it moved right next to us. Upon landing and talking with some of the other passengers, I discovered that a lot of them had caught a glimpse of the ship in the rising sun."

Dick Haymes had a strong feeling about the UFO. He revealed how he sensed that whoever was maneuvering the huge "mothership" had only peaceful intentions. "It was definitely friendly! I believe that the only way we'll get our world to pull together and stop all the warring factions is to get into outer space and meet up with the valiant and benevolent entities who operate these aerodynamically perfect vessels."

Dick Haymes (September 13, 1918 – March 28, 1980)

# SHIRLEY MACLAINE MEETS THE PLEIADIANS

## UFOs – NO LAUGHING MATTER

The brunt of many a joke, UFOs may be a "belly laugh" to some, but even many of those funnymen who make their living doing standup or slapstick are aware of the fact that, in all honesty, UFOs are no laughing matter. If you don't believe me, just ask the likes of Robert Klein, Soupy Sales and social activist Dick Gregory. And, perhaps most of all, one of the greatest comedians of all time – Jackie Gleason – would assuredly add his two cents worth if he were still alive and could talk about what just happened to be one of his very favorite subjects.

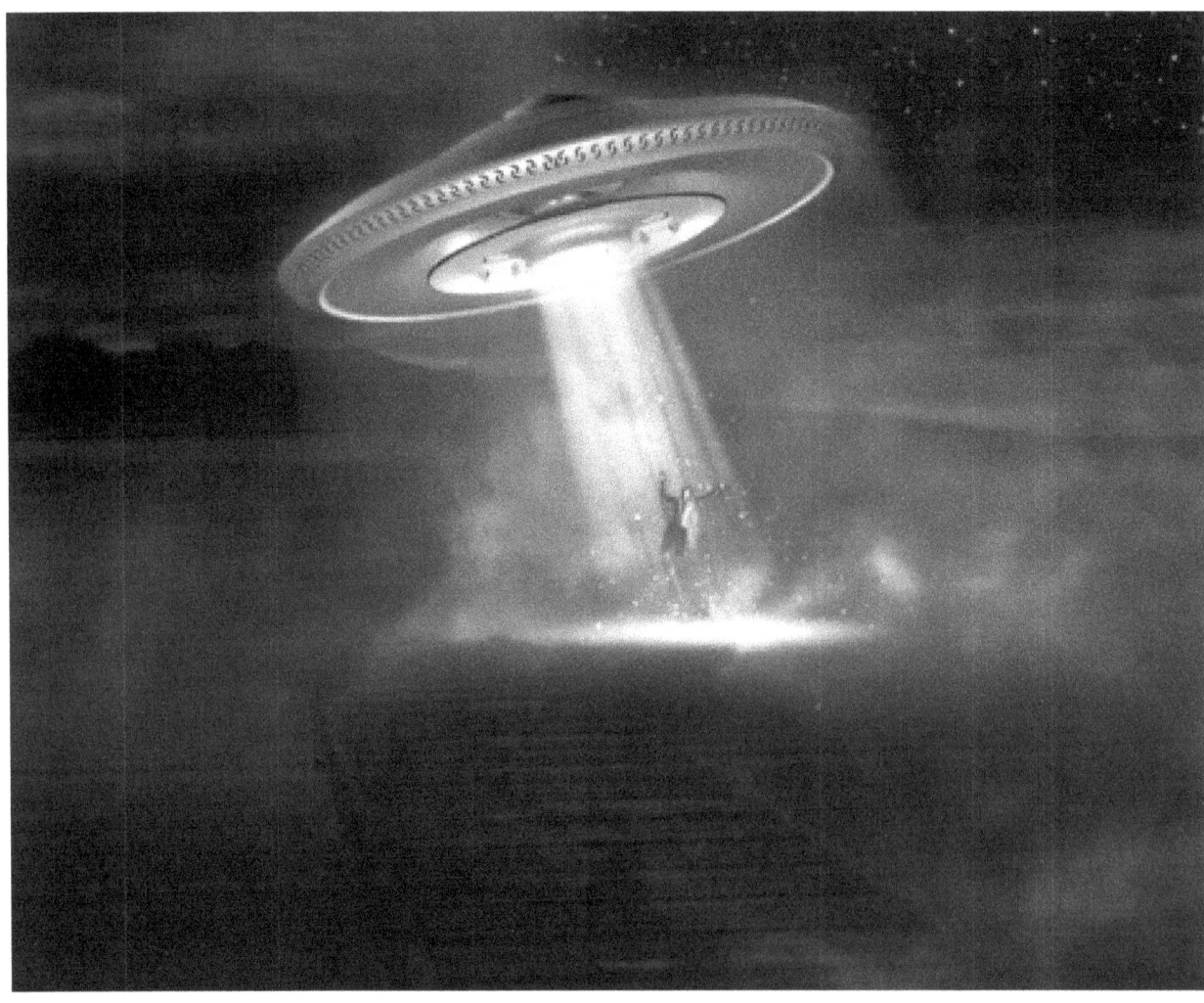

# SHIRLEY MACLAINE MEETS THE PLEIADIANS

## "AND AWAY WE GO" WITH JACKIE GLEASON

Way back in the mid-1960s, I got a letter in the mail from Jackie Gleason Productions, Hollywood, Florida, ordering a copy of a mimeographed booklet I had put together relating to UFOs. This, to me, was confirmation of what I had heard rumors about for a long time . . . that "the Great One" was personally involved in researching UFOs. Supposedly – and I've since found out that this is true – Gleason had one of the largest UFO and metaphysical libraries in private hands. The collection of thousands of volumes was known to stretch from floor to ceiling and included numerous rare titles.

National Enquirer 8/16/1983

In the 1950s, when Gleason was still doing his network TV show in New York, he would frequently drop into the studios of WOR Radio at 1440 Broadway to sit around an open microphone all night and exchange words with "experts" in the UFO field. A personal friend of Long John Nebel, the talk show radio pioneer, Gleason would often use harsh language to "put to rest" those incredible fanciful details of trips aboard UFOs to other planets that he personally did not "buy." And while he was not a believer in the stories told by such contactees as George Adamski and others who claimed they had been to Mars and Venus, he didn't dispute the fact that something strange was indeed flying around over our heads.

The reason for his belief was simple: Gleason had sighted UFOs on at least two occasions that he was willing to admit to in public. Both sightings took place near Miami and convinced the big man that "these were definitely not objects made on our planet. They weren't secret weapons but were solid craft." Gleason added that "on both occasions, the UFOs reflected the rays of the sun and were low enough for me to determine that they could not be explained by ordinary means."

"Okay! So he had two sightings," you might say, "but what could be the big

## SHIRLEY MACLAINE MEETS THE PLEIADIANS

deal about that?" Well, here's where the tale gets a bit wilder.

A story circulated by Gleason's ex-wife, Beverly, has Jackie actually viewing the bodies of several aliens who died when their craft crashed in the Southwest.

The story was carried originally in "The National Enquirer," and though Beverly Gleason later confirmed it to members of the press who were able to track her down, independent confirmation of Gleason's supposed experience – for the longest time – could not be obtained.

Now, with the striking revelations of a young man who knew Gleason personally, it can safely be said that such an event did take place.

Larry Warren was an Airman First Class stationed at Bentwaters Air Force Base in England (a NATO installation staffed mainly by U.S. servicemen) when an incredible series of events took place over Christmas week of 1980.

A UFO was picked up on radar and subsequently came down just outside the perimeter of the base in a dense forest. On the first of several nights of confrontation with the Unknown, three security police ventured into the area and came across an eerie-looking object hovering just above the ground. One of the MPs was mesmerized by the UFO and was unable to move for nearly an hour. While in this mental state, he received some sort of telepathic message that the craft would return.

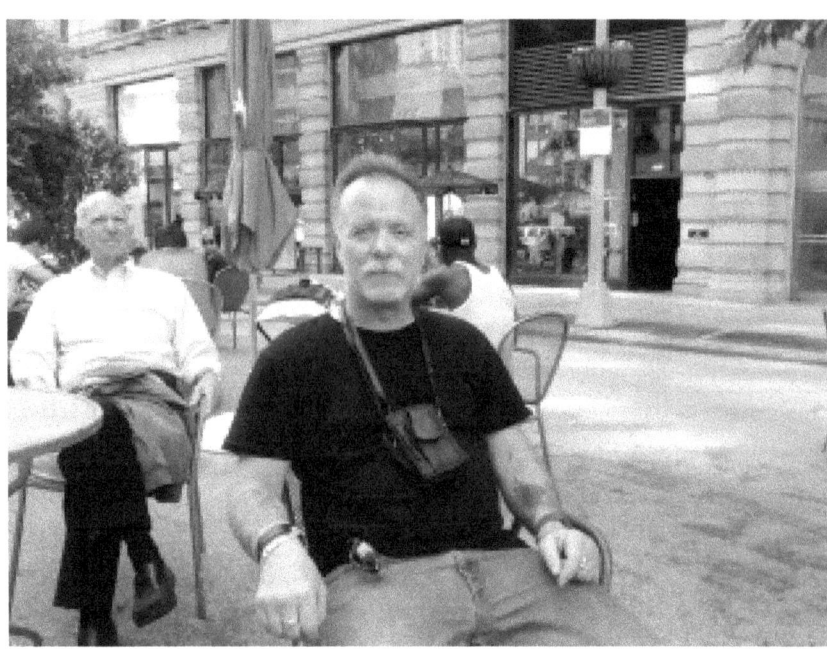

Larry Warren at the Flatiron Building

For the next few nights, up to 80 U.S. servicemen, British bobbies, as well as civilians from some nearby farms, witnessed an historic event. According to Larry Warren, who stood within feet of this craft from another world, three occupants came out of the ship and actually communicated with a high ranking member of the U.S. Air Force.

This close encounter at Bentwaters has become the subject of several books

# SHIRLEY MACLAINE MEETS THE PLEIADIANS

(see "From Out Of The Blue," Jenny Randles, Inner Light Publications) and has been given wide publicity on CNN, Home Box Office and "Unsolved Mysteries." Warren has, in a sense, become somewhat of a celebrity himself as he remains in the public eye, willing to talk about what he observed.

"Jackie Gleason was interested in hearing my story firsthand," Warren said, explaining how he met the famous comic in May, 1986. "At the time, I was living in Connecticut and both CNN and HBO had run pieces on the Bentwaters case. Through mutual friends who knew members of his family, I was told that Gleason would like to talk with me privately in his home in Westchester County. So the meeting was set for a Saturday when we would both have some time to relax."

After being formally introduced, the two men ventured into Gleason's recreation room, complete with pool table and full-size bar.

"There were hundreds of UFO books all over the place," Warren remembered, "but Jackie was quick to tell me that this was only a tiny portion of his entire collection, which was housed in his home in Florida."

For the rest of the day, UFO researcher and UFO witness exchanged information. "Gleason seemed to be very well informed on the subject," Larry says, "as he knew even the smallest details about most cases and showed me copies of the book, 'Clear Intent,' that had just been published, as well as a copy of 'Sky Crash,' a British book about Bentwaters that was published, actually, before all the details of this case were made public. I remember Gleason telling me about his own sightings of several discs in Florida and how he thought there were undersea UFOs bases out in the Bermuda Triangle."

# SHIRLEY MACLAINE MEETS THE PLEIADIANS

But it wasn't till after Warren had downed a few beers and Gleason had had a number of drinks – "his favorite Rob Roys" – that the conversation really got down to brass tacks.

"At some point, Gleason turned to me and said, 'I want to tell you something very amazing that will probably come out some day anyway. We've got 'em!' 'Got what?' I wanted to know. 'Aliens!' Gleason sputtered, catching his breath."

According to Warren, Jackie proceeded to tell him the intriguing set of circumstances that led him to the stunning conclusion that extraterrestrials have arrived on our cosmic shores.

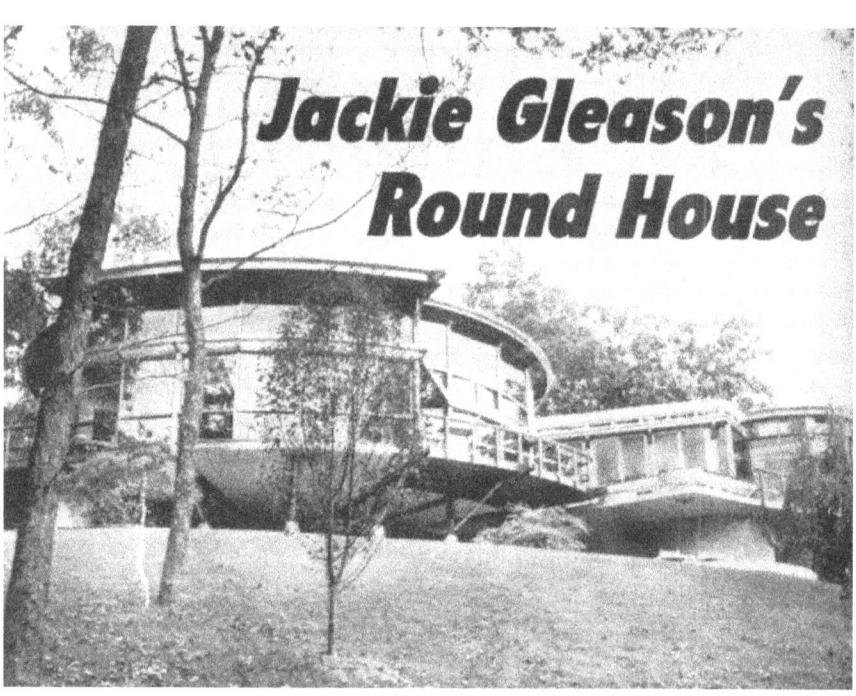

"It was back when Nixon was in office that something truly amazing happened to me," Gleason explained. "We were close golfing buddies and had been out on the golf course all day when, somewhere around the 15th hole, the subject of UFOs came up. Not many people know this, but the President shares my interest in this matter and has a large collection of books in his home on UFOs just like I do. For some reason, however, he never really took me into his confidence about what he personally knew to be true . . . one of the reasons being that he was usually surrounded by so many aides and advisers."

Later that night, matters changed radically when Richard Nixon showed up at Gleason's house around midnight. "He was all alone for a change. There were no secret service agents with him or anyone else. I said, 'Mr. President, what are you doing here?' and he said he wanted to take me someplace and show me something."

Gleason got into the President's private car and they sped off into the darkness, their destination being Homestead Air Force Base.

"I remember we got to the gate and this young MP came up to the car to

# SHIRLEY MACLAINE MEETS THE PLEIADIANS

look to see inside and his jaw seemed to drop a foot when he saw who was behind the wheel. He just sort of pointed and we headed off."

Warren says that later Gleason found out that the secret service was going absolutely crazy trying to find out where Nixon was.

"We drove to the very far end of the base in a segregated area," Gleason went on, "finally stopping near a well-guarded building. The security police saw us coming and just sort of moved back as we passed them and entered the structure.

"There were a number of labs we passed through first before we entered a section where Nixon pointed out what he said was the wreckage from a flying saucer, enclosed in several large cases." Gleason admitted that his initial reaction was that this was all a joke brought on by their earlier conversation on the golf course.

But it wasn't! As Gleason soon learned. "Next, we went into an inner chamber and there were six or eight of what looked like glass-topped Coke freezers. Inside them were the mangled remains of what I took to be children. Then, upon closer examination, I saw that some of the other figures looked quite old. Most of them were terribly mangled as if they had been in an accident."

According to Larry Warren's testimony regarding his lengthy conversation with Gleason, the comic said, "All in all, it was a very pathetic sight. At one point, the President had tears in his eyes, and finally I realized that this was not his way of trying to be humorous."

Warren tried to pin down Gleason for additional information as to how the

# SHIRLEY MACLAINE MEETS THE PLEIADIANS

military had managed to obtain the wreckage and alien corpses. He wanted to know if they might possibly be from the crash of a disc near Roswell, New Mexico, which had been spoken of so often in the literature. "But Jackie could only shake his head and say he didn't know for sure, since President Nixon didn't really fill him in on too many of the details surrounding this very weird display. Gleason did give me a bit more information on the beings themselves.

"He said they were very small, no more than three feet tall. Had grayish-colored skin and slanted eyes that were very deeply set. I forget whether he said they had three or four fingers on each hand, but they definitely were not human . . . of this he was most certain!"

For three weeks following his trip with Nixon to Homestead Air Force Base, the world famous entertainer couldn't sleep and couldn't eat. "Jackie told me that he was very traumatized by all of this. He just couldn't understand why our government wouldn't tell the public all they knew about UFOs and space visitors. He said he even drank more heavily than usual until he could regain some of his composure and come back down to everyday reality."

Larry Warren is convinced that Gleason wasn't lying to him.

"You could tell that he was very sincere; he took the whole affair very seriously, and I could tell that he wanted to get the matter off his chest, and this was why he was telling me all of this."

And, as far as Larry Warren was concerned, the Great One's personal testimony only added extra credibility to his own firsthand experience with aliens while he was in the service.

"Jackie felt just like I do that the government needs to 'come clean' and tell us all it knows about space visitors. It's time they stopped lying to the public and release all the evidence they have. When they do, then we'll all be able to see the same things the late Jackie Gleason did!"

Hopefully this day may arrive soon.

John Herbert "Jackie" Gleason (February 26, 1916 – June 24, 1987)

# SHIRLEY MACLAINE MEETS THE PLEIADIANS

**DICK GREGORY: THE GOVERNMENT'S COVERING UP**

Dick Gregory is a true crusader – a champion of human rights. Sometimes thought of as the country's top black humorist, the tall, slim satirist is a vocal fighter, a nonviolent man who will back any legitimate cause and see to it that the underdog is heard just as loud and clear as anyone else.

To set the record straight, Gregory loves America, but he does want to see things improve. "This is the only country in the world," Dick says, "where a man can grow up in a ghetto, go to the worst schools, be forced to ride in the back of a bus, then get $5,000 a week to talk about it."

Dick Gregory is certain there are UFOs! He's seen them! And even photographed them. (He used to carry around a picture he took of a formation of UFOs in his wallet!) But he doesn't like to talk too much about his own experience because he feels there is great potential for manipulation when it comes to UFOs. In fact, he seems to back the idea put forward by some UFOlogists (including the late former Naval Intelligence Officer, William Cooper) that a "Secret Government" exists that is really in control of what we are allowed to think and believe regarding a lot of matters.

"Whether they know it or not, most of our elected officials are just pawns," Gregory insists. "Big money is really in control and is trying to foster the idea of a one-world government. And I'm not talking about the small-change people like Rockefeller. I'm talking about the big boys, those like the Rothschilds . . . those that run the international banking corporations."

Asked if he thinks this "Secret Government" actually meets and plots what is going to happen on a global basis, Gregory answered in the affirmative. "Sure they do! They plot 60 to 70 years in advance . . . they try to raise families to take over the dynasties, but if their youngsters turn out wrong, they try to get them out of the way."

Gregory says he finds it very strange that, within the last few years, information is starting to be leaked to the public regarding UFOs.

"I mean, there are a lot of folks that once worked in the government that had gone on record as saying these objects never existed, and now they turn around and admit there is something to it after all. I really don't want to be a part of this [manipulation factor], but I do think it is legitimate. There is a lot of information that is going to come out soon that will convince the public there are flying saucers, but it's just part of this new conspiracy to formulate a one-world government through creating dummy UFOs."

As far as beings coming from other planets to assist our world, Gregory says he wishes it were true, but remains skeptical. "I don't doubt that they might be ours, or they might be the real thing. I would say it's a sad day if somebody from outer space is fooling around with our planet. They've really got to be out of it. If they only would say something – help clean up the pollution or something."

Dick says that he does know of a man in the Baltimore area who has invented a spacecraft that works on some advanced principle of physics. "It's supposed to run on nothing but air. I don't believe the government will ever allow him to fly this device. It would put the large gasoline companies out of business, and this they won't allow."

Pressed further on the matter of why he does not like to speak on the topic of UFOs, Gregory maintains that celebrities are often used as part of a "controlling factor."

"I think those in 'charge' of things will go around and get celebrities – those in the public eye – to support the contention that there are actually flying saucers coming here. People will listen to personalities. Even the FBI printed an article in

## SHIRLEY MACLAINE MEETS THE PLEIADIANS

one of their newsletters on what law enforcement agents should do if a UFO is sighted in the community. A former astronomer who was with the Air Force in the early days of their UFO investigation ended up heading his own 'private' agency after years of denying their existence. So, yes, I had a sighting, and, yes, I believe in UFOs, but they would like to use me to their advantage and I don't want to let them!"

# SHIRLEY MACLAINE MEETS THE PLEIADIANS

## ROBERT KLEIN'S SIGHTING OF SIX CIGAR-SHAPED UFOs

Comic Robert Klein makes his living by being funny. Yet he revealed during the course of a conversation that he is extremely serious when it comes to his sighting of a UFO.

Klein says he finds the concept of interplanetary visitors to be an engrossing subject. It is, he verified, an area of much controversy that has fascinated him for many years – going back to when he had a UFO sighting of his own.

"It was during the summer of 1957," Klein confided in complete candor. "I was only 15 at the time, but believe you me, my recollection of the event is as strong today as when it happened."

Relaxing and taking a long draw from his pipe, the well-known humorist began reminiscing about the details of his experience:

"My parents had sent me to a camp in Kent, Connecticut, for the summer. On this particular occasion, there were about 25 of us guys killing time just fooling around, playing baseball or something. Before I knew what was happening, a group of my buddies were craning their heads skyward and jointly pointing excitedly at something. Following the direction of their stare, I immediately saw what had captured their attention. There in plain view were these six cigar-shaped objects moving by at an extremely high altitude.

"They were in formation, one right behind another, traveling in and out between the cloud layers. Strange as it may seem, they made absolutely no noise. I mean, not a sound. They were just coasting along as if they hadn't a care in the world. As hard as we tried, we couldn't make out any great detail, because they were so high up. Seventy to eighty thousand feet, I would estimate. But because of their great brilliance, caused by the reflection of the sun, we could definitely ascertain their shape as being elongated. Sort of like a car, but blunt at both ends. They must really have been exceedingly large and traveling pretty fast because they went out of viewing range after several minutes. How something this size could travel at such great speeds and not make any noise is beyond my understanding. They defied all the laws of physics."

Klein makes it quite clear that he is not an expert on the subject. "I don't want people to get the wrong impression and to think that Robert Klein goes around seeing flying saucers all the time," he declared. "That happened quite a few years ago and I've never seen anything like them before or since. In fact, I couldn't swear that what we observed was an armada of interstellar space ships. That's only speculation. But, at the same time, we were so startled over what was transpiring that we moved quickly to call the nearest military installation, a Naval base, to report what all of us had seen. A representative of our group, the only one present who wasn't speechless or tongue-tied, spoke for several minutes to a high official at the base. Apparently, he took us very seriously and even admitted that other reports had been received at about the same time. Despite an obviously concerned attitude on their part, they never did call back to explain what it was we had been so privileged to see. But I'm told it's really par for the course, as I understand the government has a tight-lipped policy about such things as flying saucers."

When asked to speculate on what they might have seen, Klein says if they weren't from outer space, then perhaps they were a top secret form of military aircraft. "Since this was during the early days of our own space program, the Air Force might have been testing out a new jet aircraft or rocket. It's hard to say for certain. They certainly didn't behave in the manner of any conventional military or commercial plane that I am familiar with."

As for life on other planets, Klein says the universe no doubt teems with many life forms. "We don't know what we will find out there until we have explored it more fully," the New York-raised actor/comedian went on. "On the other hand, I don't feel that we have been visited as often as people might think. I think we're far too boring for them to come down. We're not interesting enough. If anyone really wants to contact us, they can. We have lots of signals going out and have the equipment to receive any message beamed our way." Klein added, on a more positive note: "Of course, they (these interplanetary 'visitors') might be frightened of our normally hostile attitude toward anything unusual or unknown. They might be afraid we would contain them in jail or even shoot them should they attempt to land and make themselves known. There's always this doomsday destructive feeling on our part, that any creature from outer space would have the same kind of traits that we have; thus they would have to be hostile."

In conclusion, Klein admits that he is fascinated by the possibilities and enjoys speculating on the subject. "We should, as an intelligent species, try to find out all we can about ourselves and the surrounding cosmos. This would include

# SHIRLEY MACLAINE MEETS THE PLEIADIANS

visitors from afar who might make Earth a stopping-off point in their travels. I strongly believe there is a rational explanation for the majority of UFO sightings, but there is also quite a bit about which we know nothing and a lot that remains unexplained. I must, in all honesty, put my own UFO sightings into this category."

## A BIT OF LEVITY WITH "UNCLE MILTIE"

Milton Berle let out a hardy but friendly laugh when the subject of UFOs was brought up. When asked if he'd ever seen any, the veteran funnyman chuckled. "No, only during my act. On several occasions, members of the audience have thrown saucers and plates – all kinds of dinnerware – at me!"

Becoming serious for a moment, "Uncle Miltie," as he is known to his adoring fans, confessed that he sincerely believes in the possibility of UFOs. "Something is up there. People have been seeing something strange." As for life on other planets, "Yes, I do believe in that, too," he commented.

While his busy schedule does not usually permit the entertainer time to look up at the sky, Berle did promise to relay any sightings he might have.

Milton Berle (July 12, 1908 – March 27, 2002)

# SHIRLEY MACLAINE MEETS THE PLEIADIANS

## SOUPY SALES: THEY WALK AMONGST US!

Soupy Sales was born Milton Supman on January 8, 1926, in Franklinton, North Carolina, at about three in the afternoon. "Although," as he tells it, "I always thought I was born around 10:00 in the morning. But, then again, my mother wouldn't want me to be born in the morning. See, like at 3:00 PM, she's been up, had her coffee..."

As for how he got his stage name, Soupy explains that, "In those days everybody had a nickname. And they used to mispronounce mine. They called me 'Soupman,' 'Soupbone,' and then all of a sudden cut it short and it became Soupy. Sales was taken from Chic Sales, a very funny comedian. In fact, the funny thing was my kids were like seven or eight at the time when one day their principal called up and said, 'Your boys have been absent for some 20-odd days.' I said, 'Where could kids go?' What happened, they were calling the name Supman and my boys never knew their name was that and so they would never answer. So I said, 'Can't you just remember that?' And they said, 'We don't do things that way.' So I went to court and legally became Soupy Sales."

Though he intersperses even the most serious subjects with bits of humor here and there, Soupy seriously contends that he knows enough about ESP to realize that he has it.

"Numbers seem to be most prevalent with me. I can stand at the crap table and watch people shoot and I can usually tell in advance when the number eleven is going to roll out. I can go to the races and, despite the odds, usually know what horse to bet on and he will win. When fall comes around, I can go over the new TV schedule and instinctively know which shows will get the axe and which will be successful."

Because of this extra sensory ability, Soupy Sales maintains he can intuitively tell if someone is around who is not from this planet.

# SHIRLEY MACLAINE MEETS THE PLEIADIANS

"I just don't know why anyone would think that life could only happen over here in our part of the universe. I cannot believe that there is not life on other planets. The only thing that bothers me is why they have never gotten in touch with us on a wide scale. Usually it's the rural farmer or a lonely fisherman who's contacted. But then again, they could be afraid of getting mugged!"

Though he has never had a UFO sighting as such, Soupy is convinced that aliens are here already, walking amongst us. "I definitely think there are a few people running around today who are from another planet. There is just something about them. I can tell in their face and in their eyes."

Asked for a further explanation, Soupy pressed on. "It's something about their eyes and the wrinkles and the structure of their eyes and the whole eye area that allows me to tell them apart from Earthlings."

Soupy says you can run into them anywhere, "in elevators, in shopping malls and possibly even in my audiences when I'm performing."

As for humankind meeting these aliens in space, Soupy feels "there are a lot of people on this Earth who should be put on another planet. It would do them, and us, a world of good. You never know what the flight might do to them. There are a lot of bad cats around."

Soupy Sales (January 8, 1926 – October 22, 2009)

# SHIRLEY MACLAINE MEETS THE PLEIADIANS

## EMMETT KELLY, JR.: ANCIENT ASTRONAUTS TO UNEARTHLY OBJECTS

America's most popular clown for years has been Emmett Kelly, Jr. A versatile performer, Kelly's one-ring circus travels the country hitting shopping centers and theatrical arenas, featuring a poodle in a G-string, a free-for-all wrestling match with a 700 pound black bear and dozens of acrobats.

When not entertaining under the Big Top, Kelly makes his home in Johnson City, Tennessee, where he does a lot of reading on archaeology and lost civilizations. He has become quite an expert on Egyptology and can read ancient hieroglyphics. "There's a lot scholars aren't telling us," Kelly said as I sat in his circus trailer at the end of a rigorous day. "There's one story I've been able to decipher which tells of the only woman pharaoh ever. Her name was Ha-chep-sut. The wall of her burial tomb tells about the adventures of her lifetime. It tells about a trip she took from Alexandria by boat to the continent of Atlantis. She got back in her boat and sailed to another land mass, crossed over a mountain range and visited a colony in Mu before setting sail again for Atlantis and eventually returning to Alexandria."

Wanting to know if there was any evidence that space visitors were involved in Egyptian culture, Kelly announced that there was a good possibility of this. "I'm a firm believer in the UFO cover-up. And the reason for the government's policy is simple enough. If they told us the truth they'd have to rewrite every science book around the world."

Kelly further stated that, over the years, he has had the opportunity "to sit with some big people and discuss UFOs." This in addition to having several sightings of his own to mull over.

Emmett allowed as how it's really very hard to recall when he first became interested in UFOs.

"I'd been hearing about

them for years, but never saw one until 1959, while attending the annual 200 mile boat race around Elkhart Lake in Wisconsin. We were all sleeping out in our cars and on the ground in sleeping bags and it had just gotten dark. The sun had just gone over the hills and we're all standing and sitting around, about eight of us yacking away, when one of the guys suddenly says, 'Oh, look there's the moon.' With that we all looked to the north and, sure enough, there's the moon – it was hovering, a round, domed globe. And we go on talking and one of the other guys says, 'Hey, that can't be the moon, cause the moon's over there.' And, sure enough, the second guy was right, and we said, 'Then what the hell is that thing?'"

The eyewitnesses all agreed that the object was a solid globe, gold in color. "It wasn't radiating light or anything. It was just a perfect round outline up in the sky. We looked at it for about 20 minutes or so, and then it started to move slowly eastward out toward Lake Michigan. We didn't know what the hell it was or what it was doing. I don't think we even tried to connect it to flying saucers, except on the 6:00 AM news, a Milwaukee radio announcer was saying that over 2,000 telephone calls had been received that night at the station, the Sheriff's Department and at the state Highway Patrol headquarters, and that nobody knew what the object was."

As it turns out, Kelly's next sighting will always remain fixed in his mind, as it took place on November 22, 1963, the same day President Kennedy was assassinated.

"I was en route from Jackson City, Tennessee, to Johnstown, Pennsylvania, and had pulled off to one of those rest stop areas where the trucks pull into. I was driving a Dodge convertible at the time and I turned the heater on full blast and tucked up a pillow and was ready to take a cat nap when this giant fiery thing comes hurtling down. Where it came from or where it went I never did find out. I have no idea what it was. It had a streak in back of it, a solid green streak, and it looked like it had some white color in it and some green and it looked sort of like aluminum. I don't know how far away it was when, all of a sudden, it just exploded. The car shook, but there was no sound, and I've never been able to understand that particular phenomenon."

# SHIRLEY MACLAINE MEETS THE PLEIADIANS

## THE BROWN MOUNTAIN LIGHTS

Being an inquisitive person, Emmett Kelly, Jr., is prone to investigate most matters if they seem too far-fetched to be believed out of hand. A case in point is the mysterious lights that have been seen for hundreds of years along the ridges and valleys of North Carolina's Brown Mountain, located about 15 miles north of the town of Morganton.

Here, long before the white man had reached the shores of America, the Indians reported seeing these strange glowing orbs weave and bob about the mountain peaks without any apparent source. The Cherokee and Catawba feel they were the braves of the two tribes killed in a big battle many moons ago, while others have come to accept them as some form of natural, but unexplained, "Earth lights," while many others feel they may be some form of intelligence from outer space.

Witnesses have watched the lights make fairly incredible maneuvers, such as butting into each other and bouncing around like basket balls. One observer tracked them at speeds of almost 100 miles per hour. Another individual – a gentleman by the name of Ralph Lael – contends that he actually established contact with the lights and that they live beneath the mountains in deep caverns and originate from Venus.

For the most part, during certain seasons at least, the lights appear fairly regularly and have become part of the lore of the area. Tourists have traveled from thousands of miles (including this author) to bear witness to the unexplained

# SHIRLEY MACLAINE MEETS THE PLEIADIANS

phenomena. Among the travelers is Emmett, who sizes up his experiences at Brown Mountain this way:

"Looking downward and across at Brown Mountain from Highway 181, we've seen all these lights come and go. Dim and brighten up. One time, there were three red lights on the mountain, one in the middle and one on both ends. If you go over there in the daytime, you can't see them. But they are there at night. From a vantage point looking downhill from a lodge that is just about to the top of Vesuvius Ridge, you can see this great granite section of the mountain that contains no shrubbery, just straight granite. Someone pointed out these lights and said to take a good look at them. I saw two amber ones together. Not real bright, but just steady amber. Then there were four red ones in straight columns, the tops of which were blinking, alternating red. There were also three red lights in a straight line and, at the base of these, there were four amber lights so straight you could lay a ruler out across them."

Waiting to see if they showed any signs of having an intelligence behind them, Emmett proceeded to try and signal them. "I got this powerful flashlight out of the car. I was in the Navy and I remembered how to send an SOS – which is, oddly enough, the only thing I can recall about the International Morse Code. I put the flashlight on my chin to get a steady aim and I'm standing there and pointing the light right through a clump of little trees. And I go dit-dit-dit-dit-dit with the button, when all of a sudden these two amber lights lit up real bright. I thought to myself, my God, I've never seen them that bright. And in between and just above a little white light comes on that was so brilliant that it reminded me of those carbon arcs on the battleships and carriers from my Navy days. In fact, they were like candles compared to this light. I've never seen anything so bright and penetrating in my entire life. And it sent in real rapid succession SOS-SOS-SOS and went out. We got scared and got into the car and took off, afraid that some UFO or flying saucer was going to come after us."

Getting their nerve back a few days later, Emmett and one of the ladies that had been among the group decided they wanted to try and reach the exact spot where they had seen the lights flare up.

"We had to park the car and hike for a while as there was only a jeep trail and that only went about a third of the way. Finally we reached this granite place, and I'm walking ahead of the person who is with me and all of a sudden I hear something moving nearby. We stood still and it sounded like someone walking on a 50 gallon oil drum that was empty, very hollow. I don't know if it was coming from beneath the mountain, but when we knocked on some of the rocks, it didn't duplicate what we had heard. We climbed all over that granite spot looking for breaks in the sides of the walls, but never came across any.

# SHIRLEY MACLAINE MEETS THE PLEIADIANS

"Apparently, there have been at least two different scientific teams from the federal government down there; one from the Smithsonian Institute, and the other sponsored by the Department of Agriculture. Neither could find anything unusual, even though they had all the sophisticated scientific equipment. I've always felt there might be an underground UFO base in Brown Mountain, but it's 'wired' in such a way that if anything gets near these openings, they close up for their own protection."

Emmett Kelly, Jr. (November 13, 1923 – November 29, 2006)

# SHIRLEY MACLAINE MEETS THE PLEIADIANS

## MUHAMMAD ALI: KING OF THE UFO WATCHERS

Of all the famous folks I've spent time with discussing UFOs and theories about extraterrestrial civilizations and life in outer space, no one seems to know more about the subject – at least from a firsthand point of view – than retired heavyweight boxing champion Muhammad Ali. Thus, Ali deserves an entire chapter for himself.

I'll never forget the first time I went to visit Ali at his home in Cherry Hill, New Jersey. I remember thinking to myself, "What a place! This looks more like a Holiday Inn than somebody's residence." There was a long, circular driveway paved with massive cobblestones with four or five classic cars parked in front of an adjoining garage that would be any collector's dream. Ali owned them all! Even here where the wealthy reside, it was hard to believe that few would ever attain the financial plateau reached by their most prominent neighbor. Towering well above six feet, I had first met the most famous prizefighter of all one morning around 5:00 AM as he sprinted along the trail that leads into Manhattan's Central Park around 80th Street. His long-time friend and trainer, Angelo Dundee, warned me that Ali wanted to talk and jog at the same time, as he was getting into shape to fight then-arch rival Oscar Bonavena.

I looked at my own less-than-perfect physique, wondering whether I could keep up with Ali's pace, even for a short distance.

As luck had it, Ali didn't plan on doing any heavy sprinting. After introducing myself and giving Ali a brief rundown on what I wanted this opportunity to speak to him about, we began to trot and chat simultaneously – fortunately at a speed that, though taxing, I could maintain.

The "knockout" king had been working out in the park on previous morn-

# SHIRLEY MACLAINE MEETS THE PLEIADIANS

ings and had made the news by claiming to have seen not one, but two UFOs moving over New York City. Both in the park and later in his home, Ali would tell the same story to all those willing to listen.

"I happened to look up just before dawn, as I often do while running, and there hovering above us was this brilliant light hanging as if by an invisible thread. At first I thought it was a beacon projected from a helicopter," Ali explained, "but moments later a similar object passed in front of us." The second UFO had a glowing red trail behind it.

"I brought it to the attention of my trainer, who was standing nearby. We watched them come from behind the skyline and move slowly across the sky for at least 15 minutes. The best I can describe the sighting is to say they were just round and big." Ali says he later found out there were other UFO sightings made that same night, "including a report from a pilot about to land at Newark Airport."

A number of reporters traveling with the Champ jumped on the story and it was picked up by the wire services, though Ali was concerned that these re-

Photo www.Uri-Geller.com

ports made it sound as if the subject were to be treated as a joke. He wanted to let me know right from the starting bell that he was quite serious about what he had seen. "This is no joke. All my friends here saw it."

Ali added that this was by no means his only encounter with a UFO. "Actually, I've seen them many times before. I've had 16 sightings total to date," he said as he headed toward his limousine. I was prepared to bid him goodbye, but he waved me over and said he wouldn't mind talking further.

"I have a few more stories you'll definitely find of interest. Why not come over to the hotel and we'll discuss these things some more."

When I arrived at his hotel suite sometime later along with Global Communications correspondent Harold Salkin, Ali was trying to relax. He was flat on his stomach talking a mile a minute to a small group that had gathered while at the same time getting a massage and rubdown from one of his personal aides.

Trying to cram as many words and thoughts into each sentence seems to be his method for getting a particular message across.

"Hey, I wanted you to check out these paintings. The champ's an artist you know."

He motioned to four or five medium-sized canvasses. "I'm quite good, I've been told" he went on, rapping to no one in particular but everyone in general. It was easy to see how the public always got the impression that Ali's a braggart. He is, but it's all part of the hype that made him the most talked about – and highly-paid – boxer in the annals of prize fighting.

Now he looked directly at me. "I thought you would find this really fascinating," he remarked. "In my painting, I brush in the number of the round I'm going to win my next bout by. See this one with the number three in it? I did that a few weeks prior to pounding Jerry Quarry into the mat. It happened exactly as I predicted."

During his career, Ali had long been known for his poetic flights in which he foretold the round his opponent would be knocked out in or otherwise defeated. Some of his divination was accurate; other times . . . well. But his paintings all contained the right round number.

"Remarkable?" One reporter was heard to mumble under his breath that he wasn't sure our host hadn't airbrushed the correct round numbers in after his successful ring appearances. (Some people will just never believe, I thought to myself.)

After testing the credibility of the group further, Ali went from predictions and poetry to UFOs. "You know those objects we discussed in the park? I've mentioned this to no one before, but they've been watching me for some time now!"

"When?" "Where?" "Why?" We all queried at the same moment.

"Many times, in the early morning hours, if you look up in the sky you can

# SHIRLEY MACLAINE MEETS THE PLEIADIANS

see them playing tag between the stars, really high up. I've had a good number of sightings myself. The closest one happened when a cigar-shaped ship hovered briefly over a car I was a passenger in one night driving north on the New Jersey Turnpike. What a sight that was. We could see the shadow made by the UFO as it passed over the pavement of the road in the light of the full moon." His trainer put down the bottle of rubbing alcohol; Ali raised himself on his elbows.

Ali's voice shifted to a more confidential tone. "I don't like to talk about this much, but we all seem to be open-minded here. One day, walking through the Florida Everglades, I saw this ship land and, as I watched, a door slid open and a ramp projected itself onto the ground. Out stepped a human-looking figure more than seven feet tall who proceeded to walk down the ramp and stand in front of me.

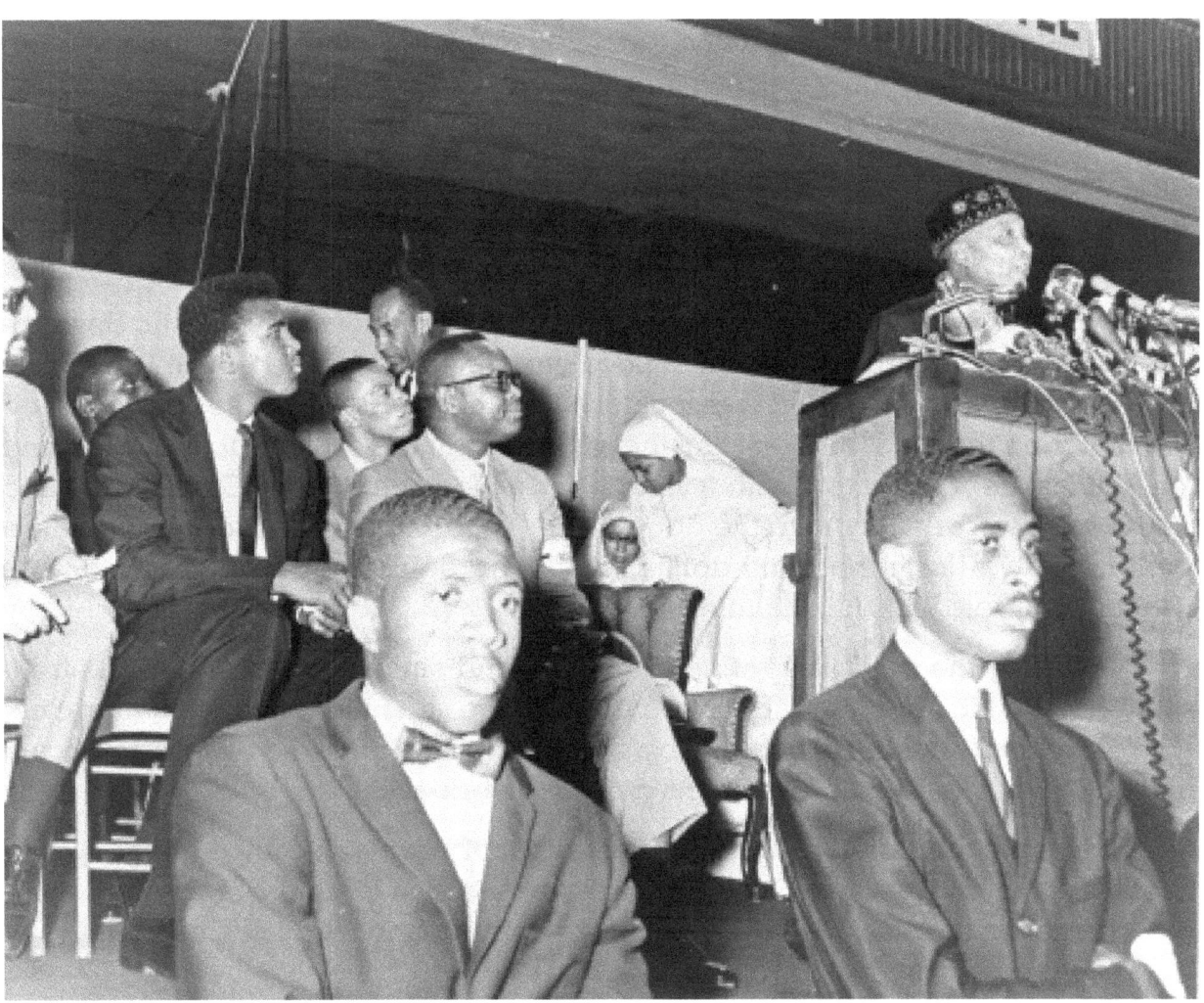

Cassius Clay lstens intently to the Prophet Elijah Muhammad

# SHIRLEY MACLAINE MEETS THE PLEIADIANS

"'Muhammad,' he said, 'You will beat Sonny Liston in . . .'"

The room filled with laughter. What had sounded at first like it could have been an honest account of an Ali fantasy was really another of Ali's famous put-ons.

After a last round of stories, Ali excused himself and headed for the shower. "Be sure to call me at home," he said, grasping my hand, into which he placed a slip of paper with his unlisted phone number. "I just bought a new house and would like to you to see it."

Three weeks later I called and a soft, feminine voice answered, introducing herself as Mrs. Ali. Muhammad took the phone a few seconds later: "You sure Joe Frazer didn't tell you to call?" he shouted in jest. All I had to do was mention UFOs, and Ali knew who I was.

"Listen, I'll be back in around ten days, so come down and bring some photos, slides, films, anything you have on saucers, okay? I'll even tell you what they are, if you're interested enough."

Promising to bring all the material I could carry, we concluded the brief conversation. On the appointed day, I piled everything I could possibly carry into the car, and, with a few friends, headed for southern New Jersey.

We hardly knew what to expect, having read various journalistic descriptions of Muhammad Ali's new home. Locating the house was a breeze (everyone in Cherry Hill knew where it was located). The house itself was set back a good 500 feet from the road, hidden from the mainstream, but obvious to those looking for Ali's estate. (I equate it with trying to hide Madison Square Garden on 32nd Street in New York City.) On the edge of the property sat a large mobile house trailer, easily a forty-thousand dollar score. Parked in the drive was Ali's Rolls Royce, complete with TV and telephone.

Ringing the bell brought no response, and since signs of life in the front section were nil, our entourage hiked through the soft mud to the back entrance. Knocking loudly, we were greeted by a smiling black man who ushered us down into an elaborately set up basement-den-and-work-area.

Here sat the "king," gabbing to a roomful of people, mostly teenagers from nearby communities. "Joe Frazer better worry 'cause when I get finished, he'll wish he never insulted me." Ali was using his time-honored trick of turning the truth around to make his opponent look bad.

"Hey, here are my UFO men. What did you bring with you?" he smiled. I explained that we had brought along some motion picture film of flying saucers taken in West Virginia.

# SHIRLEY MACLAINE MEETS THE PLEIADIANS

"We'll plug in the projector and let's see what they look like." There was never any question in his mind about their being real or not; he's a stone cold believer. At Ali's request, we ran the film three times while he pointed out the physical characteristics on these video saucers that were similar or identical to the ones he observed in real life.

When we completed the screening, Ali asked if we could have copies made for him.

"I'd like to show them at my college lectures. UFOs tie in with what my teacher, Elijah Muhammad, says." To back up his point, he produced a copy of a book, "Message To The Black Man In America." Thumbing through the clothbound volume, he stopped about midway. Under the heading, "Battle in the Sky is Near," Ali read us the following passages: "The vision of Ezekiel's wheel in the sky is true if carefully understood. There is a similar wheel in the sky today which very well answers the description of Ezekiel's vision. The similar Ezekiel's wheel is a masterpiece of mechanics. Maybe I should not say the wheel is similar to Ezekiel's vision, but that Ezekiel's vision has become a reality.

"The present wheel-shaped plane known as the Mother of Planes is one-half mile by a half mile and is the largest mechanical manmade object in the sky. It is a small human planet made for the purpose of destroying the present world of the enemies of Allah. The cost to build such a plane is staggering! The finest brains were used to build it. It is capable of staying in outer space six to twelve months at a time without coming into the Earth's gravity. It carries fifteen hundred bombing planes with the deadliest explosives – the type used in bringing up mountains on the Earth. The very same method is to be used in the destruction of the world.

"The small circular-made planes called flying saucers, which are so much talked of being seen, could be from this Mother Plane."

After closing the book, Ali concluded our discussion of UFOs and indicated to the dozen or so persons seated around that it was time to leave. He pulled me aside and asked if I was interested in seeing the rest of the house. "I got it at a real bargain," he said proudly. "Originally it was priced at $750,000, but I got it for nearly half." (Just imagine as I write this, years later, how much that house would be worth at today's inflated prices!)

Walking up the semi-spiral staircase connecting the basement with the first floor, we stepped into the dining area that is built around an outdoor patio, enclosed on all four sides with glass, behind which two frisky dogs romped. I could see Ali's eyes glow as he pointed out items of interest. "The crystal chandeliers cost me only $25,000. Can you believe that?"

Looking at them, I could.

# SHIRLEY MACLAINE MEETS THE PLEIADIANS

Escorted out of the dining room, we were then shown his wife's and children's personal quarters. "Notice the black velvet wallpaper. I got that at a real buy. Bet you've never seen anything like this," Ali challenged, pointing to gold bathroom textures.

Indeed, I hadn't and I suspect neither have many other people. Next, the exclusive set of silver and chinaware were brought out and we were allowed to examine it. I could not even guess the cost of something like this. But from the way Muhammad talked about everything, I'm sure he got the best of the deal.

A tour of the grounds surrounding the house completed the inspection, and I bid Ali farewell. My impressions at that point were mostly positive. I felt an affinity for him, for he has a warmth and glow his public image does not convey. I couldn't wait to get together for Round Two and find out more about Ali's interest in UFOs.

## THE SECOND ROUND

Some time passed before I was to see Ali again, which is to be expected, considering the fact that he was in such demand all over the world as a champion prize fighter, a celebrity and a peacemaker who always felt that, because of his status, he had the opportunity to help mend fences and bring about a better Earth.

He's one of the few well-recognized figures who is comfortable whether he is speaking with a group of ghetto kids, being interviewed on national television or dining with presidents or kings. Regardless of the circumstances, he has always been permitted to get his message across because he is Muhammad Ali.

One of his messages happens to involve UFOs. Ali even went so far one time as to break away from a pre-planned conversation on the Johnny Carson Show to bring up a subject that "The Tonight Show" host seemed to have little interest in discussing.

Our next "confrontation" was at Ali's training camp high in the Pocono Mountains of Pennsylvania at Dear Lake. This time I went along with an entire entourage, including my old friend Harold Salkin, health writer Herbert Bailey and super psychic Uri Geller.

In addition to finding out more about Ali's UFO experiences (there were several sightings that had transpired since we last met), Ali expressed interest in meeting the young Israeli sensitive who was said to have the power to bend metal utensils and make objects disappear and reappear upon command.

For the record, Geller put on quite a show that afternoon. I remember him standing in the outside doorway of one of the buildings on the camp site with Ali's ex-wife, Belinda. Clasping her hand in his, Uri asked her to tell him when she felt anything unusual. After a minute or two, she commented that she felt her ring getting warm. After another minute or two, she commented that she felt her ring getting warmer. After another minute of deep concentration, Geller removed his hand and everyone standing around – particularly Belinda – gasped out loud. Without applying any physical strength that was visible to the naked eye, the stone inside Belinda's ring had vanished from its setting and was nowhere to be found!

Hopefully it was not a valuable stone, because I do not recall it ever being returned, like all professional magicians would do as part of their act. Later, Uri was talking with one of Ali's sparring partners when he asked if he could demonstrate his powers again. He held a very heavy religious medallion that was around the boxer's neck and, by merely touching it – and without pressing down his hand – Geller made a considerable impression in the medallion with his fingertip. Again everyone was impressed, as there was no "logical explanation" as to how this extraordinary feat was accomplished.

Meanwhile, back in the main house, Muhammad Ali was doing some fancy "trick work" of his very own. It turns out that the champ is a bit of a magician himself and thinks he can do everything Geller can do with sleight of hand. He did accomplish an impressive rope trick where a piece of thick hemp was sliced in two pieces, only to have it turn back into a single length of rope. Apparently some of Ali's professional magician friends had told Ali that Geller was not "the real thing" and to be leery of what he was able to accomplish.

Be that as it may, once the "magical" interlude part of our visit was out of the way, Ali happily returned to the topic of UFOs, which he seemed genuinely more comfortable with than psychic phenomena.

"Remember how I told you about Elijah Muhammad's belief in a large mothership circling the Earth? Well, I think this is what I observed recently over my training camp here."

Prodded into giving additional details, Ali seemed willing to talk about this sighting, which had taken place over a two-night period on a Friday and Saturday during the summer.

"I had been training for three hours in the afternoon, getting ready to do battle with George Foreman. After a light supper, I decided to take a stroll around the grounds. Around 9:00 PM – it had just gotten dark – I walked up a gravel path that runs along back of our log cabin gym.

"The nighttime sky was as picturesque as one of my poems," he interjected. "The sun had been down for only a short while, and so the sky was still quite light."

Suddenly, seemingly from out of nowhere, Ali's eyes caught a glimpse of a bright glowing orb off in the distance. "At first I thought this flicker was the North Star rising in the heavens. However, within moments, I could tell I was watching something out of the ordinary."

Ali went on, talking with unusual candor. "Before I could blink my eyes, this 'light' had come down toward the mountains until it hovered right above the valley here. I knew I couldn't be dreaming. Sure 'nough, it was still there. This had to be one of those big ships they talk about! The UFO was streamlined and shaped sort of like a cigar, but blunt on both ends. I couldn't see any windows or anything, but I'm certain there must have been people onboard."

I asked how he knew it wasn't a helicopter or an airplane. Ali said that the object acted like no conventional aircraft he was familiar with. "First, it would stand still, and then move about, jumping from one portion of the sky to another. From time to time, it would speed away, up to the far reaches of the heavens, and then, minutes later, it would come down toward us again. It did this numerous times during the two hours I watched it."

Upon first hearing Ali tell the story, a skeptical individual might suspect he was pulling your leg a bit. But, no, as usual the champ seemed sincere enough. In fact, as usual, he shied away from talking about his experiences unless there was someone around to verify them. This time was no exception. Ali says the nocturnal visitor came back to haunt the skies above his mountaintop retreat at the identical hour the next evening.

"For two more hours, until 11:00, I watched this 'stranger' maneuver about. It was really somethin' to see," Ali related. With him on the second evening was business manager Gene Kilroy.

"I never paid too much attention to Muhammad when he talked about these things. I chalked it up to a vivid imagination. But I know there was something mighty peculiar happening over the camp that night. I looked up and saw this thing – this UFO – doing acrobatics up among the stars. The sighting changed my previous opinion concerning UFOs," Kilroy conceded.

During our next – and final – formal meeting, Ali only had a few minutes to spare, as he was flying to the West Coast on a promotional tour. Wiping his brow with a towel – he had just gone four rounds with a hard-slugging sparring partner – Ali said he found it a lot easier to live with UFOs than ever before.

"I always speak my mind, since I found out that so many other people have had similar sightings. I've spent a lot of time in the last few years lecturing to college campuses around the country and I find students are open-minded toward the existence of things like this. I hope others will listen in the future as I'm convinced UFOs are of tremendous importance to the whole world."

# SHIRLEY MACLAINE MEETS THE PLEIADIANS

## DIRECTORS, PRODUCERS AND A GLAMOROUS MODEL

Many other "movers and shakers," people outside of your normally thought of Hollywood stars and celebrities, have experienced relevant UFO phenomena touching their lives, both positively and in an adverse manner. There is a growing feeling among many UFO investigators that some of Tinsel Town's most prolific producers and directors are actually tuning into a sort of "cosmic radio band," helping to further the aims of our alien friends (or foes) by getting their message across via the medium of motion pictures and television, affecting the attitudes and beliefs of millions of people on a global scale – thus, in essence, circumventing the policy of government officials who refuse to tell the public the truth.

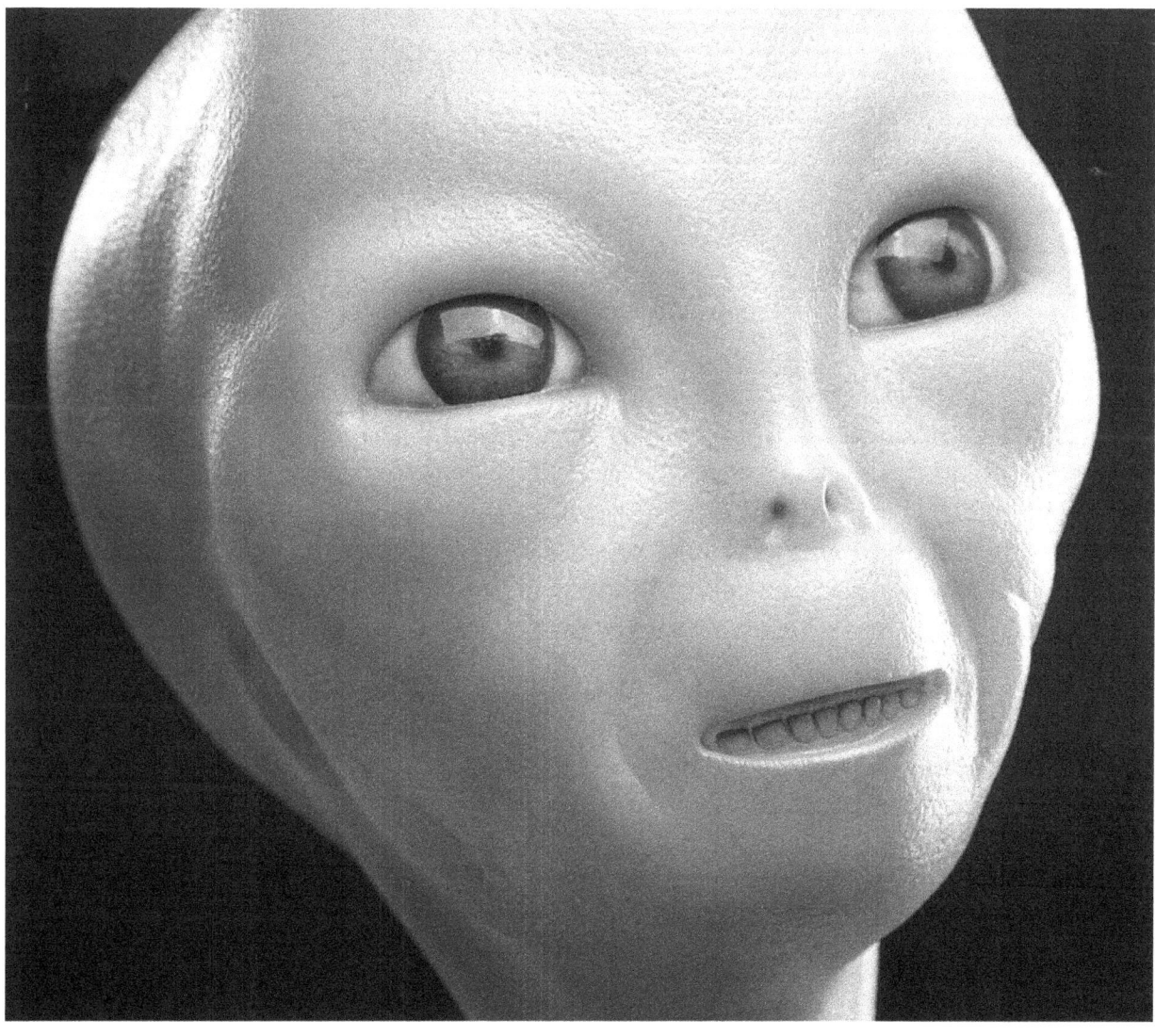

# SHIRLEY MACLAINE MEETS THE PLEIADIANS

**STEVEN SPIELBERG'S OWN "CLOSE ENCOUNTER"**

Steven Spielberg's "Close Encounters of the Third Kind," and, several years later, his presentation of "E.T. The Extraterrestrial," are important, popular movies that focused their attention on the reality of extraterrestrial visitors. Both films hover among the top box office draws of all time, grossing billions. It's hard to estimate, but a good guess would be that a majority of the world's population have viewed either one or both of these films during the course of their original theatrical release or on video and television.

What made "Close Encounters" and "E.T." so popular was the fact that they were not presented as wild-eyed science fiction tales, but as a slice of reality – something that could happen to a close friend or even a member of our own family. Unlike science fiction films of the past, these two modern classics were not pure fantasy but instead dealt realistically with the subject. "Close Encounters," for example, was perhaps the first movie to portray in an intelligent manner what contact with aliens might actually be like.

The UFO occupants were not presented as ray gun-toting monsters bent on conquering Terra Firma. Instead, they were portrayed in a benevolent light, seen as friendly creatures eager to share the mysteries of the universe with all of us.

In this respect, sociologists and academic community members agree that both motion pictures had a great impact, opening the minds of millions to the possibility of intelligent life existing on other planets, and that these civilizations could contact us at any moment – if, indeed, they haven't already, as Spielberg seems convinced they have! When asked what he thought the primary attraction of these films was, Dr. Berthold Schwarz, a highly-respected psychiatrist, made these comments: "'Close Encounters' and 'E.T.' had a built-in missionary zeal. There has been a great latent fascination with UFOs for a long time. 'Close Encounters,' in particular, acted like a charge; it ignited the spark to get the whole subject going in flames. People talked to their friends about the film; they became very excited. It definitely filled a need, and the way Columbia handled the film's advance publicity, keeping it all secretive, burying the news, only helped to create more of a curiosity. Instead of really covering up, it only served to generate more interest in the finished film."

### GUIDED SINCE AN EARLY AGE

It almost seems that Steven Spielberg was being "prepared" from an early age to be the guiding force behind such a monumental film, one that may well represent a true breakthrough in science. "One night at the age of five," Spielberg reveals, "my father rushed into my bedroom and wrapped me up in a blanket. We went out to the car and drove to a nearby clearing where several hundred people were already gathered. He spread the blanket out on the ground and pointed to the sky, indicating that I should look up. There was a beautiful meteorite display that night, and I can still remember those incredible points of light just crisscrossing the sky. And, while I was terribly frightened, at the same time I was tremendously attracted to the source, to what was causing them."

Several years later, Spielberg's parents bought him a telescope, and he spent hours looking up at the heavens, wondering if intelligent life existed out there among the Stars.

The next incident that brought Spielberg closer to the realization that we are not alone came in his early teens. Unfortunately, the memory lingers as a sad one, for, being sick, he was unable to go on a camping trip organized by his Boy Scout troop. Upon returning from a weekend in the Arizona desert, his scout companions told him how a round, "blood-red object, rising up behind the sagebrush and then shooting off into space" had startled them out of a sound sleep in the middle of the night. "I've been brooding about not having been there ever since that day," grumbled one of the world's most acclaimed movie makers. "I felt so left out that I was mad at myself for weeks afterwards."

# SHIRLEY MACLAINE MEETS THE PLEIADIANS

## THE EERIE MYSTERY SURROUNDING THE "MOTHERSHIP"

Three times the specially constructed four-foot model that, through the wizardry of special effects, takes on the colossal dimensions of the huge "mothership" that lands on top of the Devil's Tower in Wyoming, and from which emerge the aliens, had to be scrapped.

The first model was built to look like an upside-down pyramid. This unconventional looking UFO was shelved when it was realized that the craft was aerodynamically unsound; based upon the laws of physics, it could not possibly travel through the vacuum of space.

Thus, an estimated quarter-million-dollar prop had to be relegated to a backlot garbage heap.

The second model of the mothership was a huge sphere with thousands of ports and docking stations. This model also could not be used because it looked almost exactly like the Death Star in "Star Wars." At the time the model was being constructed "Star Wars" had not yet been released. After seeing the George Lucas production, one of Spielberg's assistants reported back to him the striking similarity, and everyone involved in "Close Encounters" agreed that this second mothership could not be used, either, for fear that the public would think that they had ripped their idea off from the phenomenally successful "Star Wars." (It is important to note that Spielberg and Lucas are not truly rivals but are actually long-time friends who have worked together on such projects as the "Indiana Jones" films.)

# SHIRLEY MACLAINE MEETS THE PLEIADIANS

The third model, as constructed by special effects wizard Douglas Trumbull, was the one eventually decided upon. On the screen, this magnificent vessel of light appears as a floating city, a majestic chandelier of cosmic proportions. It is a mind-blowing sight, one that many viewers find absolutely breathtaking.

The strange thing about the mothership, as far as director Spielberg was concerned, is that though he did not see the model until it was totally completed, when it was finally shown to him he was shocked to discover that it resembled to perfection the type of UFO he had repeatedly seen in his dreams. Says Spielberg, "I had many times dreamed of a huge craft just like the one that lands at the Devil's Tower. It was amazing to me when I saw the UFO Doug Trumbull had constructed, that it was exactly like the one I had dreamt about, time and time again."

## MORE STRANGE DREAMS

During the course of an interview, Steven Spielberg revealed further that he had many such dreams that seemed to be "directed" at him for some unknown purpose. "These dreams seemed as real as any true-to-life experience, as if I were awake. They involved the same thing – my bedroom window and something odd in the sky. Somehow these dreams gave me a living sample of what it would be like to have a real UFO experience. They set a mood – a tone if you will – for my film. Each dream – or encounter – was more vivid than the one before, and each was very seductive. I would wake up angry that what had happened was simply a dream, because it seemed to be real. When it was over, I became upset because I wanted to know so much more."

The question remains, who was trying to "teach" Steven Spielberg? Was it the aliens that he depicted so realistically in "Close Encounters"? There are many involved with the film who will openly admit that "eerie forces" were at play on the set.

## PERFORMERS FELT THE FORCE

Actress Teri Garr, who portrays the wife of Roy Neary, the power lineman whose life is drastically affected by a close encounter, insists that she kept looking over her shoulder, so strong was her feeling that some "invisible force" was

# SHIRLEY MACLAINE MEETS THE PLEIADIANS

on the set, helping with the film. "I kept looking around and thinking, 'There must be greater forces than us here, and they want us to do everything their way!'"

Melinda Dillon played the mother of Barry, the four-year-old boy kidnapped in "Close Encounters" by aliens. She is not above admitting that she might have been "chosen" for the part by the UFOnauts. Something, she senses, guided her to the role, and Melinda believes it might somehow be related to a close encounter she, herself, experienced several years ago.

Her encounter, she reveals, may actually have been responsible for curing a serious ailment that had been plaguing her body, causing great pain.

"My back was giving me a great deal of trouble," Melinda recalls. "I had been going to the doctor for cortisone shots, but that didn't even help to stop the pain. At night my back would swell up and it was impossible for me to fall asleep. It got to the point where I would just lie awake in bed feeling miserable and crying."

One night, while living in Malibu, California, the pain got so bad that Melinda was forced to call her physician at a very late hour. "All I got was his answering service, so I had to go to bed nearly paralyzed."

Gary Guffey

In bed, she prayed that the pain would go away, and, as if in answer to her prayers, something happened that night that she doesn't fully understand even to this day. Melinda, who had rented an apartment overlooking the ocean, since she thought the fresh air might give her some relief from the pain, awoke at around 4:00 AM and was drawn to the window as if in a trance.

"There was this orange light out over the ocean. I stared at it for a while, and it was as if it was saying to me, 'Come with us. Come with us.' Mentally, I said I wouldn't. I told them to go away and leave me alone. But I stood in the window for more than an hour. I returned to bed and didn't get up until 10:00 the next morning. On reflection, I remember that as I stood by the window, there was very little pain; it was very soothing."

Referring to this mind-expanding experience, Melinda says there was a sense of communicating "between them and me. It wasn't like anything in this dimension that I can explain."

Two weeks after her sighting, the attractive performer had just returned home from picking up her unemployment check when she found a package on the kitchen table. It was a script from Steven Spielberg's office. Since she was not expecting any screen offers, she moved the parcel to one side, figuring it was meant for her roommate. It was not until hours later that she realized its significance.

Melinda Dillon can't help but suspect that her part in the film "Close Encounters" was "divinely inspired." She took the part without hesitation, and today she's glad she did, for besides being in a highly successful picture, she doesn't have that nagging backache any longer.

There is every reason to believe the beings aboard the UFO that she saw outside of her window in Malibu were somehow responsible for her miraculous recovery.

### SIGHTINGS ON THE SET

On several occasions during the filming of "Close Encounters," members of the cast saw strange objects cascading across the horizon that they could not explain and which they believe might have been UFOs. As reported in "The Enquirer," Spielberg was among a group of observers when four objects, flying at a very high altitude, zigzagged across the sky.

"It was one of the most thrilling moments of his life," Paul Drake, a cameraman, later noted. "He was really excited and stood there for several minutes, pointing them out to others until they finally sailed out of view."

Later, Spielberg was told that he had seen a satellite, but those who were at the scene and who witnessed the phenomenon firsthand do not agree with the "official" explanation. The objects were blinking a multitude of colors – red, white and yellow. "They were," stated one source, "acting in a very erratic manner that would eliminate the possibility of the objects having been any orbiting machin-

## SHIRLEY MACLAINE MEETS THE PLEIADIANS

ery put up by an earthly nation."

In addition to the sighting of what might have been an armada of UFOs, strange cloud formations, strikingly similar to those seen in the film (in which UFOs hide) were noticed over the Mobile, Alabama, aircraft hangar where much of the filming took place. Everyone present on the set was said to have remarked at the unnatural appearance of these "clouds."

The evidence indicates that UFOs were keeping a watchful eye on the filming of "Close Encounters" to make certain everything went along on schedule.

### A FAR-REACHING EFFECT

And while it may be quite some time before the total impact of "Close Encounters" is felt, it has already had a dramatic effect, not only on the public, but on world leaders as well, the only film ever to generate such a far-reaching global reaction.

President Jimmy Carter, for example, asked that a print of "Close Encounters" be shipped to the White House for a private screening before it was even released for theatrical showing.

Shortly after viewing the film, President Carter asked that NASA reopen the government's investigation of the flying saucer phenomenon. NASA has since stated that they are now willing to view any evidence that might tend to prove that UFOs are physical craft from other planets.

Likewise, the Honorable Eric M. Gairy, the now-ousted Prime Minister of Grenada (an island nation located in the Caribbean), addressed the United Nations General Assembly. Shortly after the release of "Close Encounters," he told members of this world body that they should take UFOs seriously. He requested that the U.N. set up a communications network through which important data concerning UFOs could be rapidly exchanged on an international basis.

Gairy also asked that the U.N. declare 1978 the "International Year of Unidentified Flying Objects," and join Grenada in issuing postage stamps commemorating great moments in UFO research. And it was Gairy who distributed 300 tickets for a special screening of "Close Encounters" to other diplomats who wished to be brought up to date on the subject.

**THE FORCE OF A RELIGIOUS EXPERIENCE**

It is to the average man on the street, however, that the effect of "Close Encounters" seems to be the greatest. Many of those who have entered the theater expecting to see another "Star Wars" have left feeling as if they were part of some great cosmic awareness. Many viewers describe their reaction to the film in almost religious terms. Even cynical film critics who have "seen it all" are left in awe at what Steven Spielberg has created.

To ultra-sophisticated New York movie reviewers like Rob Banker, "'Close Encounters' is the most exciting movie I've ever seen. Probably also the best. More exciting than 'Jaws,' more important than 'Star Wars,' less pretentious than '2001.' And beyond those three magnificent films, there is nothing – absolutely nothing – to compare 'Close Encounters' to." To Banker, being confronted by the aliens in this movie can be related to having a vision of God. "I left the theater in a state of grace. That's never happened to me in a movie house before – or anywhere else public."

A colleague, Art Gatti, couldn't agree more. "The ecstasy in 'Close Encounters' permeates your pores," states the experienced journalist. "Its sensuality gradually overwhelms you. One more than sees. You leave anticipating seeing the sky. A joyfulness clings like the memory of no movie would."

# SHIRLEY MACLAINE MEETS THE PLEIADIANS

### AMAZING PSYCHIC POWERS REPORTED

According to Jeffrey Goodman, the former editor of a nationally distributed UFO magazine, at the time of the film's release he received numerous phone calls and visits from people who have returned from viewing "Close Encounters" only to discover that they have developed amazing powers they had apparently never possessed before.

"One woman from Los Angeles told me that she was in the kitchen preparing a midnight snack when suddenly the refrigerator door opened by itself and the light over the sink came on without her pulling the cord. She had returned from seeing 'Close Encounters' less than an hour before. Since then, objects move of their own accord, and the TV set has turned itself on in the presence of both her husband and friends on several occasions, just by her walking into the living room. She's convinced that somehow she developed these abilities after viewing the film.

"A man from Ohio, after viewing 'Close Encounters,' found that he could bend silverware much in the same manner as Israeli super psychic Uri Geller. All he had to do was stroke a spoon or a fork lightly with his fingertips and the metal could curl up as if the utensils were made out of a soft, pliable material.

"Several individuals purport that they are now able to read the thoughts of others. This greatly enhanced ESP came about only after they had been to see 'Close Encounters.'

"There was something about the film that prompted a change in consciousness, actually altered a person's awareness and enabled him or her to accomplish amazing psychic feats they never even dreamed of before," states editor Goodman.

### SPACE ALIENS MAY HAVE HELPED IN THE MAKING OF THE FILM

Though quite a number of years have passed, there is still a general feeling among those who participated in the making of "Close Encounters" that the film was "helped along" by some "outside force." In some strange way, extraterrestrial beings might have actually lent a helping hand in the preparation of this motion picture, which, probably more than any other event, alerted the general public to the startling conclusion that visitors from other worlds have been arriving here on a regular basis.

Perhaps director Spielberg helped contribute to this feeling by recruiting the late astronomer and UFO expert, Dr. J. Allen Hynek, as technical advisor to the film. (Hynek has a brief appearance on screen puffing his pipe, right near the end of the film, as the mothership is in the process of landing atop Devil's Tower.)

# SHIRLEY MACLAINE MEETS THE PLEIADIANS

Even the producers of "Close Encounters," the husband and wife team of Julia and Michael Phillips (hardened Hollywood veterans whose previous credits included "The Sting" and "Taxi Driver") admit there were times when the filming seemed to have been taken out of their hands and guided from afar.

"Sometimes I had the feeling," Julia maintains, "that we were telepathically implanted with this movie to get the world ready for meeting THEM!"

And these are very strong words coming from such a talented and creative individual. From the very beginning, Julia and Michael knew this would be a highly successful venture, one they most certainly wanted to be associated with. "As Steven outlined the film, it was more than a story about UFOs and a government cover-up of the whole UFO matter. I knew it was Steven's feeling, and we share it, that there is something happening up there, and we should be told about it."

The Phillips and others connected with "Close Encounters" remain surprised to this day at how smoothly the project got off the ground. Columbia Pictures took to the idea of the film immediately, before they had even seen a partial script. And the amazing thing is that the idea for "Close Encounters" came about a whole year before "Jaws" was released. At that point, Steven Spielberg had no track record to indicate that he was worthy of being trusted with $20 million dollars to direct such an elaborate undertaking.

Yet, according to Julia and Michael Phillips, negotiations with Columbia went surprisingly well, and the necessary money was appropriated in record time.

Was some "power" influencing the big brass of Columbia? Those connected with this motion picture are not about to scoff at such an idea. According to special effects expert Douglas Trumbull, who masterminded the construction of the UFOs in "Close Encounters," "There were many times when the studio could have said,

# SHIRLEY MACLAINE MEETS THE PLEIADIANS

J. Allen Hynek cameo shot on the set of "Close Encounters."

'Hell, we're not going to spend a penny more,' or 'We don't understand what you're trying to do,' yet they didn't take this attitude; they just let Steven do what he wanted, which is totally unheard of."

It could easily be said that Steven Spielberg started a trend in Hollywood. For decades UFOs could not be portrayed on the silver screen unless their occupants were destroying entire cities or dragging away screaming Earth women to repopulate some dying planet at the far reaches of the galaxy. All that has abruptly changed now as Hollywood's movie backers realize that a "realistic approach" may be a more profitable one. In this vein, the Budd Hopkins book, "Intruders," was presented to television audiences with the help of screenwriter Tracy Torme, who later headed up a $20 million dollar project to bring the Travis Walton abduction story to moviegoers in the 1993 feature film, "Fire in the Sky."

In addition, several UFO books have been optioned and are in various stages of production, to say nothing of the persistent rumor that may be confirmed when you read this, that Oliver Stone is busy scripting a UFO film that could easily be as explosive as "JFK" turned out to be.

The late Dr. John Mack, a psychiatrist, Harvard University Medical School professor and author of two books on alien abduction, declared that possibly "more than a million persons in the United States alone may have been abducted" and taken to be examined by aliens! "It's disturbing. I don't have an explanation. But I know they've undergone a powerful experience of being intruded upon and traumatized..."

Julia Phillips (April 7, 1944 – January 1, 2002)

John E. Mack, M.D. (October 4, 1929 – September 27, 2004)

# SHIRLEY MACLAINE MEETS THE PLEIADIANS

**PETER BOGDANOVICH: WAS IT JUST A "SHOOTING STAR"?**

According to a close friend, one of Hollywood's finest film directors will never forget the night he saw something that resembled a "shooting star," though it acted quite strange and "out of place."

The encounter is recounted for us by actor Ray Girardin, who was appearing in the soap series "General Hospital" when we spoke to him. According to Girardin, he was driving with Bogdanovich when they noticed an intensely bright light in the sky.

"Our initial reaction was that the object was a shooting star, but then it surprised us both by stopping dead in the sky and hovering in one spot for 30 seconds or more. During that half minute, while it remained stationary, the object's color changed from white to pink."

Slowly the craft began to pick up speed and drifted away from the witnesses.

"It halted its forward movement once more, then flew off in an instant over the distant horizon," says Girardin, who insists he has no idea what it was they saw.

"We didn't report our observation because we felt nobody would believe us. At the time, we did mention what we had seen to some of the other people in the cast, but they simply scoffed at our story."

# SHIRLEY MACLAINE MEETS THE PLEIADIANS

## CLAUDIA WEILL AND A "FLATTENED FOOTBALL" OVER WESTCHESTER

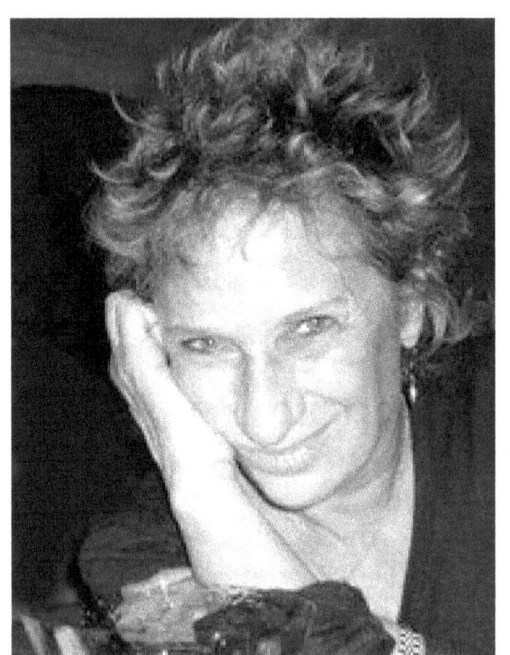

While still quite young by Hollywood standards, Claudia Weill was one of the top award-winning women in the film industry. She has produced, directed, filmed, and edited such major motion pictures as "The Other Half of the Sky – A China Memoir," featuring actress Shirley MacLaine.

In an interview, Claudia talked about the time she observed a flying saucer while driving from New York City toward her home in Westchester. It was, she recalls, about 3:00 AM, and the night was warm and the sky clear.

"I was alone in my convertible with the top down, affording me a clear view of the starry night as I drove along. I was going north on the Henry Hudson Parkway, having spent the evening at a dance in Manhattan.

"All at once, l became aware of a luminous object in the air, apparently following my car, to the rear and slightly to the right to me. I could see it as I glanced over my right shoulder. It was at a low angle, slightly higher than the line of trees along the parkway. I would judge its size to be about 12 feet long, and its distance about 50 to 75 feet away from me, although it is difficult to judge relative size and distance of an airborne object, especially at night."

Ms. Weill says the UFO was shaped like a "flattened football." It was glowing with a brilliance that seemed to come from within.

"The object was definitely solid. There were no markings or windows visible on it, and I heard no sound."

# SHIRLEY MACLAINE MEETS THE PLEIADIANS

According to the witness, the UFO appeared to be keeping pace with her vehicle. "I tested it out several times. When I slowed down, the UFO followed suit, and when I sped up, it would do the same." The UFO stayed in view for about 15 minutes and then it was gone. "I just looked around and it wasn't there any longer."

Asked about her reaction to being tailgated by a possible space visitor, Claudia had these remarks: "When I first spotted it, I was frightened, as I had never delved into the subject, and I had no idea what this thing might be or what its motives were. But as the minutes ticked by – slowly, I might add – and there were no signs of hostility, I gradually regained a calm state of mind. I then began to think logically and I came up with the idea that this was indeed a craft from outer space. I actually felt a slight elation that I was viewing one of those elusive saucers."

# SHIRLEY MACLAINE MEETS THE PLEIADIANS

Varuska photo by Helen Hovey

## VARUSKA KALWA'S MODEL EXPERIENCE

Model, poet, and singer Varuska Kalwa has long felt as though an alien intelligence has been keeping a watchful eye on her activities.

The charming and attractive former lead singer of the rock band Teknoboys has always felt she possessed heightened extrasensory abilities and that "other forces" in the universe were aware of her sensitivity, thus making it easy to "get through" to her where they might have difficulty with other individuals who are not as psychically advanced.

Her first experience took place in late summer of 1966 as she was driving to her mother's house in Lansing, Michigan. "I was driving late at night around 1:00 AM in the vicinity of Ann Arbor, when suddenly the car was engulfed in a radiant light. I felt the car being followed by something travelling in the sky. My ex-husband was with me at the time, and we were not frightened, but remained calm. Finally, after what seemed to be about 10 minutes, we took a sharp curve and the highway changed direction, and the light just disappeared into the star-filled sky." Varuska says they were traveling near high tension lines as well as being close to a marshy area, where a lot of UFO sightings seem to take place.

# SHIRLEY MACLAINE MEETS THE PLEIADIANS

During the summer of 1976, the Hollywood-based entertainer was laying outdoors on a large rock looking up into the heavens. "The night was warm and crystal clear. Suddenly, far above, somewhere around midnight, this fast moving object caught my attention. I was certain the object was not a meteorite because it stayed in view for five or six minutes and traced a strange pattern across the sky. After performing a celestial dance, it shot out of sight and was gone within seconds." Varuska was not alone at the time. "A close friend of mine was there and we witnessed the phenomenon together. Later, we commented on how we felt as if whoever was onboard the craft was trying to communicate a feeling of peace to us."

In 1977, Varuska had her first out-of-body experience. Apparently, she traveled to a strange, otherworldly city. "I was at the state where I was almost sleeping, but not quite," she recalls. "All of a sudden, I found myself above a city looking down at a bubble-like structure that covered this metropolis. Within seconds, I found myself down in the center of a very modern culture. There was green all around, and it was very sunny. I got an impression of intense peace, which has happened during all of my UFO-related experiences. I saw people, but apparently they could not see me. The beings here had very large heads, especially in the area of the forehead and brain. I stayed long enough to study the whole atmosphere of their place."

Varuska says that as fast as she had made the trip, she was back in her bed. "I was wide awake but now very tired and ready for sleep."

Varuska says her best, and most recent, UFO experience happened on December 30, 1979 en route to the Detroit Metro Airport from Lansing, Michigan, on an airport commuter bus.

"It was the time of day when light slowly turns to dusk. We were on the outskirts of Ann Arbor headed down the highway when I noticed two orange-yellow balls in the sky. They were far up and nobody else seemed to be paying any attention to them. From my angle, through the bus window, I could see them perfectly, and I could tell that they weren't conventional aircraft. After keeping pace with the bus for 15 or 20 minutes, they went straight up leaving a trail like a jet might leave. However, these objects were moving up in unison and traveling very slowly. As it turned dark, I lost sight of the objects altogether, but they did leave an impression on me I will never forget."

# SHIRLEY MACLAINE MEETS THE PLEIADIANS

## PRESIDENTS, POLITICIANS, WORLD LEADERS AND A CONQUERING GENERAL

As surprising as it may appear, despite a massive UFO cover-up, numerous presidents, politicians and world leaders have both privately and publicly expressed a deep and personal belief in the existence of UFOs – or have at least commented on them. This despite the fact that, officially, their various governments have continued to deny the reality of UFOs.

UFO follows Jimmy Carter's helicopter over Panama City.
From the Carter Presidential Library.

# SHIRLEY MACLAINE MEETS THE PLEIADIANS

## GENERAL MACARTHUR: UFOs TO INVADE EARTH!

He first became interested in UFOs when they were known as Foo Fighters. During World War II, General Douglas MacArthur learned firsthand that something pretty peculiar was going on when many Allied pilots reported their bombers were being followed on a regular basis by mysterious balls of glowing light that seemed to be under intelligent command. Initially, the reports were classified because the military suspected that the discs could be a secret German aerial device.

According to writer John Keel, MacArthur realized the significance of the matter when, during the summer of 1946, he was personally called upon to examine reports coming from Sweden and Norway of unexplained "Ghost Rockets" that seemed to be plaguing the skies over those nations. After examining hundreds of reports, he became convinced that some unearthly power was behind the observations of cigar-shaped craft that often hovered and then shot across the sky at what were then considered to be fantastic speeds. Some of the "Ghost Rockets" may have even crashed, and it's possible that MacArthur was among the first to examine wrecked alien craft.

Once in the private sector, MacArthur began to collect reports of UFOs and read up on the subject. Several times near the end of his life, he made some fairly "far-fetched" statements about unidentified flying objects.

"The nations of the world will one day have to unite, for the next war will be an interplanetary war," he was quoted as having said in October, 1955. "The nations of the Earth must someday make a common front against attack by people from other planets."

At an address he gave at West Point Military Academy in 1962, MacArthur repeated his rather bleak forecast when he stated: "We speak in terms of harnessing the cosmic energy of ultimate conflict between a united human race and the sinister forces of some other planetary galaxy."

Supposedly, it was MacArthur who first briefed Harry Truman on the importance of the Government's ongoing efforts to monitor UFO activity.

# SHIRLEY MACLAINE MEETS THE PLEIADIANS

## THE PRESIDENTS

Following the crash of a spaceship outside of Roswell, New Mexico, in July of 1947, every U.S. President has been fully informed about UFOs once he has taken office, despite the fact that before being elected, they have been kept in the dark like everyone else. And promises of some presidential candidates to be more forthcoming about UFOs after being elected have faded in the inaugural glow. Reminders of these promises later on were almost always ignored.

## PRESIDENT EISENHOWER MEETS WITH ALIENS

This story would be hard to believe except for the fact that it has been confirmed by many unimpeachable sources. One of those sources, the late Earl of Clancarty, a member of the British Parliament, stated that President Dwight D. Eisenhower met with beings from outer space in 1954.

The date was February 20, 1954. Eisenhower was vacationing at Palm Springs when he was summoned to Muroc Airfield by high military officials. Muroc is now known as Edwards Air Force Base, recently popularized as a landing field for the space shuttle.

The President had a press conference scheduled for that day but never showed up for it. There were rumors that he was ill. The official explanation was that he went to a dentist. Newsmen, however, were never able to learn which dentist treated him.

Actually, Eisenhower was driven to the California air base to meet with space aliens. According to Lord Clancarty, the incident was reported to him by a former top U.S. test pilot.

Says the Earl: "The pilot was one of six people at Eisenhower's meeting with the beings. He had been called in as a technical adviser because of his reputation and abilities as a test pilot."

The test pilot told Lord Clancarty: "Five different alien craft landed at the base. Three were saucer-shaped and two were cigar-shaped . . . and as Eisenhower and his small group watched, the aliens disembarked and approached them.

"They looked something like humans, but not exactly."

The test pilot described the beings as having human-like features, but that by our standards they were misshapen. They were the same height and weight as the average man and were able to breathe air without the use of a helmet or mask.

The test pilot reported that the aliens spoke English and wanted Eisenhower to start an education program for the people of the United States and eventually the entire world. Eisenhower allegedly replied that he didn't think the world was ready for that. The President said that his concern was that a worldwide announcement that aliens had landed would likely cause panic.

The aliens agreed with that opinion, saying that they would continue to contact isolated individuals until the people of the Earth got used to the idea of their presence.

According to the test pilot: "They demonstrated their spacecraft to the President. They showed him their ability to make themselves invisible.

"This really caused the president a lot of discomfort because none of us could see them even though we knew they were still there. The aliens then boarded their ships and departed."

The pilot told Lord Clancarty that he never told another soul about this unique meeting and that now all the others involved in the encounter are dead.

# SHIRLEY MACLAINE MEETS THE PLEIADIANS

## GERALD FORD: CONGRESSIONAL HEARINGS

Though we do not have any inkling of what President Ford did once he moved into the White House, beforehand, while a member of Congress, he struck out very boldly against those in positions of power who keep the matter of UFOs under closely guarded wraps.

After a rash of UFO sightings in his home state of Michigan, Gerald Ford made this statement: "In the firm belief that the American public deserves a better explanation than that thus far given by the Air Force, I strongly recommend that there be a committee investigation of the UFO phenomenon.

"I think we owe it to the people to establish credibility regarding UFOs and to produce the greatest possible enlightenment on this subject."

Ford proposed that either the Science of Astronautics Committee or the Armed Services Committee of the House of Representatives schedule hearings on "the subject of UFOs and invite testimony from both the Executive Branch of the government and some of the persons who claim to have seen UFOs."

# SHIRLEY MACLAINE MEETS THE PLEIADIANS

## JIMMY CARTER SEES A UFO

Before Jimmy Carter became president, he promised to unlock the secret files of the Pentagon and release all the information in the government's possession on UFOs. He went back on his word after being elected. Nobody knows the reasons why he did a policy flip-flop, but, as might be expected, theories abound concerning what has become known in certain circles as the "Cosmic Watergate."

"I don't laugh at people anymore when they say they've seen UFOs, because I've seen them myself." Future-president Jimmy Carter made that statement in September 1973 while at a speaking engagement in Dublin, Georgia. Reporters immediately pressed him to elaborate, which he did. He said that when he was campaigning for governor in the small southern Georgia town of Leary, he was standing outside the hall where he was to make a speech to members of the local Lions Club and saw a blue disc-shaped object in the sky.

Several members of the organization were with Carter when the object appeared. Carter ran a tape recorder so that his description of what he saw would be accurately recorded. He told the newsmen, "It was about 30 degrees above the horizon and looked about as large as the moon. It got smaller and changed to a reddish color and then got larger again."

Newsmen asked him for an explanation. He said: "It was a very sober occasion. It was obviously there and obviously unidentified."

Carter was quite emphatic about what he saw. His press secretary, Jody Powell, told reporters: "I remember Jimmy saying that he did in fact see a strange light, or object, at night in the sky, which did not appear to be a star or a plane or anything he could explain. If that's your definition of an unidentified flying object, then I suppose that's correct."

Powell added: "I don't think it's had any great impact on him one way or the other. I would venture to say that he probably has seen stranger and more unexplainable things than that during his time in government."

Indeed, this is a curious statement Jody Powell has made, for we do know that Jimmy must have thought the sighting important enough, as he took the time and trouble to fill out a detailed, three-page sighting report form and turn it over to a private UFO group that investigated his account. Furthermore, exactly what did Powell have in mind when he said that Carter had "probably seen stranger and more unexplainable things" during his time in office? Could it be that the former president has personally experienced something along the lines of a close encounter? Or perhaps he has even been taken to see the actual remains of a crashed UFO and its occupants that the government was said to be in possession of since the late 1940s?

**THE UNTOLD STORY**

Some experts think that the photograph is "flawed" and that there is a "rather simple explanation" for the sequence of events. Other researchers remain puzzled after all this time when it comes to a photograph taken of President Carter's military helicopter while he was visiting Panama in 1978.

"I was watching the President's helicopter take off on the way to Tocumen International Airport. He was in the country to sign the Instruments of Ratification with officials of Panama. It was an overcast day, but I was standing in what sunlight penetrated the clouds. I was taking photos of the reception party that had welcomed him at Fort Clayton, where I am employed by the U.S. Government as part of their Defense Mapping Agency Inter-American Geodesic Survey."

Ms. Linda Arosemena, in an exclusive interview with this author, revealed that she hadn't seen anything at all unusual in the sky on Saturday, June 17, at 2:20 PM, the time of President Carter's departure. But when the film was developed, there, near the helicopter with Carter in it, was a very strange Saturn-shaped object – a definite flying saucer-type craft.

"I can't account for what turned up on the negative," Ms. Arosemena declared, "but I can tell you this – I've never seen anything like it during the 14-odd years I have been working as a professional photographer."

Taken aback by what materialized on her finished print, Ms. Arosemena immediately telephoned the Panamanian offices of the Federal Aviation Administration and was put in touch with one Mr. Frank Grba, an FAA official who was totally stumped but had to admit that radar hadn't picked up anything odd at the time. "They were curious, however, and did request that I send them prints. So far, they have not contacted me officially as to what they think the object might be."

# SHIRLEY MACLAINE MEETS THE PLEIADIANS

Ms. Arosemena also revealed that she sent a print to the President in Washington, "because I thought he would want to see what I photographed." The only response she has gotten to date is a printed "form letter" thanking her for her interest in the President's trip to Panama.

The photo was taken with a Nikon camera equipped with a motor drive, using Kodak TRI-X black and white film, at 1/250 sec., f/16. The negative is exactly the same quality as the rest of the roll and the previous frame taken 10 seconds earlier shows no signs of anything peculiar. Neither the film nor the negative appear to have been tampered with and it is impossible to take a double exposure with this type of camera.

"I'm still not certain what I caught," Ms. Arosemana stated, "but the image is very clear and there have been quite a few UFO sightings in Panama lately!"

According to a front page story in Panama's "Star & Herald" newspaper, the day before, on June 16, at approximately 2:30 PM, Brenda Reilly was fishing with some friends on the causeway at Fort Amador.

Suddenly, her friend Sandra Chandler looked up and asked what the lights in the sky were. They talked about the lights being a plane or helicopter but realized that they were neither when they saw its shape. Before their other friends could come up the embankment to see it, the object vanished.

"It was spinning, moved forward and then it just disappeared," Brenda said, adding, "It was just about to rain and the sky was overcast."

Brenda drew a picture of it for her mother, Mrs. Velma Reilly, "It had a black inner oval with a dull, gray, metal-like outer oval," said the woman. "It looked very much like Linda Arosemena's photograph, except that my daughter made the sketch before the photo was even taken."

UFO activity is on the increase in Panama, though very seldom do the papers carry any information, most reports being passed on by word of mouth.

One report making the rounds is that, along the coast on one New Year's Eve, both Americans as well as Panamanians observed a brilliant orange globe that bedazzled and stunned the many eyewitnesses. On another occasion, an employee at the Panama Canal Locks working the late shift was shocked into speechlessness by a glowing sphere that appeared out of nowhere.

"Unfortunately, notes Linda Arosemena, "there is no official agency to report these sightings to." The issue of the "Star & Herald" that carried her photo asked readers of the paper who might have seen anything "unusual" to step forward and issue a report.

# SHIRLEY MACLAINE MEETS THE PLEIADIANS

"The paper sent me a couple of color snapshots taken by a serviceman who did have a sighting some weeks before. The object in his prints is not as clearly defined as mine, but you can tell what he saw was neither an airplane or balloon."

The fact that strange objects often appear on film while being invisible to the human eye is not so unusual, as anyone who has studied UFOs can tell you. In several instances, mysterious objects appeared on film but were not visible to the human eye at the time the pictures were taken. There is a general feeling that UFOs are capable of rearranging their atomic structure and dematerializing into other dimensions, thus making it possible to travel through space and time much faster than the speed of light.

In addition, it was not until sometime later that an American working as a teacher in Panama came forward to say that he had seen videotapes showing a UFO following Carter's Presidential helicopter. The video showed a UFO and it was taken around the time that Carter was taking off, adding credence to the still photograph. In fact, as far as I'm concerned, the photo taken by Ms. Arosemena looks quite legitimate. Unfortunately we have no way to get in touch with Jimmy Carter for a comment.

His Royal Highness, Prince Philip of England, has long been known as a collector of UFO literature. Those, in fact, who have been inside his private quarters insist the Prince has a large map hanging on his wall upon which he has pinpointed the location of UFO activity worldwide. A firm believer in even the "farther out" contact cases, the Prince once sent a note through his Secretary, Lord Rupert Nevill, thanking the author of this book for placing at his disposal several books and magazines. "His Royal Highness is most grateful to you for doing this and looks forward very much to reading it all," came the reply on royal stationery.

# SHIRLEY MACLAINE MEETS THE PLEIADIANS

## RONALD REAGAN'S "ALIEN THREAT"

I first got wind of President Reagan's interest in UFOs from none other than Steve Allen, with whom journalist Harold Salkin, a close associate, had spoken to over the phone after the famed celebrity had brought up the matter on his radio show. According to Allen, a very well-known show business personality (since identified as Lucille Ball) had thrown a party in Hollywood to which the Reagans had been invited.

As they sat down to dinner, it was noticed that the then-Governor of California had not arrived, though he had been expected much earlier.

About a half hour into the main course, Ronald and Nancy showed up but were visibly shaken. They told those present that they had seen a UFO while driving down the coast and had slowed down to watch its movements.

No additional information about this sighting was ever forthcoming (there was one other in which Reagan's private plane was followed by a blinding light), but it no doubt was to weigh heavily on the mind of the President because later on he was to make some rather startling pronouncements about an interplanetary invasion.

Near the conclusion of his speech before the United Nations General Assembly on September 21, 1987, Reagan "spooked" everyone by flatly stating: "In our obsession with antagonisms of the moment, we often forget how much unites all the members of humanity. Perhaps we need some outside, universal threat to make us recognize this common bond. I occasionally think, how quickly our differences worldwide would vanish if we were facing an alien threat from outside this world." He went on to suggest that an alien force "might already be amongst us!"

# SHIRLEY MACLAINE MEETS THE PLEIADIANS

Reagan also brought up the same general topic when he met with Mikhail Gorbachev in Geneva. "I told the Russian leader how I thought his task and mine might be easier if there was a threat to this world from some other species from another planet, outside in the universe. We'd forget all the little local differences that we have between our countries."

Another remark can be found in an article written by senior editor Fred Barnes of "The New Republic." Apparently, Barnes was near enough to overhear a conversation between Reagan and Russian Foreign Minister Eduard Shevardnadze in which the President wondered out loud, "What would happen if the world faced an 'alien threat' from outer space? Don't you think the United States and the Soviet Union would join together?" Shevardnadze said, "Absolutely, yes," adding, "And we wouldn't need our defense ministers to meet (to discuss what to do)."

## ADMIRAL HYMAN RICKOVER: THE LORD'S MANY "OTHER WORLDS"

It was reported on CBS TV's popular "60 Minutes" program that in front of Congress the much admired Admiral Hyman Rickover was said to have stated: "We can go to church every Sunday and pray, but the Lord has many demands made on Him from many other worlds, and in the eyes of the Lord we are not the most important thing in the universe!"

# SHIRLEY MACLAINE MEETS THE PLEIADIANS

## FERDINAND E. MARCOS, UFOs AND THE EX-PRESIDENT OF THE PHILIPPINES

Now it's time we turned our attention elsewhere, outside of our own United States. At the time this statement was made, the now long-deposed President of the Philippines, Ferdinand E. Marcos, was still the leader of that nation.

"The possibility of our planet's receiving visitors from outer space is, I am certain, not remote in the face of the wonders that we, right here, have witnessed; indeed, it is a thought, an idea, that brings intense and magical excitement which I, for one, would not unduly set aside until all avenues of the pros and cons have been examined.

"I am often staggered by the thought of the vastness of our universe and the massive secrets the skies hold, which we on this earth have barely scratched. Since I am of an adventurous bent, I shall not be the first to say that it is not impossible for other planets to be inhabited, nor that people in outer space, or whatever creatures they are, do not have the capability which Earth people are now developing to travel through space and perhaps discover other planets."

(Did anyone ever consider that the aliens want Mrs. Marcos' shoes?)

## ROBERT F. KENNEDY – CARD CARRYING MEMBER

In a letter to researcher Gray Barker, the late Senator wrote: "As you know, I am a card carrying member of the Amalgamated Flying Saucer Clubs of America. Therefore, like many other people, I am interested in the phenomenon of flying saucers. It is a fascinating subject that has initiated both scientific fiction fantasies and serious scientific research. I watch with great interest all reports of unidentified flying objects, and I hope that someday we will know more about this intriguing subject. I favor more research regarding this matter and I hope that, once and for all, we can determine the true facts about flying saucers."

# SHIRLEY MACLAINE MEETS THE PLEIADIANS

## THE EARL OF CLANCARTY INVITES ALIENS TO SPEAK BEFORE PARLIAMENT

I am honored to have been invited to the House of Lords to speak before a small group of around 50 individuals consisting of members of Parliament who have long been pressing to get the British government to end its silence on the matter of UFOs and to air what they know openly and truthfully to the British public.

The invitation was made by the late Earl of Clancarty, Mr. Brinsley Le Poer Trench, who has been a harsh critic of his government's policy for many years and who continues to seek support from those in positions of power within the British hierarchy.

And while the Earl of Clancarty has not been successful so far in overturning Her Majesty's current UFO stand, he has become somewhat of a "sticky wicket" – a thorn in the side of the ruling officials, constantly pushing for change.

After my presentation, made in a secluded chamber within the honored halls of the House of Lords, I was invited back to the Earl's London estate for dinner. And what started out to be light conversation ended up as a serious interview on UFOlogical issues.

BECKLEY: How did you start to get the ball rolling on the question of UFOs in the House of Lords?

EARL OF CLANCARTY: I took my seat in June, 1976, and, a month after, I made my maiden speech, which wasn't on UFOs but had to do with the state of our nation. Then I started sounding a few of the other Lords out and found that quite a number were interested in the topic. In our country, if you want to find out something from one of our leaders, you can put it in writing or ask a question in the chamber. If you do both you must get a double answer. My questions led me to believe that there was a cover-up here in this country. I asked Her Majesty's government several questions which dealt with a statement made on French radio to the effect that the French Ministry was reviewing a large number of UFO cases and the better ones were being passed down to the Center for Space Studies, which is loosely the equivalent of your NASA. In light of this fact, I wanted to know what our government was doing about the situation.

BECKLEY: Did you get a response?

EARL OF CLANCARTY: I got a reply from Lord Winterbottom of the Labor Party, who was speaking on behalf of the Ministry of Defense. Lord Winterbottom said he had "never heard of the broadcast." He added that "We would only be interested if there was a threat to the United Kingdom." Next I questioned Her Majesty's government about what role our police were playing in the matter, since, in France, law enforcement officials are known to play a key part in interviewing witnesses. This time I got a reply from Lord Harris who was then a Minister of State for the Home Office who, of course, look after the police in England. He said he also hadn't heard of the French radio broadcast where this was discussed and said that the police are not investigating anything, but, if they were called upon to do so, they would do so with their customary vigor.

As it so happened, I was invited by Scotland Yard to give a talk on UFOs some years later and I happened to mention my letter from Lord Harris. Hands went up all over the place. Our law enforcement officials wanted to know why Lord Harris wasn't familiar with the fact that, prior to 1977, the police had investigated thousands of cases and thousands since. Not only have our police investigated cases, but they have been involved many times as witnesses.

I was determined to find out all I could and set the record straight. I followed up with additional correspondence. I pointed out that in France there is a group whose initials are GPEN, which is actually funded by the government, and didn't Her Majesty know that there was a book written by the head of the group detailing a number of unexplainable incidents involving UFOs? Again I got a response from Lord Winterbottom, who said that he would look into the matter further and get back to me. Awhile later, a reply came that they had found the original transcript and that the broadcast had taken place.

BECKLEY: They were giving you the old run-around, as we would say in America.

EARL OF CLANCARTY: This set me off but good. The next thing I did was introduce a debate in the chamber of the House of Lords. This debate went very well. In total, 14 speakers took part. The Earl of Kimberly, who is a member of our group now, was my main supporter. True, some people were talking against UFOs and some in favor of the subject, but there was no ridicule. It was treated with respect. As the result of a suggestion that I made during the debate, we now have gotten a House of Lords UFO study group. It has over thirty members.

BECKLEY: Can you name some of the members for us?

EARL OF CLANCARTY: Some of the members who were here this afternoon to listen to your talk included Lord Oakchester, the honorary secretary of our group; the retired Admiral of the Fleet, Lord Hill Norton, who was the Chief of Defense; Lord Gainsford; Lord Grey; Lord Rennick, and Lord Rudgby.

BECKLEY: At this point in time, what is the group seeking to do? Will there be a proposal made to Her Majesty?

EARL OF CLANCARTY: Up to now, including yourself, Timothy, we have had 19 guest speakers. Some have come from the U.S., one from Canada. We had three from Europe, one from Spain, Italy, Denmark, and the rest from England, including the well-known astronomer Fred Hael. Some of our members know a great deal about the subject, while others are less informed. For that reason, we felt it would be a good idea to have guest speakers give their points of view. The other day, we had a closed meeting which gave members of the group the opportunity to discuss the matter amongst themselves. We discussed quite frankly the cover-up in various countries, but we didn't put it like that on our notice boards. Instead, we said we had discussed "the attitudes of governments" to the UFO phenomenon. Lord Kimberly took part and told us about a remarkable telephone conversation with our Minister of Defense. Lord Hill Norton spoke about 20 minutes about how something had to be done. Afterwards, some of us got together and thought we ought to take the matter further into the chamber where the business of the country is conducted and to ask more questions and perhaps to engage in another debate. This time we want the authorities to come clean and tell us the truth about UFOs.

BECKLEY: What do you think the British government knows? What are they keeping a secret?

EARL OF CLANCARTY: I'm sure they've got records of reports going back any number of years. What we want to do is to get material released. The whole thing is, we haven't got what you have in the U.S., a Freedom of Information Act. So we can't sue the intelligence department or the military or whoever it is. What we can do is get the government to come clean. I'm sure they've got plenty of reports. There are reasons for the cover-up. The original one, I think, has to do with panic, but also a number of countries might be trying to get hold of an alien spacecraft in operational condition, or in good order, not a crashed, smashed one.

# SHIRLEY MACLAINE MEETS THE PLEIADIANS

BECKLEY: Do you think that the British government has a crashed UFO?

EARL OF CLANCARTY: It's possible, but I wouldn't know. I couldn't give you a good answer to that one. But I think that if one country were to get hold of one and were actually able to make more of them, that particular country would rule the world. That, of course, is the reason that a particular government would have a cover-up. Another possible reason for a cover-up is that if they are using a free electromagnetic method of propulsion, this would be a blow for a lot of industries, the nuclear industry, electrical, oil, and coal. It would be a good thing, because a lot of these industries are causing pollution. Another possible reason for the cover-up is that I think the government is aware that aliens have bases on the Earth from which they operate and look at them; for instance, the Russian nuclear bases in Siberia, and in the same way, look at nuclear power stations in North America. This is information that was released, as you know, to "Ground Saucer Watch," because they sued the CIA under the Freedom of Information Act and the Pentagon had to release the documents.

BECKLEY: Do you think that there is an international cover-up? Do you think the various governments have exchanged information amongst themselves?

EARL OF CLANCARTY: I think it's highly possible. At one time, they were working together, exchanging information about gravity in space, the Russians and the Americans. Whether they still do, I don't know. What I think is important is that we make contact with the aliens. One reason why I think the aliens are watching all these bases, nuclear bases and whatever in different countries, is because they are so concerned about us. They think that we may have a catastrophe ahead of us, a nuclear war or something that will destroy our civilization. I go along with Morris Chattalane and his book, "Our Ancestors Came From Out of Space." They started coming sixty thousand years ago and have been coming ever since.

BECKLEY: You were one of the first to write about extraterrestrials in ancient history. You found a lot of references in the Bible, in Genesis.

EARL OF CLANCARTY: Yes, indeed, because Elijah was taken up in what they called a whirlwind. They used to call these UFOs whirlwinds and sometimes clouds. Yes, there are a lot of Biblical references.

BECKLEY: In fact, haven't you theorized in one of your books, "The Sky People," that civilization, as we know it, actually began on another planet, and Adam and Eve came to earth in a spaceship?

EARL OF CLANCARTY: Yes, I think that Adam and Eve were meant as the plural; in other words, as the male and the female. I think when they came here, they were put here in different ways. Sometimes they mutated with an earlier race here and brought about a more advanced one. That was supposed to have hap-

## SHIRLEY MACLAINE MEETS THE PLEIADIANS

pened when the aliens mutated with Neanderthal man and the result was Cro-Magnon man.

All of the countries have had their traditions of what we now call UFOs for thousands of years. The Chinese and Japanese, South Americans and Hopi Indians, the Scandinavians and the Celts and the Irish, all have them in their traditions. They are concerned about us because they put us here, probably not just this one race. There are thousands and thousands of advanced civilizations in this galaxy that are communicating with each other. That would help to explain the different races that we have here on this planet, including the yellow, the red, white and the black. I think that many of them have come here from different civilizations and helped to colonize this planet. I think that they are basically friendly.

Brinsley Le Poer Trench, the 8th Earl of Clancarty (September 18, 1911 – May 8, 1995)

# SHIRLEY MACLAINE MEETS THE PLEIADIANS

## ASTRONAUTS, AN ANTHROPOLOGIST AND AN ACE AVIATOR

As it turns out, you don't have to be a "Liberace" to enjoy the privilege of seeing or believing in UFOs. Though there are not currently many men or women of letters who are willing to risk their careers by coming "out of the closet" and proclaiming UFOs as being real, a few courageous souls have ventured forth, though the stakes for personal humiliation among their peers remains high.

So here are a few statements, interviews and quotes from those of a scientific or academic background whose names should not be totally obscure. We feel that this chapter offers a fitting conclusion to show the world that many of those whom we have come to love and trust know there is more to this vast universe than just heaven and the earth below our feet.

# SHIRLEY MACLAINE MEETS THE PLEIADIANS

## GORDON COOPER: A MISSING FILM AND CRASHED FLYING DISCS

Every schoolchild in America knows who Gordon Cooper is. But, for those of us who have been away from the classroom for a while, to refresh your memory, Cooper was one of America's original astronauts. He helped pioneer this country's space exploration efforts when, aboard a tiny space capsule known as Mercury 7, Cooper orbited the Earth for 34 hours, proving that man could live outside our atmosphere for prolonged periods. His patriotism, bravery and respectability go without saying, so when the "space traveler" telephoned me to check on some statements he had heard I had been attributing to him during the course of several interviews, I used the opportunity to "clear the air" and "set the record straight."

Though he had not heard the program himself, an associate had told Cooper that during a conversation on some radio station (for which I have long since forgotten the call letters), I had supposedly claimed that the astronaut had actually examined alien bodies lying on a morgue slab. I almost had to laugh at this wild accusation, since it was stretching the truth quite a bit – but maybe not all that far. For while I had never said anything of the sort, I did recall the subject of crashed spaceships being discussed with Gordon Cooper in a positive light, while he was being interviewed by Merv Griffin on the latter's now-defunct nationally televised talk show. Indeed, recalling the broadcast, I knew that Cooper had probably shocked many viewers by speaking for over five minutes on a topic that is often considered to be too bizarre for polite conversation.

In the early 1950s, Cooper was assigned to a jet fighter group in Germany. While stationed there, he remembers very vividly the week an entire formation of circular objects passed over the Air Base on an almost daily basis.

"The first day, a weatherman spotted some strange objects flying at high altitude and, before long, the entire fighter group was out looking at these groups

# SHIRLEY MACLAINE MEETS THE PLEIADIANS

of objects coming over,"

Cooper recalls telling details of what was to turn out to be an eye-opening episode for him. "But, unlike jet fighters, they would stop in their forward velocity and change 90-degrees, sometimes in the middle of their flight path."

Within the next few days, Cooper and his men were climbing higher and higher in their jets, trying in vain to get close to these strange, otherworldly craft.

"We could never get close enough to pin them down, but they were round in shape and very metallic looking," Cooper said.

UFOs were to continue to haunt him when the Air Force colonel was transferred several years later to Edwards Air Force Base Flight Test Center in the California desert. What happened one afternoon while he was on duty at this military base is evidence enough that the government definitely does keep a hell of a lot of secrets when it comes to UFOs!

The incident took place in the late 1950s, either 1957 or 1958 as Cooper can best recall, and, to this day, the photographic evidence of an actual UFO touching down upon the Earth is being kept under wraps.

During this period, Cooper was a Project Manager at Edwards Air Force Base, just three or four years before entering America's space program. After lunch this particular day, Cooper had assigned a team of photographers to an area of the vast dry lake beds near Edwards.

In a taped interview with UFOlogist Lee Speigel, the former Astronaut disclosed that while the crew was out there, they spotted a strange-looking craft above the lake bed and began to film it.

Cooper says the object was very definitely "hovering above the ground. And then it slowly came down and sat on the lake bed for a few minutes." All during this time, the motion picture cameras were filming away.

"There were varied estimates by the cameramen on what the actual size of the object was," Cooper said, "but they all agreed that it was at least the size of a vehicle that would carry normal-sized people in it."

Col. Cooper was not fortunate

# SHIRLEY MACLAINE MEETS THE PLEIADIANS

enough to be outside at the time of this incredible encounter, but he did see the films as soon as they were rushed through the development process.

"It was a typical circular-shaped UFO," he recollects. "Not too many people saw it, because it took off at quite a sharp angle and just climbed straight on out of sight!"

Cooper admits he didn't take any kind of poll to determine who had seen the craft, "because there were always strange things flying around in the air over Edwards." This is a statement Lee Speigel was able to verify through his own research efforts, having obtained closely guarded tapes of conversations between military pilots circling the base and their commanding officers in the flight tower, tracking the presence of unknown objects.

"People just didn't ask a lot of questions about things they saw and couldn't understand," notes Cooper, who adds that it was a lot simpler to look the other way, shrug one's shoulders, and chalk up what had been seen to "just another experimental aircraft that must have been developed at another area of the air base."

But what about the photographic proof – the motion picture footage – that was taken? "I think it was definitely a UFO," Cooper affirmed, as he makes no bones about it. "However, where it (the object) came from and who was in it is hard to determine, because it didn't stay around long enough to discuss the matter. There wasn't even time to send out a welcoming committee!"

After he had reviewed the film at least a dozen times, the footage was quickly forwarded to Washington. Cooper no doubt expected to get a reply in a few weeks' time as to what his men had seen and photographed, but there was no word, and the movie vanished, never to surface again.

"I'm sure that there's a great deal of information up in Washington, if only somebody could just find it," as Cooper so diplomatically put it, offering his theory that "I don't think a great deal of UFO information was ever classified. As a rule, if you really want to keep something a secret, you don't classify it! I'm sure that a lot

## SHIRLEY MACLAINE MEETS THE PLEIADIANS

of that stuff was probably just thrown into a file someplace in Washington and forgotten. I'm certain that there are roomfuls of such films that have things in them that people don't even know about. As soon as you classify something, every Congressman in the U.S. tries to get ahold of it and broadcasts it all over the country. Our classification system isn't always the best way to keep something a secret."

Colonel Gordon Cooper at the United Nations

On coast-to-coast television, Cooper some years ago made a blockbuster statement that had the telephone lines tied up the next day, as viewers telephoned the stations that carry the syndicated "Merv Griffin Show," anxious to find out if their ears had been playing tricks on them the night before.

Toward the end of the talk show host's interview with the former astronaut, Merv broke into a secretive tone of voice right on the air and aimed a hundred thousand dollar question at his guest: "There is a story going around, Gordon, that a spaceship did land in middle America and there were occupants, and members of our government were able to keep one of the occupants alive for a period of time. They've seen the metal of the aircraft and they know what the people look like. Is that a credible story?"

For all intents and purposes, Cooper should have laughed, for assuredly such a speculative story belongs in the category of science fiction or space fan-

# SHIRLEY MACLAINE MEETS THE PLEIADIANS

tasy. But Gordon Cooper kept a straight face when he replied: "I think it's fairly credible. I would like to see the time when all qualified people could really work together to properly investigate these stories and either refute or prove them."

The bombshell had been dropped. Cooper went on to say that, from the various reports of UFO contacts and abductions he had been privy to, he was convinced that the occupants of this crashed UFO were "probably not that different from what we are," that they are almost totally humanoid (i.e., have two arms, two legs, a torso and readily identifiable facial features) in appearance.

Taken aback by what Cooper had said over the national airwaves, Lee Speigel telephoned Cooper's office the following morning and managed to get past his private secretary, though others in the media were getting the cold shoulder.

"Cooper admitted to me that he could have revealed more on the air, but he decided not to play his entire hand because he felt certain that some 'official eyebrows were going to get raised.'"

Gordon Cooper (March 6, 1927 – October 4, 2004)

# SHIRLEY MACLAINE MEETS THE PLEIADIANS
## JAMES McDIVITT'S "SWITCHED PHOTOS"

During a Gemini flight, Major James McDivitt had a strange experience that involved taking various photographs of a mysterious object.

Several years ago, I attended a conference in Manhattan at which McDivitt briefly told about what went on in space, though the astronaut warned that just because he could not explain what it was he saw, he wasn't about to claim that alien creatures were looking in the space capsule window.

According to his testimony, he and fellow space traveler Ed White were over Hawaii. "I was looking out the port when I saw this mysterious sphere. I was holding a hand-held camera and was able to take five frames of film. From what I could tell, the object resembled a beer can with a cylinder protruding from the top of it."

Because of McDivitt's reluctance to reveal more details of his sighting, it was necessary for me to scrutinize with a fine tooth comb the daily NASA voice transcription logs of the conversations between ground control at Cape Kennedy and Gemini 4. According to what I found, at 6:55 on the 21st orbit, Mission Control gave the following report:

"This is Gemini Control. We are now 30 hours and nine minutes into the mission. Spacecraft Gemini 4 has just completed a pass over the state on its 20th orbit. In voice communication with Gus Grissom, spacecraft communicator, Command Pilot Jim McDivitt reported he had sighted another object in space. He described it only as an object that appeared to have big arms sticking out. He said he took some motion pictures of this object but was having some difficulty because of the sun."

A few seconds later, it was asked whether McDivitt was still looking "at that

# SHIRLEY MACLAINE MEETS THE PLEIADIANS

thing out there." His reply was, "No, I've lost it. It had big arms sticking out of it. I only had it for just a minute. I got a couple of pictures of it with the movie camera and one with the Hasselblad. But I was in free drift and before I could get the control back, I drifted into the sun and lost it."

Minutes passed before Mission Control said it was checking with the Space Detection and Tracking System to locate the object McDivitt reported. A later investigation showed that the nearest object in space would have been slightly more than 1,200 miles away from the craft.

Forty minutes after Mission Control released its report, it told newsmen it was having extreme problems communicating with the spacemen because of an unexplained power failure that had occurred onboard the tracking ship, the Coastal Sentry Quebec. The difficulty was quickly corrected, although no explanation for the blackout was offered.

The day after the sighting, the matter was still being taken into consideration by the best minds at NASA. Though the theory that the object was a satellite was being offered, nobody seemed to take that conclusion as a definite explanation. This is a verbatim transcript of the communication between Gemini 4 and Ground Control regarding the UFO report:

MISSION CONTROL: Could you give us an estimate as to how far that 'satellite' was from you yesterday?

SPACECRAFT: I couldn't really tell; it looked like quite a large object. It looked like I was approaching it rather rapidly. I'd say 10 miles or so.

MISSION CONTROL: Ten miles?

SPACECRAFT: That would be a guess. It was close enough that I could see . . .

MISSION CONTROL: See what?

SPACECRAFT: (Garbled transmission)

MISSION CONTROL: You're coming off pretty badly there. I couldn't read that.

SPACECRAFT: OK.

MISSION CONTROL: That came through good.

SPACECRAFT: All right, I said I got close enough to . . . (Abrupt halt in conversation as Mission Control voice breaks over that of astronaut)

MISSION CONTROL: Close enough to it to what? The nearest we can tell, there wasn't anything that close to you. Pegasus was about 1,200 miles away.

# SHIRLEY MACLAINE MEETS THE PLEIADIANS

SPACECRAFT: No, not quite that close. That far away.

MISSION CONTROL: Pretty good eyeball, all right.

SPACECRAFT: I took a picture. I just hope it comes out.

MISSION CONTROL: So do we.

Even the next day the subject was not put to rest as McDivitt contradicted what he had been told when he said, "No, it couldn't have been a distance of 1,200 miles away" (where the Pegasus satellite would have been at the time), but more likely was only "between 10 to 20 miles," from the Gemini 4 space ship.

But the big kicker was yet to come. When the photos were developed by NASA and shown to him, McDivitt was additionally puzzled, for he immediately realized that these were not the pictures he had taken. "I spent time looking through all the frames of all the photographs taken on the flight and there wasn't anything in there that looked like what I had taken."

Those who have studied UFOs feel that NASA might have successfully switched photos or at least quietly done away with those that might have shown more detail and proven it was not a satellite.

# SHIRLEY MACLAINE MEETS THE PLEIADIANS
## EDGAR MITCHELL: SCIENCE OF THE MIND

Following his trip into space and his walking upon the moon, astronaut Edgar Mitchell began a spiritual journey that took him into many highly uncharted regions. Like some of his fellow astronauts, Mitchell claims he felt closer to God while in space and had a spiritual awakening.

Returning to Earth, the astronaut founded his own center for higher awareness and even began to explore the realm of parapsychology. In public statements, Mitchell confessed that he no longer doubted the existence of UFOs. "It's not whether I believe they are real or not, but we still have to find out where they are coming from." A theory that he espouses is that at least some UFOs may belong in the category of "mental phenomena" and that our study of the mind could provide us with a lot of answers.

As to whether or not they are intelligently controlled, Mitchell didn't hesitate for a minute when he said, "Yes! I am sure that there is intelligent control somewhere behind them."

According to Dr. Garry Henderson, a senior research scientist at General Dynamics Corporation, just about all of our astronauts have seen and even photographed UFOs. He insists that NASA has files bulging with pictures.

Following a recent event, the Prophets Conference, Dr. Edgar Mitchell responded to the quest of UFOs by saying: ". . . in our briefing of the Joint Chiefs of Staff Intelligence Group, it became very clear to us that they were naive. They did not really know any more about this effort than we do, if as much. That is because, as Bob Dean pointed out earlier, most of the people in government were not in government when I retired twenty five years ago, they are younger people. The files going back fifty years just no longer exist. They've either been purged, compromised or whatever. They don't exist. So when we blame government for not being forthright, they really don't have anything to be forthright about, at least at that level.

# SHIRLEY MACLAINE MEETS THE PLEIADIANS

"Now, somewhere there's knowledgeable people, and Steven has ferreted out quite a few of them. And in my own efforts in talking with these folks, and talking with government, the question often comes up as to how they could have kept this a secret for so long. And friends they haven't. It's been around us all the time, but it has been denied, and obscured.

"I often like to state the condition, the story, the myth if you will, about Columbus coming here and some of the Indians not seeing the ships simply because it was not in their collective consciousness and their repertoire, they at least didn't want to see them. Much of what we're seeing now is what many people don't want to see either. There's been a massive effort at creating that, of denying the obvious, of saying that you're not seeing what's sitting right in front of you right now, thus causing doubt in your own mind. It's amazingly effective.

"So, documentation and evidence, that is probably the smoking gun type of evidence, has been totally compromised by saying that it's simply not true. So it is not true that they (government) have kept the secret. They haven't kept the secret, but it has been totally compromised by misinformation and disinformation.

"Now, for my own experience, I have had no firsthand experience like so many of you. I have not encountered a UFO, and we did not have them trailing us as far as we know, going to the moon. We didn't meet anyone on the moon. We did it just like we said we did. For the last twenty-five years we have dealt with the issue of, on one hand, the flat-earthers who said, 'you didn't go anywhere, it was all filmed out here in the desert,' and on the other hand, another fringe that said, 'yes you have been there, but you were followed. You were in contact with UFOs. There were beings on the moon that you met and had contact with.'

"Well, that's not true either. So, we have walked between these two extremes of misinformation, disinformation and pure ignorance. We did what we said we did, and I want to assure you, from that period up until the current time, NASA was one of the organizations ignorant of this type of activity. And the prevailing wisdom in NASA (at-the-time) was that we didn't even think about it. It was a ridiculous idea that we would encounter beings on the moon.

"However, in the last twenty-five years since that time, I became quite knowledgeable and became friends with Allan Hynek. I know and work with Jacques Vallee consistently now, and I have known the gentlemen on this stage, Bob Dean and Steven Greer for a few years. For me with all the evidence, it's not a matter of believing, it's a matter of the preponderance of evidence, and the evidence keeps building. The sightings keep happening.

"So it is clear that if they are ET, and I will question some of the sightings as to if they are ET, they are making their presence known. I also think that the prevalence in the modern era of so many events—the sightings, the continual mutilation events, the so-called abduction events—that we are looking at likely reversed engineered technology in the hands of humans that are not under government control or any type of high level control. I find that quite alarming.

"With regard to the technology itself, I work with folks who do know what is in our technological data base and what is available to modern armies. The so-called ET technology, the ability to have silent engines and flying machines that make no sound, flying machines that have the characteristics that are consistent with reproduction of UFO sightings, are not in any nation's arsenal, but they do exist. So if there are back engineered technologies existing, they are probably in the hands of this group of individuals, formerly government, formerly perhaps intelligence, formerly, under private sector control with some sort of oversight by military or by government.

"But this (oversight) is likely no longer the case as a result of this access denied category that is now operating. I call it a clandestine group. The technology is not in our military arsenals anywhere in the world, but it does exist, and to me that's quite disconcerting.

"I do work with a number of groups. We do know about some of the things that the technologies are used for, and I want to assure you that these technologies are not that far beyond our current state of knowledge. Now understanding it scientifically, understanding how it can be, is a long way from having a fully developed usable technology.

"But if in our knowledge we can understand how it has to be in order to create that technology, we're not that far away. So I want to assure you that we're not talking about technologies that are so farfetched that we can't understand them. They're just beyond the technological horizon.

"I want to tell you that it doesn't appear we need to be using ultra-dimensions and wormholes, etc., for this. It looks like our three dimensional or four dimensional space-time universe is about what it appears to be, and that we can operate within that space-time universe with these types of technologies. We have tended, like the ancients of old, to have invented myths about too many dimensions and time travel, wormhole travel, etc., and it doesn't look like that's necessary to explain what we're seeing."

# SHIRLEY MACLAINE MEETS THE PLEIADIANS

## DR. BRIAN O'LEARY'S NIGHTTIME INTRUDERS

Receiving his Ph.D. in astronomy at the University of California at Berkeley, Dr. Brian O'Leary was trained by NASA to be a part of their manned Mars missions before budget cuts postponed the project indefinitely. Having read about the "red planet" as a youth, O'Leary was fascinated with the fourth planet from our sun, and he entered the astronaut training program determined to set his foot on another world besides our own.

One weekend, at a personal growth seminar, he received his first inkling that the universe of reality is not always the way science says it should be. Surprisingly, he was able to pick up personal information, apparently through mental telepathy or clairvoyance, from a woman he had never met previously and knew nothing about. His newfound, extrasensory gift led the astronaut on a search for answers to many cosmic questions and was responsible for his becoming involved in investigating paranormal phenomena.

At a press conference in 1991, O'Leary voiced his opinion that Congress should look into the matter of UFOs and support research in this area. Said O'Leary: "Gallup Polls through the years indicate that over 80% of Americans now believe that the UFO phenomenon is real – up from 40% in 1966.

"We hear allegations that the government has been covering up much UFO

# SHIRLEY MACLAINE MEETS THE PLEIADIANS

information since the Roswell incident in 1947. Research on the UFO phenomenon is in disarray in large part because of divisive disagreements within the UFO community and the government as to what is the truth. Also, UFO research remains unsupported by the government and as a result is often amateurish.

"I am not an insider and I do not know the truth of the matter of alleged UFO cover-ups. What I do know from my own experience and from scientific investigations and experiments is that UFO phenomena and a range of other paranormal events (ESP, near-death experience, etc.) are part of our reality – as incredible as it may seem. These phenomena are not all hoaxes, as the skeptics claim. Polls show that two-thirds of all Americans have claimed to have had at least one paranormal experience.

"The truth about UFOs may be painful for us to face, and this might provide a continuing rationale for the government to maintain secrecy. But the truth will and must be known eventually. Continuing our denials and fears, in my opinion, is only adding to the problem. We are all in this together.

"In a time of opening our relations with the Soviet Union, we have the potential for radically demilitarizing our foreign policy reallocating those resources toward preserving our planet and opening ourselves to the Global Village. Part of that new reality is embracing the unknown and the possibility that we have visitors beyond Earth or beyond our dimensions of time and space. We must enter our new openness in peace and without recrimination.

"Our government of the people, by the people and for the people needs to be involved in the process not as a hostile, separate secret unit. I therefore advocate an orderly, non-vindictive Congressional investigation of UFOs and a change in government policy on supporting research into these and other paranormal phenomena.

"The late philosopher, Joseph Campbell, once said that we are living in a time in which our ignorance and our complacency about the unknown are coming to an end. It is time we let go of our fears and evolve into a higher awareness of ourselves and our place in the universe."

In regard to his own personal UFO experiences, they took place in the upstate New York cabin of Whitley Strieber, the popular author whose book "Communion" hit the top of "The New York Times" bestseller list and detailed close encounters with bug-eyed aliens who "invaded" his residence around midnight on numerous occasions.

Describing what happened, Dr. O'Leary says that, in May 1987, he was an overnight guest of the Striebers. Upon going to bed, he felt as if he had been "drugged without the use of anesthesia," though he had not even had a drink in weeks. O'Leary says he had to fight to stay awake, so strong was the feeling that he was being "pulled under" by some strange force. "To stay awake, I started to recite a particular meditation I am fond of, but my words trailed off to oblivion. I couldn't move."

A companion sleeping in the same room that night recalls awakening several times to find that she also was unable to move as bright lights filled the room coming from an unknown source.

"Yet we had turned out the lights before going to sleep, and the lights were out when we woke up in the morning."

Venturing down to breakfast, the astronaut/astronomer found that others staying overnight had experienced a similar state of being. "To this day, we do not know who drugged us or who turned on the lights. But the experience was a very real one. Later I learned that much of what transpired is a common aspect of the UFO phenomena."

Dr. Brian O'Leary (January 27, 1940 – July 28, 2001)

## EUGENE CERNAN: CONSTRUCTED BY OTHER CIVILIZATIONS

Eugene A. Cernan was Commander of the Apollo 17 mission to the moon. While in space, he says he had the opportunity to ponder the mysteries of the universe and he feels that exploring space can tell us not only lots about ourselves but about the future of humankind. He believes that our present civilization is not the only highly technological one that has ever existed on our planet. "Maybe infinity goes backward as well as it does forward, and maybe the moon can tell us something about the existence of some ancient civilization, not necessarily on Earth, nor necessarily on the moon, but possibly within our own universe, and give us insight into what reality is all about." As for UFOs, Cernan does think they might come from space.

# SHIRLEY MACLAINE MEETS THE PLEIADIANS

## MARGARET MEAD: AN ANTHROPOLOGIST TALKS ABOUT UFOs

"Yes! There are UFOs," stated anthropologist Margaret Mead before her death. In a passionate plea, the inquisitive scientist noted that "even the most cautious and painstaking investigation does not explain away the phenomenon. This much, at least, we have to accept."

Mead's own studies have shown that "thousands of sightings have been reported, and not only by individuals alone at night who are faced with the terrifying spectacle of a shining disc hovering soundlessly over the trees or touching the ground and then suddenly taking off vertically with a tremendous burst of speed. Pilots have continually reported sightings, and sometimes several planes have given chase – always unsuccessfully. Persons unknown to one another have described identical phenomena seen in the same night – or daylight – sky. Radar tracings are not uncommon either, and occasionally fleeting views have been captured by cameras."

# SHIRLEY MACLAINE MEETS THE PLEIADIANS

What did the internationally renowned anthropologist think flying saucers might be? She never reached any conclusions and remained as objective as possible. She did give credence to the late Dr. Carl Jung's theories. "Jung neither rejected nor accepted the reality of UFOs," she explained.

"What he suggested was that there is also a psychological component – what he called a 'living myth' or a 'visionary rumor' that is potentially shared by all human beings in a period of great change and deep anxiety about the future. UFOs, Jung speculated, might be a worldwide visualized projection of our uneasy psychic state, but he also postulates that the two unknowns – UFOs and our human visualized projections – may simply 'coincide in a meaningful manner.'"

But suppose UFOs are real and that they do come from other planets and star systems, as many people claim? How can we account for the fact that they haven't openly contacted any government here on earth or landed en masse? Ms. Mead never let this worry her, as she fit these questions into the "scheme of things" without any difficulty.

"The most likely explanation, it seems to me, is that they are simply watching what we are up to – that a responsible society outside our solar system is keeping an eye on us, in order to see that we don't set in motion a chain reaction that might have repercussions far outside our solar system. It is plausible to attribute to extraterrestrial creatures such intentions – as plausible as any that we ourselves at present are capable of imagining."

Margaret Mead (December 16, 1901 – November 15, 1978)

# SHIRLEY MACLAINE MEETS THE PLEIADIANS

**JOHN LEAR'S "ALIEN TERROR" BELOW**

His is one of the strangest scenarios to emerge from the study of UFOlogy. Indeed, it is an incredible tale that seems almost "out of place" in this work, and, to many, perhaps too frightening to tell.

One cannot help but be impressed with the name John Lear. After all, his late father, William, was the famous aviation pioneer who built the Lear Aircraft Company, which currently provides thousands of those fancy corporate jet planes and boasts untold millions in defense contracts from the Pentagon.

Lear – the son – is also highly regarded in aviation circles, having flown a variety of over 150 test aircraft and winning every award granted by the Federal Aviation Administration.

For a long time, John Lear had little or no interest in UFOs; he hadn't thought terribly much about the subject, which seemed "way out" to him. Then he chanced to talk to a friend who had been stationed in England when a UFO touched down at a military complex there and was seen by U.S. servicemen on duty, small creatures and all. Intrigued, Lear began asking around and found some of his former associates in the CIA – for whom he had flown any number of missions – willing to confirm that government leaders knew a great deal more about UFOs and space aliens than the public was being told.

Lear discovered to his utter amazement that the U.S. military actually possessed craft from outer space and that some of the vehicles were even in partially working order. Apparently, the Americans had initially gotten their hands on these extraterrestrial disc-shaped devices as far back as the late 1940s, upon recovery of the wreckage of a downed saucer that the Nazis had somehow captured during World War II.

Apparently, some of the lethal "death weapons" we subsequently developed were based on facets of this interplanetary technology.

Furthermore, Lear believes any number of flying discs "fell" into our hand when they crashed in the southwest in the late 1940s and early 50s. Scattered around the various crash sites were the bodies of small humanoid beings, the EBEs. At least one alien was found still alive, and he, along with his badly burned buddies, was flown to Wright-Patterson Air Force Base in Dayton, Ohio, home of the infamous "Hangar 18", with their final destination the so-called "Blue Room," which the likes of former Senator Barry Goldwater have not been permitted to penetrate.

Lear's scenario also includes the suspicion that the government has made secret deals with aliens, actually exchanging humans for advanced technical data. Supposedly, the government was to be provided a list of those being abducted so they could maintain a vigil over them after their experience to make sure that they were not being harmed in any way.

Unfortunately, the aliens took advantage of the situation, taking away tens of thousands for God knows what purpose, and implanting small transmitters inside their brains that can be activated for some sinister "mission" at some prearranged future moment.

"The United States Government has been in business with little gray extraterrestrials for about 20 years," declares Lear in an "Open Paper to UFO Researchers."

"In July of 1952, a panicked government watched helplessly as a squadron of 'flying saucers' flew over Washington, D.C., and buzzed the White House, the Capitol Building and the Pentagon. It took all the imagination and intimidation the government could muster to force that incident out of the memory of the public. Thousands of sightings occurred during the Korean War and several more saucers were retrieved by the Air Force. Some were stored at Wright-Patterson Air Force Base, some were stored at Air Force bases near the location of the crash site. One saucer was so enormous and the logistic problems in transportation so enormous that it was buried at a crash site and remains there today.

# SHIRLEY MACLAINE MEETS THE PLEIADIANS

"On April 30, 1964, the first communication between those aliens and the U.S. government took place at Holloman Air Force Base in New Mexico. Three saucers landed at a prearranged area and a meeting was held between the aliens and intelligence officers of the U.S. Government.

"During the period of 1969-1971, MJ-12, representing the U.S. Government, made a deal with these creatures, called EBEs (Extraterrestrial Biological Entities, named by Detley Bronk, original MJ-12 member and 6th President of Johns Hopkins University).

"The 'deal' was that in exchange for 'technology' that they would provide to us, we agreed to 'ignore' the abductions that were going on and suppress information on the cattle mutilations. The EBEs assured MJ-12 that the abductions (usually lasting about 2 hours) were merely the ongoing monitoring of developing civilizations. In fact, the purposes for the abductions turned out to be:

"(1) Insertion of a 3mm spherical device through the nasal cavity of the abductee into the brain. The device is used for the biological monitoring, tracking, and control of the abductee.

"(2) Implementation of Posthypnotic Suggestion to carry out a specific activity during a specific time period, the actuation of which will occur within the next two to five years.

"(3) Termination of some people so that they could function as living sources for biological material and substances.

"(4) Termination of individuals who represent a threat to the continuation of their activity.

"(5) Effect genetic engineering experiments.

"(6) Impregnation of human females and early termination of pregnancies to secure the crossbred infant.

"The U.S. Government was not initially aware of the far-reaching consequences of their 'deal.' They were led to believe that the abductions were essentially benign and since they figured the abductions would probably go on anyway whether they agreed or not, they merely insisted that a current list of abductees be submitted, on a periodic basis, to the National Security Council.

"After the initial agreement, Groom Lake, outside Las Vegas, one of the nation's most secret test centers, was closed for a period of about a year, sometime between about 1972 and 1974, and a huge underground facility was constructed for and with the help of the EBEs.

"The 'bargained for' technology was set in place but could only be operated by the EBEs themselves. Needless to say, the advanced technology could not be used against the EBEs themselves, even if needed. During the period between 1979 and 1983, it became increasingly obvious that things were not going as planned.

"It became known that many more people (in the thousands) were being abducted than were listed on the official abduction lists. In addition, it became obvious that some, not all, but some of the nation's missing children had been used for secretions and other parts required by the aliens.

"In 1979, there was an altercation of sorts at the Dulce laboratory in New Mexico. A special armed forces unit was called in to try and free a number of people trapped in the facility who had become aware of what was really going on.

"According to one source, 66 of the soldiers were killed and our people were not freed. By 1984, MJ-12 must have been in stark terror at the mistake they had made in dealing with the EBEs. They had subtly promoted 'Close Encounters of the Third Kind' and 'E.T.' to get the public used to 'odd looking' aliens that were compassionate, benevolent and very much our 'space brothers.' MJ-12 'sold' the EBEs to the public and were now faced with the fact that quite the opposite was true. In addition, a plan was formulated in 1968 to make the public aware of the existence of aliens on Earth over the next 20 years, to culminate with several documentaries to be released during the 1985-1987 period of time.

"These documentaries would explain the history and intentions of the EBEs. The discovery of the 'Grand Deception' put the entire plans, hopes and dreams into utter confusion and panic.

"The EBEs have a type of recording device that has recorded all of Earth's history and can display it in the form of a hologram. This hologram can be filmed, but, because of the way holograms work, does not come out very clear on movie film or videotape. The crucifixion of Christ on the Mount of Olives has allegedly been put on film to show the public.

"The EBEs claim to have created Christ, which, in view of the 'Grand Deception,' could be an effort to disrupt traditional values for undetermined reasons. Another videotape allegedly in existence is an interview with an EBE. Since EBEs communicate telepathically, an Air Force Colonel serves as an interpreter.

"Just before the stock market correction in October of 1987, several newsmen had been invited to Washington, D.C., to personally film the EBE in a similar type interview and distribute the film to the public. Apparently, because of the correction in the market, it was felt the timing was not propitious. In any case, it certainly seems like an odd method to inform the public of extraterrestrials, but it would be in keeping with the actions of a panicked organization who at this point

# SHIRLEY MACLAINE MEETS THE PLEIADIANS

in time doesn't know which way to turn.

"If the government felt they were being forced to acknowledge the existence of aliens on Earth because of the overwhelming evidence, such as the October and November sightings in Wytheville, Virginia and such books as "Night Siege" (Hynek, J. Allen; Imbrogno, Phillip J.; Pratt, Bob: Ballantine Books, Random House, New York), and taking into consideration the 'Grand Deception' and obviously hostile intentions of the EBEs, it might be expedient for MJ-12 to admit the EBE.s but conceal the information on the mutilations and abductions. If MJ-12 and researcher William Moore, who first disclosed the existence of MJ-12 to the public, were in some kind of agreement, then it would be beneficial to Moore to toe the party line. For example, MJ-12 would say, 'Here are some more genuine documents . . . but remember . . . no talking about the mutilations or abductions.' This would be beneficial to Moore as it would supply the evidence to support his theory that ETs exist but deny the truths about the ETs. However, if Moore was indeed working for MJ-12, he would follow the party line anyway . . . admitting the ETs, but pooh-poohing the mutilations and abductions.

"Now you ask, 'Why haven't I heard about any of this?' Who do you think you would hear it from? Dan Rather? Tom Brokaw? Sam Donaldson? Wrong. These people just read the news, they don't find it. They have lackeys who call and interview witnesses and verify statements on stories coming over the wire (either AP or UPI). It's not like Dan Rather would go down to Wytheville, Virginia, and dig into why there were four thousand reported sightings in October and November of 1987. Better that Tom Brokaw or someone else should risk their credibility on this type of story. Tom Brokaw? Tom wants Sam Donaldson to risk his credibility. No one, but no one, is going to risk their neck on such outlandish ideas, regardless of how many people report sightings of 900 foot objects running them off the road.

"In the case of the Wytheville sightings, dozens of vans with NASA lettered on the side failed to interest newsmen. And those that asked questions were informed that NASA was doing a weather survey. Well then, you ask, what about our scientists? What about Carl Sagan? Isaac Asimov? Arthur C. Clarke? Wouldn't they have known? If Carl Sagan knows then he is committing a great fraud through the solicitation of memberships in the Planetary Society, 'to search for extraterrestrial intelligence.'

"Another charade into which the U.S. Government dumps millions of dollars every year is the radio telescope in Arecibo, Puerto Rico, operated by Cornell University with – guess who? – Carl Sagan. Cornell is ostensibly searching for signals from Outer Space, a sign, maybe, that somebody is out there. It is hard to believe that relatively intelligent astronomers like Sagan could be so ignorant.

# SHIRLEY MACLAINE MEETS THE PLEIADIANS

What about the late Isaac Asimov? Surely the most prolific science fiction writer of all time would have guessed during his lifetime that there must be an enormous cover-up? Maybe, but if he knows he's not saying. Perhaps he's afraid that 'Foundation' and 'Empire' will turn out to be inaccurate.

"What about Arthur C. Clarke? Surely the most technically accurate of science fiction writers with very close ties to NASA would have at least a hint of what's really going on. Again, if so, he isn't talking. In a recent science fiction survey, Clarke estimates that contact with extraterrestrial intelligent life would not occur before the 21st Century. If the government won't tell us the truth and the major networks won't even give it serious consideration, then what is the big picture, anyway?

"Are the EBEs, having done a hundred thousand or more abductions (possibly millions worldwide), building an untold number of secret underground bases (Groom Lake, Nevada; Sunspot, Datil; Roswell, and Pine Town, New Mexico, just to name a few) getting ready to return to wherever they came from? Or, from the obvious preparations, are we to assume that they are getting ready for a big move? Or is the more sinister and most probable situation that the invasion is essentially complete and it is all over but the screaming?

"A well-planned invasion of Earth for its resources and benefits would not begin with mass landings of ray gun-equipped aliens. A properly planned and executed invasion by a civilization thousands and probably hundreds of thousands of years in advance of us would most likely be complete before even a handful of people (say 12?) realized what was happening. No fuss, no muss. The best advice I can give you is this: Next time you see a flying saucer and are awed by its obvious display of technology and gorgeous lights of pure color – RUN LIKE HELL!"

In summary, Mr. Lear contends that our government has for over 40 years been concealing from the public a "horrible truth" concerning an "invasion" of Earth by EBEs. He alleges that the U.S. government has conducted "business with little gray extraterrestrials for about 20 years," i.e., we were "sold" by MJ-12 to the aliens in exchange for technology and to preserve our democracy. He contends that our government agreed to ignore human/cattle abductions and mutilations, but that the deeply sinister purposes of these activities were not completely understood by MJ-12 until about 1984.

Still unexplained are the EBE's reason(s) to do business with the most powerful nation on Earth when they could covertly continue their activities in the Third World without concern, or why these advanced and powerful aliens would even want or require our "agreement" to continue their activities. Lear cites the history of UFOlogy in the 1940s and 50s, contending that several crashed saucers and at

# SHIRLEY MACLAINE MEETS THE PLEIADIANS

least three live aliens have been captured and hidden by the government. But would such a powerful adversary permit humans to hold, study and possibly copy crashed saucers or permit us to keep captured aliens? Or would they simply take them back?

The EBEs are said to suffer from an atrophied digestive system which requires that they sustain themselves by absorbing through the skin a solution made from certain enzyme/hormonal secretions derived from cattle and humans and collected by ghoulish cattle and human mutilations. The various body parts said to be obtained in this manner are then supposed to be taken for processing to various hidden laboratories jointly maintained by the aliens and CIA in the Southwestern U.S.

Mr. Lear maintains that a 20-year plan for release of UFO information to the public (including the history and intentions of the EBEs), to be completed by 1987-88, was terminated when the "horrible truth" became apparent. Indeed, during the first year of the Carter Administration, various media sources, including Walter Cronkite on the "CBS Evening News" and "U.S. News and World Report," reported that before the end of that year the administration was to release UFO information of a "startling" nature. The information was never released. He contends that "Star Wars" is in reality a defensive response to the EBEs, not Soviet nuclear missiles, but does not explain why the EBEs permit us to continue with SDI studies if they pose a threat to them.

What follows is a transcript of a conversation between Lear and the National Fringe Sciences Bulletin Board.

QUESTION: You just mentioned that there were 70 other species in contact with this world, of which four were overt. Are they aware of the EBEs?

LEAR: Yes, they are. The types I will mention are listed in a USAF Academy Physics book called Introductory Space Science Volume 2.B. I refer to Chapter 13, about page 8, which lists the ones that are most seen. They are the EBEs, the "blondes" (also called the Nordics). They look just like us but are invariably blond-haired and blue-eyed. Don't know where they come from but they do not interact with us except for a few abductions now and then.

We also have a species that is similar to us in appearance, but they are about seven feet tall and the main difference is that their eyes wrap around the head a little more than ours. Another type listed is a small species about four feet tall, very hairy and extremely strong for their size. We don't know where these guys come from either. All this was in the aforementioned text which was withdrawn by the Air Force in the early 70s from the book. But there are several people that have the original book.

# SHIRLEY MACLAINE MEETS THE PLEIADIANS

The EBEs are about the only ones where we are pretty sure where they come from and that is Zeta Reticuli 1 & 2, a binary star system visible only from the southern hemisphere, spectral class of G2 and 38 light years from here. It is possible that they use some form of the Einstein Rosen Bridge theory (wormholes in space) to get here. We know all this from the work that Marjorie Fish did in the early 70s.

There is a good article about it in "Astronomy Magazine," December, 1974. There was also a reprint of this article in 1976 which had all the comments and rebuttals, and rebuttals to rebuttals, by Carl Sagan, Bob Schaefer etc., etc.

QUESTION: I remember reading about the characterizations of ETs that you have described about 25 years ago. I also recall a book by a George Adamski regarding these golden haired aliens. In "The Interrupted Journey," I believe it was Betty Hill that under hypnosis revealed many of the invasive techniques used on abductees. Also, perhaps it was in the article on the Zeta Reticuli Incident that a woman under hypnosis reconstructed a 3D model of the Zeta Star system with the relative positions of the other stars as they would have appeared as established by computer modeling. I guess one of the primary questions is, if there are other forms visiting and/or interacting with humans, are they completely insensitive to these "arrangements" put out by the EBEs with the government?

LEAR: This may be hard to swallow, but it's my information from government sources that the blondes adhere to a universal law of noninterference, and even though the EBEs are not doing us any favors, that they, the blondes, will not do anything about it unless the EBEs do something that will affect another part of the universe. Back to Adamski. He has been labeled as a fraud; however, like all things, nothing is all black or all white. Some of his stuff was true. But it's hard to separate which stuff.

He claimed that the blondes came from Venus or Mars, which is highly, highly unlikely. As far as the map, it was drawn by Betty Hill under hypnosis in 2D. It was Marjorie Fish that did the interpretation to bring it into 3D.

QUESTION: I'm curious also as to the government's plans, if any, to deal with an uprising of EBEs should that eventuality occur. Or would the technological gap make such an attempt untenable?

LEAR: It's my understanding that we have already lost the battle. This is the reason why MJ-12 is in such a panic. They had a lot of well-laid plans to inform us, and when the deception was confirmed about 1984, it was all out the window. Back to Betty Hill for a minute. Under hypnosis, she recalled being given a pregnancy test. A needle was inserted in her stomach. She recalls saying that this was like no pregnancy test here on Earth (1962).

# SHIRLEY MACLAINE MEETS THE PLEIADIANS

Amniocentesis was developed around 1972-1973 and uses the exact same procedures. In 1986, a British doctor had given an amniocentesis to a woman and was looking at the fluid under a microscope. He saw a tiny speck and started enlarging it. When he got it big enough to see, what he found was what looked like a computer chip attached to one of the chromosomes. This doctor and six others wrote an open letter in "Nature Magazine," one of Britain's most respected scientific journals, along with a picture of the chip, and asked for any doctor or scientist anywhere that could help explain what they were seeing.

QUESTION: Recently, in the INF treaty negotiations, Gorbachev indicated that despite prior claims, they too were working on an SDI program. Is there any connection between our program and theirs? And, if the battle is lost, why are these attempts being made?

LEAR: I wish I knew the answer to that. Several rumors have come out of the test site recently and one of them was that every test shot this year has been to make a giant room. The shots are very clean and as soon as everything subsides they move in equipment to make walls, ceiling, floors and various levels.

QUESTION: Several critics have highlighted the apparent discrepancies between our medical technology and that of the EBEs as to synthesizing plasma material. Also, technological gaps between our cultures suggest that solicitation of indigenous humans for their undertakings seems akin to asking help from chimpanzees. My analogy. What about these concerns?

LEAR: All of these questions are valid and show a lot of thought. All I know is what I wrote. It's very hard to speculate the reasons why or why not a species almost a billion years older than us would do anything. This is not a cop-out. I just don't know and don't want to guess. It's my understanding from those "in the know" (and as late as one week ago) that the situation is "ominous."

The Roswell crash was the first recovered flying saucer crash in the U.S. Bill Moore located 90 material witnesses to the crash. It was near Corona, N.M., and a few months ago I interviewed Mrs. Procter, near whose ranch this thing crashed. Four bodies were recovered.

There is one person still alive at this moment who helped Mac Brazel drag some of the wreckage to the shed. He and Brazel were approached at that time by (I know it's hard to believe, but the guy is going to come forward soon) an alien who told them both to keep their mouths shut. He is the last guy alive that was directly connected with that retrieval.

The last guy to die was Major Jesse Marcel, the intelligence officer at Roswell who went out and helped pick up the wreckage. Before he died a few years ago, he went public with his account, which was that the crash was not a balloon or a

# SHIRLEY MACLAINE MEETS THE PLEIADIANS

radar reflector or an airplane. He didn't state what it was, but said it was not of this Earth. I have a transcript of the cassette tape of his memories of picking up the wreckage.

QUESTION: Of course, any information you have will be helpful. What of yourself? Why are you coming forward now, particularly, placing the spotlight on yourself? Aren't you concerned that there may be some sort of repercussions from the government regarding the stir this has caused and will continue to cause?

LEAR: Let me say that five years ago I wouldn't have gotten away with this, but things are so screwed up now that one voice talking to . . . what 50? 100? . . . people can't make any possible difference. Also, if something was going to happen, it would have happened a few weeks ago. I wrote Dr. Lew Allen, Director of J.P.L. and also an MJ-12 member, that I was going to do a story on his participation in MJ-12, particularly because J.P.L. employed 8,000 people in the Southern California area. I also enclosed a copy of my hypothesis. Dr. Allen has a reputation of responding to all mail in a very prompt manner. But me? I didn't hear anything. Not even a "John Lear, you must be crazy." He wrote a letter to Max Fiebleman of Los Angeles on the 18th of December. Max had sent him a copy of the Hudson Valley video and asked Dr. Allen to look at it. Dr. Allen responded that he had taken a quick glance but did not have the time for anything more and on the basis of what he saw determined that it was a blimp.

He also wished Max a Merry Christmas.

Now . . . this is one of the world's greatest scientists? Not interested in that Hudson Valley videotape? Gimme a break. I would be very surprised if some kind of statement from the government is not forthcoming within the year, more probably within six months and possibly much sooner. That's about all I can speculate from the information I am getting.

# SHIRLEY MACLAINE MEETS THE PLEIADIANS

**SEAN CASTEEL**

Sean Casteel has written about UFOs, alien abduction, and related phenomena since 1989 when he interviewed Whitley Strieber, around the time that the movie version of "Communion" was released. He was a contributor for several years to UFO UNIVERSE and was eventually given the title of Associate Editor. Later he began to write special reports and books for both of Tim Beckley's publishing companies, Inner Light Publications and Global Communications. The books he has written include "UFOs, Prophecy and the End of Time," "The Heretic's UFO Guidebook" and "Signs and Symbols of the Second Coming." His work has also been published in the U.K., Italy, Romania and Australia.

# SHIRLEY MACLAINE MEETS THE PLEIADIANS

**PHOTOGRAPHERS**

**HELEN HOVEY**

Award winning photographer Helen Hovey began her career as a photographer by photographing a bevy of rock stars from the orchestra pit of Manhattan's historical landmark The Academy of Music, a 3000 seat vaudeville theater on Manhattan's lower east side.

Helen was born, and raised in New York City. Helen preferred working the rock 'n' roll scene of the 70s. Her portfolio includes private photo sessions with: Dr. John, Edgar Winter and guitarist Ronnie Montrose, to name only a few. Helen specialized in rock action photography. In her portfolio, one can find the lead singer of Humble Pie, Steve Marriott, Marc Bolan (from T. Rex), Rod Stewart, David Bowie, Led Zeppelin, The Grateful Dead, The New Riders of The Purple Sage, Kingfish and Bob Dylan. Several years ago, Helen won two Kodak International Awards in the black & white category. One of the photos, of model Varusika Kalwa, can be found in this work.

After almost 25 years of working in the music industry, Helen recently retired to Southern California to catch some sun and write her memoirs.

Individual photographs as well as a series of collectable cards are available. Helen can be contacted through her Face Book page – ref=ts"https://www.facebook.com/helen.hovey?fref=ts

# SHIRLEY MACLAINE MEETS THE PLEIADIANS

**DINA REGINE**

Dina Regine is a photographer, a recording artist and a songwriter who is a long time member in good standing of the New York artist and celebrity scene. She first met publisher/author Tim Beckley while he was operating out of a huge loft on Manhattan's 14th Street, which was then the home of the New York School of Occult Arts and Sciences. Beckley had placed an ad in "The Village Voice" looking for photographers to accompany him while he interviewed some of the top rock stars of the day for a variety of music magazines he was affiliated with.

Among those rockers who grace Dina's portfolio are: Keith Richards, Mick Jagger, Alice Cooper, Led Zeppelin, James Taylor, Leon Russell and guitarist Ace Frehley of KISS, whose UFO experiences are detailed in this work. Her photographs have been seen in numerous publications/books, record covers and galleries, as well as in two museum collections. Her DJ clientele reads like a who's who in the entertainment and art world.

A musician in her own right, Dina has performed both in bands as well as having established herself as a solo artist. In November 2014, "Right On, Alright," produced by Regine and Nik Chinboukas, hit the streets. Steven Van Zandt picked the opening track "Gotta Tell You" for his TV series "Lilyhammer," and, in January 2015, he welcomed "Gotta Tell You" to the "Underground Garage" on SiriusXM as "The Coolest Song In The World." Her video for the first single, "Dial My Number," was also Video of the Day on the "Underground Garage." "Broken" was in the top 100 pick in "New York Music Daily" for 2014, and "Fences" was in the top six pick for December 2014. "The Aquarian Weekly," who called her album "a vintage-fueled ride," picked Dina as an act to watch in 2015. Right On, Alright!

Recording available on http://dinareginemusic.wazala.com/

as well as Amazon and Itunes

http://dinaregine.com/

http://www.dinareginephotography.com/

# SHIRLEY MACLAINE MEETS THE PLEIADIANS

Above: Celebrity rock photographer Helen Hovey and author Tim Beckley are besieged by UFOs on a road trip to Area 51.

Left: A-listers Dina Regine and Tim Beckley were famous long before there was a TMZ.

# SHIRLEY MACLAINE MEETS THE PLEIADIANS

## TIMOTHY GREEN BECKLEY - UFO & Paranormal Pioneer

Tim Beckley has had so many careers that even his own girlfriend doesn't know what he does for a living . . .

Timothy Green Beckley has been described as the Hunter S. Thompson of UFOlogy by the editor of "UFO Magazine," Nancy Birnes.

Since an early age his life has more or less revolved around the paranormal.

At the age of three his life was saved by an invisible force. The house he was raised in was thought to be haunted. His grandfather saw a headless horseman.

Beckley also underwent out-of-body experiences starting at age six, saw his first of three UFOs when he was but ten, and has had two more sightings since – including an attempt to communicate with one of these objects.

Tim grew up listening to the only all night talk show in the country that revolved around the strange and unexplained. Long John Nebel's guests included the early UFO contactees who claimed to have visited other planets and built time machines in the desert. Tim was fascinated by everything that went bump in the night – or even in the daylight for that matter. Years later, Tim was to appear on Long John's show numerous times and over the years has been a frequent guest on hundreds of programs which have come and gone just like ghosts in the night. He is a popular guest on Coast to Coast AM. Has appeared on William Shatner's "Weird Or What?" And an episode of "UFO Hunters" regarding the dreaded Men In Black. He has his own podcast, "Unraveling The Secrets" and "Mr. UFOs Secret Files," a new YouTube channel.

Tim started his career as a writer early on. At age 14, he purchased a mimeograph machine and began to publish the "Interplanetary News Service Report." Over the years he has written over 25 books on everything from rock music to the secret MJ-12 papers. He has been a stringer for the national tabloids, such as "The Enquirer" and editor of over 30 different magazines (most of which never lasted more than a couple of issues). His longest running effort was the newsstand publication UFO UNIVERSE, which went for 11 years. Today he is the president of Inner Light/Global Communications and editor of "The Conspiracy Journal" and "Bizarre Bazaar."

He is one of the few Americans ever to be invited to speak before closed door meetings on UFOs presided over by the late Earl of Clancarty at the House of Lords in England. He visited Loch Ness in Scotland while in the U.K. and went home with a belief that Nessie was somehow connected with dragons of mythology as well as strange discs engraved on cathedrals and ghostly phenomenon.

The Inner Light Publications and Global Communications' catalog of books and video titles now number over 200, including the works of Tim Swartz, Sean Casteel, T. Lobsang Rampa, Commander X, Brad Steiger, John Keel, Tracy Twyman, Wendelle Stevens and a host of many other authors.

He probably knows more about the history of the UFO movement since the early 1950s than anyone today. Because of his fair and balanced approach, he made friends

## SHIRLEY MACLAINE MEETS THE PLEIADIANS

with everyone regardless of whether or not he personally believed their stories.

Tim is known among horror movie fans as Mr. Creepo. When asked his major cinema influences, he mentions Nancy Reagan as having gotten him involved as a horror host. During the heyday of double features and Time Square grind houses, he worked as a movie review critic as well as a publicist for several small film companies. His recent efforts include "Skin Eating Jungle Vampires" and "Blood Sucking Vampire Freaks."

Check out the show he co hosts with Carla Anderson at

www.UnravelingTheSecrets.Com   on www.PSN-Radio.com

His YouTube channels are

Mr UFOs Secret Files  and Tim Beckley

MrUFO8@hotmail.com

# SHIRLEY MACLAINE MEETS THE PLEIADIANS

**CONTACT US FOR A FREE MAGAZINE SUBSCRIPTION**

To receive our FREE catalog and Conspiracy Journal
please send us your name, and address to:
TIMOTHY G BECKLEY, BOX 753, NEW BRUNSWICK, NJ. 08903
Or you may e mail us at:
MrUFO8@hotmail.com

Conspiracy Journal
PRODUCTIONS

www.ingramcontent.com/pod-product-compliance
Lightning Source LLC
Chambersburg PA
CBHW081916170426
43200CB00014B/2745